The Christian Story

The Christian Story

A Narrative Interpretation
of Basic Christian Doctrine

by
Gabriel Fackre

William B. Eerdmans Publishing Company
Grand Rapids, Michigan

Library of Congress Cataloging in Publication Data

Fackre, Gabriel J.
    The Christian story.

    1. Theory, Doctrinal. I. Title.
BT75.2.F33   230   78-15087
ISBN 0-8028-1735-1

To Our Children
Bonnie, Gabrielle, Judy, Skye, Kirk, and Gary

Acknowledgments

The seminar table and theological guild are testing places for such a book as this. The rigorous academic scrutiny received there has greatly helped me. But it is working clergy and laity engaged in mission who have provided the most intense learning laboratory for this kind of presentation of basic Christian doctrine. The material made its initial tentative appearance at a Theological Event for United Church of Christ clergy at Craigville, Massachusetts, and took more developed form in the Perkins Lectures at First Methodist Church, Wichita Falls, Texas. Thereafter it received various elaborations and emendations in clergy conferences at La Foret, Colorado, and Deering, New Hampshire; among laity at the Iowa School of the Church; with new Baptist pastors in Maine and missionary sisters at Maryknoll, New York; with members of First Congregational Church, UCC in San Francisco; the First Baptist and Old South Churches in Boston; and in my own congregation, Eliot Church, Newton, Massachusetts, and with its pastor Herbert Davis. One or another of these chapters of the Story have been explored with colleagues in the Boston Theological Society, with students and faculty in courses and lectureships at the School of Theology at Claremont, Perkins School of Theology, Austin Presbyterian Theological Seminary, Bangor Theological Seminary, Lancaster Theological Seminary, Boston College, in the Christology Seminar of the Divinity School, Cambridge University, and with my classes and colleagues at Andover Newton Theological School. A crucial partner in theological conversation is my family—always my wife, Dot, and now increasingly our children.

I am indebted to Kay Coughlin, faculty secretary at Andover Newton for her persistence and competence in working with the manuscript in its many permutations, and to Gary and Gabrielle Jenkins for their preparation of the Index.

Unless otherwise noted the biblical quotations are from the *New English Bible With the Apocrypha* (Oxford University Press and Cambridge University Press, 1970).

Contents

Introduction

This is a book for those struggling with the question, "What is the Christian faith?" The answer given here unfolds in the form of a story. Basic beliefs are interpreted as chapters in the biography of God. We call the narrative "a translation," for whenever the Christian Story is told with the hope of being heard, it is done in the language of a given time and place.

Both the confusions and possibilities of this particular time and place warrant the telling and hearing. The din of competing religious claims perplexes both the seeker and the ordinary churchgoer. New cults, movements, and religious superstars appear almost daily on the television screen or street corner to hawk their wares. The pious novelty may carry the label "Christian," or very self-consciously reject that identity and offer in its place either a secular nostrum or some import from the East. Who are *we* vis-à-vis these things, and how do we sort and sift their contentions? Confusion is compounded by the hard ethical choices moderns must make, from abortion and euthanasia, ecology and energy, to racial and ethnic justice, hunger, poverty, and war. While one cannot draw a straight line from basic Christian beliefs to particular stands on these questions, it is true that a knowledge of the Christian Story illumines them and points in a direction where answers may be found.

If the perplexities of the hour argue for the clarification of faith, its possibilities make that task even more urgent. Within some segments of the faith community there is a rising self-confidence about Christian identity, and a corresponding determination to celebrate and share it. Hence the current interest in evangelism. But if we are to get the story *out,* we must first get the story *straight.*

It is important for the Christian community to get the Story straight also because the world is aggressively telling its own tale. Assailed by its messages on every side, it is tempting to believe they are true: that we live on the "mean streets" of the violent and promiscuous film or in the vapid bourgeois suburb of the television commercial, or that we await the impending holocaust without hope or God, on the one hand, or on the other, that we can confidently expect that the virtue and wisdom of the race assures upward mobility for all toward a Disneyland of joy and plenty. To these half-truths and full fictions must be juxtaposed another scenario. It will be strange to the ears and eyes of modernity, a counter-word and counter-vision. The task of Christian Story-telling is to keep alive this set of counter-perceptions so the Church may be what it is and see what it is called to see, rather than be made over in the image of the regnant culture.

This book, therefore, is for those in the community of believers whose intuitions tell them that it is time to repossess their own core visions. As we engage here in the task of recovery and retranslation, we use some of the long-lost language and enter some of the forgotten cob-webbed passageways of ancient Christian thought. The arcane and the underground of Atonement theories and eschatological motifs require an intensity of interest in the fundaments, a theological will and way. This is not a book for browsers. It is for the student of faith, either clergy or lay—particularly those responsible for forming the community of counter-perceptions—who in private study or classroom dialogue is ready for intellectual struggle with ultimate concerns. The religious gurus and philosophical sages avidly read by the frequenter of the shopping mall bookstore expect as much from their devotees. And now the laity of the Church in their pleas for Bible study and examination of the faith issues are sending the message: "No more pap and gruel! Give us some meat." There is work expected here, mastication and digestion. Not the work, however, of the professional cook or connoisseur. The volume carries virtually no footnotes, the apparatus of scholarship is modest, and the exposition of each chapter of the Story is by no means thorough. Further, there are undeveloped themes and neglected areas and assertions that demand much more adequate defense, all of which reflect the author's own struggle and inadequacies, as well as the incommensurability of the project with the space chosen to encompass it. It is the intent of the author that this overview of Christian belief be followed by separate volumes on each basic Christian doctrine. In these individual inquiries deeper probes will be made and the important work of documentation done. What is here suggestive will be there more exhaustive. Despite all that, this study of the range of Christian doctrine grows out of extensive research and long-time reflection and makes its own demands of comprehension.

While this book is primarily "from faith to faith" it can be hoped that just as an interesting building project in mid-city attracts its sidewalk superintendents, so the Church when it is about its business of constructing its basic faith may attract some interested onlookers. Good systematics may be the best apologetics.

My own first perception of both the need and readiness for exploration of the faith prompted a modest effort several years ago in metaphorical Storytelling, "Dawn People." This short tale of the deeds of God from creation to consummation, told in the imagery of light, found its way into the mission training programs of several denominations, onto film, and into the preparatory materials of the Nairobi Assembly of the World Council of Churches. The reception given "Dawn People" strengthened my conviction that work on basic Christian faith needed desperately to be done. While metaphor is a particularly apt way of grasping and communicating faith, as today's exponents of "metaphorical theology" point out, it is also necessary to distill *meaning* from metaphor. Indeed something is always lost in the distillation, for rich imagery, especially in religion, puts us in touch with reality in a way that the more ascetic language of theology cannot. The parables of Jesus, the images of the prophets, the atonement pictures of Paul, and the eschatological symbols of John make that clear. But there is a "truth of the symbol" as well as "symbolic truth," as the philosopher of language, Wilbur Urban, long ago pointed out. We have the obligation to say what we mean as well as sing what we say.

This book explores the meaning in the metaphors. And it does so in a certain orderly way, attempting to see Christian faith as a network of beliefs. As such, it is an effort in *systematic* theology. A frightening phrase! Some reject even the possibility of that kind of careful articulation today, declaring that theology is too much in disarray to be any more than bits and pieces. Others are put off by the hint of over-rationalization in a time when the experiential and visceral are so much to the fore. Extensive testing of the materials of this book among students, clergy, and laity makes me believe otherwise. This is a ripe time for going beyond both timid *ad hoc* theologizing and too easy acquiescence to the feeling fads of the day. Mindlessness is no Christian virtue. But this volume is obviously not an architectonic presentation of Christian belief. It is an outline of the rudiments of faith, a "mini-systematic," for those who want a working knowledge of the reference points of Christian conviction.

CORING

Martin Marty suggests that the task of the Church has to do with both "coring and caring." Clarity about the ABC's of faith, telling the Christian Story, is what we are about here, the *coring* mandate. But is there really a core of Christian faith? The bewildering variety of current assertions as to what Christianity really consists of seems to indicate otherwise. Moreover, both the biblical scholar and the church historian regularly point out the diversity of belief in both Scripture and Christian tradition. There seems to be a multiplicity of stories rather than *a* Christian Story. The strong sense of relativity that marks our time, the assumption that what we believe is rooted and shaped by who we are and where we come from, makes any talk about a common core suspect. Pluralism is the order of the day. The most that many are willing to affirm is a theology from a particular ethnic, sexual, geographic, or social-economic perspective.

The truth in this perspectival view of Christian belief we shall attempt to honor in our conception of this effort as *a translation*. It is a recounting of the Christian Story from one angle of vision, not from a God's-eye point of view. Its language and accents are those of a particular time and place. We shall examine what this idiom is in the next section on the *how* of theology.

However, we do not assume here that basic Christian belief is mired in one's stream of history, nor can it be servile before pluralism. There is an out-thereness of biblical truth which is to be seen, whatever the angle of vision, and however our view of it is affected by the glasses we are wearing. There is an object with which our subjectivity deals. There is a Story which our translation seeks to communicate. There is a hard core of affirmation at the center of our perceptions and interpretations.

In times of perplexity and possibility in Christian history renewed efforts are made both to locate the outlines of this Story and to translate it into the concerns and language of the day. In the second century when the Church was beset by pressures from within and without to set forth its identity, there emerged a "rule of faith," a simple statement of the fundamentals for those making a first profession of faith, and for the general purpose of distinguishing between the basic Christian vision and its distortions. Later, this time in the midst of debate about the uniqueness of Christ, the Council of Nicea drew up some definitive articles of belief. From these two epochs of clarification we have the Apostles' Creed and the Nicene Creed. Subsequent eras produced their own statements of the Story. All bear the marks of the time in which they were formed, from the substance philosophy that influences ancient confessions to the masculine language that dates many modern credos. But the translations and accommodations circle around and return to a core of conviction. It is made up of refrains that run through the charter of the Christian religion, the Bible, and recur in the classic and contemporary formulations of faith. They represent the abiding skeletal framework for the flesh and blood of any statement of faith.

In the most elementary of terms these refrains are the chapter headings of the Christian Story: Creation, Fall, Covenant, Christ, Church, Salvation, Consummation, with their Prologue and Epilogue, God. These are the acts in the Christian drama, the chapters in the Story, the exposition of which constitutes the beliefs of the Christian faith. They might be diagramed simply by the varied relationship of two lines representing the main characters in this story, God and the world:

God brings the world into being, the stretching of one line toward the other as captured in Michelangelo's painting of God's reach toward Adam, Creation:

The response of the world is the rejection of the divine invitation, the Fall, the juxtaposition of the lines:

The re-call of God, the new reach of the Creator toward creation, takes place in the Covenant with Israel:

The depth of human alienation requires a correspondingly deep plunge into a resisting world issuing in the suffering Love at the center of human history, Jesus Christ.

The New Age from Christ to the End is the time of the Church, salvation, and consummation, when that drama through which we now are living thrusts toward the intended unity of God and the world.

Described in the language we shall use to translate the Christian Story, the saga so portrayed runs from the *reach* of vision toward reality, through *the polarization* of vision and reality, the *connection* of vision and reality, the *intersection* of vision and reality, to the *convergence* of vision and reality. And the fundamental beliefs of the Christian faith we shall explore in terms of the chapters of this tale: Prologue, Creation, Fall, Covenant, Jesus Christ, Church, Salvation, Consummation, Epilogue.

That there is a God who creates, reconciles, and redeems the world is the Storyline in its bare bones. But there is a body of belief as well as a skeletal structure. The creation of the world by God entails a conviction about the goodness of nature, the dignity of humanity, and the freedom to respond to the divine invitation. The fall of the world means the abuse of the freedom granted to us, with effects everywhere to be seen in the estrangements in humanity and the groaning of creation. The liberation and reconciliation of a broken world mean a covenant to bind up the wounds, an Incarnation to deal firsthand with recalcitrance, a struggling, suffering, death, and resurrection that bring at-one-ment to alienation, the birth of a community that participates in and serves the new freedom and points to the healing power released into history and the cosmos, and the promise of a coming of the final victory for the purposes of God. This is the flesh and blood that covers the bones. To know who we are is to be familiar with this body of faith as it is set forth in the biblical language and preserved in the tradition of the church universal. The work of theology is the exploration of the *what* of the matter.

TRANSLATION

When this core Christian Story is told in a given time and place, it is always related in the language of that setting. The worldview of the era and its particular issues and sensibilities shape how the narrative is set forth and heard. That version of the Story will also influence the accent given to one or another chapter, as well as the manner in which the message in its entirety is communicated. In the science of an earlier century the *how* and *when* of creation and consummation will be conceived in a fashion very different from the cosmology of this day. And in the society of another time and place the issues that are to the fore may be quite different from our own, calling forth from the body of Christian belief different themes and adapting the thought forms of the time to express those themes. We shall speak more about this in discussing the perspective from which the Story is viewed. The crucial task of translation is to find ways in each generation and location to bring the basic convictions of the Christian faith into the thought world of its hearers. Following the analogy of the human organism, the body must be clothed, fed, and housed with materials available in the land in which it seeks to live.

Translation does not mean rewriting the Christian Story. In the zeal to be understood it is sometimes tempting to make this strange Tale fit snugly into the stories with which the new land is already familiar. When this happens, faith's perceptions of life, death, and destiny become just another way of saying what is already believed by the philosophy, politics, economics, science, poetry, and common sense of a particular time and place. We thus eliminate the radical, the disturbing, the unmanageable in the Christian faith by fitting it into our terms. The awesome biography of God becomes our autobiography. The Stranger settles in as a pliant citizen of our country who not only knows our language but also adopts our ways.

While requiring translation, the Gospel is always distanced from our ways, always a norm to which we are accountable, never subservient to our agenda. To know this critical line between translation and accommodation is the art of authentic communication.

Packed into the word *translation* is much more than the idea of a verbal crossover. Translation surely includes the employment of other terms to convey the meaning of the Christian saga. But this language is rooted in profound experience. To tell the Christian Story in one way rather than another is to ask the hearer to relate it to the agonies and ecstasies that have marked the era in which we live and to connect it with deeply shared premises and perceptions. As the recounting of the Story in its biblical form strives for inclusiveness of all its chapters, so this translation attempts to be an ecumenical one that honors the richness of contemporary experience. Thus when "freedom" is referred to as a way of understanding one aspect of the vision God has for the world, it includes liberation from the enslavements experienced in our time by the black, the poor, the woman, the Third World, the "in-the-middle" citizen, the liberation of the individual from personal and spiritual oppressions that characterize our era, and beyond that the freedom of nature from its technological tyrants.

Whether one's translation of the Gospel is really heard and understood by those who speak the intended language depends on how deeply the translator is really immersed in that world and has learned its idiom. Has the communicator lived and suffered and rejoiced alongside those with whom the word of faith is being shared? Telling the Christian Story *of* liberation is best done from *within* the contemporary struggles for liberation.

To strive for an ecumenical translation is particularly demanding. One cannot be a native of all the lands in which one seeks to live—black, red, white, brown, female, male, young, old, First, Second, Third, and Fourth Worlds. That fact, and the heightened sense of particularity which characterizes contemporary Christian thought, has produced a spate of perspectival theologies—black, feminist, Third World. While our finitude precludes what eternity promises—"neither male nor female"—the universal vision of the Kingdom calls us to participate as deeply as possible in the places where that Kingdom is making its presence felt. While we cannot *be* native, we can *go* native. We can do our theology in and with those who are struggling to be free and reconciled. When that involvement takes place, the reflection that rises out of it bears the marks of authenticity. And when that engagement is wide-ranging, then the catholicity of experience is productive of ecumenical translation.

Translation means that we go native, "in all things *but* faith and morals." This addendum from classical missionary lore distinguishes translation from accommodation. Because the freedom of the Kingdom of God is not just another word for the going perception of freedom—current liberation movements, whether political, personal, or ecological—the effort to translate means the need to transmute as well. Thus freedom becomes, in translation, liberation from *sin* and *death,* as well as liberation from the political, social, and economic powers of evil that afflict a generation. Authentic translation finds the points of contact with contemporary sensibility, but it also seeks to enlarge the meanings of the language of the new land by infusion of fresh perception from the biblical faith.

What then is the systematic theology we undertake in these pages? It is ordered reflection that seeks to elaborate and render intelligible the faith of the Christian community. It is the explication and interpretation of the chapters of the Christian Story.

Whether we both state and translate the Christian Story responsibly depends on how we go about our task. The matter of procedure, the "how to," is the question of theological method. This is more than the way we arrange the subject matter. In that simplest sense we use here the story form of organizing Christian belief. We employ a narrative method of theology. More basically, method has to do with what we rely upon for setting forth the Christian faith. What are the sources and standards of Christian belief? How do we *get to* the Christian faith? This is the question *of authority*. Because of the erosion today of some of the traditional religious centers of authority—the Bible and the chief spokespersons of the church or traditions—the issue of authority has become an insistent one. In fact a good deal of contemporary theology is so preoccupied with this question that its attention to the *what* beyond the *how* is minimal. While this book gives primary attention to the what of Christian belief, it must also honor the importance in our day of the issues of authority and its tandem question *revelation*. Authority deals with the identity and revelation with the veracity of the Christian faith. We cannot discuss one without assumptions about and references to the other, but they are distinguishable aspects of the question of theological method. We begin here with an inquiry into the authority for the Story we have to tell.

AUTHORITY

What are the authoritative materials for the work of theology? Where do we go for the Story we have to tell? How do we pursue the goal of communicating the Christian faith in the language and thought forms of our time?

There are five elements to the answer we give to that question in these pages. 1) First and fundamentally, we go to the *source* of the Story, the Scriptures of the Old and New Testaments. 2) As an aid in interpreting the Scriptures we make use of a *resource,* the life and lore of the Church, or the traditions of the Christian community. 3) Whatever exploration is made of source and resource goes on in the *setting* of the world of our experience. 4) Informing and organizing the matter in which we relate source, resource, and setting is our angle of vision or *perspective.* 5) The *goal* at which we aim is the faithful and intelligible articulation of the Gospel. Describing these in terms of our narrative image, we may say that our goal is to tell the Story, our source is the Storybook, our resource is the Storytellers, our setting is Storyland, and our perspective is the translation key. The elements in this authority structure can be portrayed in this way.

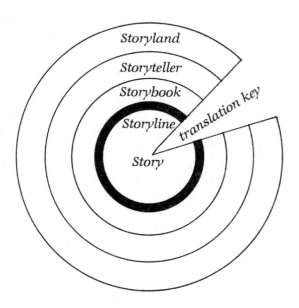

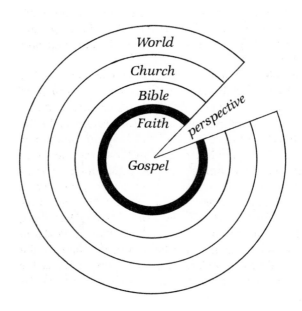

Let us take a closer look at the circles and components and at how they are related to each other.

The Bible as Source

The ultimate source of the Christian Story is the Scriptures of the Old and New Testaments. (The apocryphal material is "edifying for the people of God," as ecumenical statements have it.) Our theological work begins and ends in this canon, which emerged in the early centuries from the Christian community as it struggled with its identity, and which it has since maintained as the fundamental reference point of Christian doctrine.

The authority of the Bible rests in its testimony to the decisive events in the faith narrative. Here we learn about both their happening and their meaning. In its role as recorder and interpreter, the Bible is part of these redemptive events themselves. As such, the Scriptures are agents of liberation and reconciliation, and therefore the work of the Spirit (Rom. 16:25–26). The relationship of inspiration to revelation we shall investigate in the following section. For the time being, we note that the authority of the Scripture is grounded in its gift of disclosure.

The authority of disclosure is inseparable from the nature of what is disclosed. The Storybook exists to tell the Story (II Tim. 3:15–16). It is not an encyclopedia of general knowledge authoritative in matters of physics and chemistry, astronomy and geology, sociology and psychology. It borrows the language and thought forms of its own time to state the Christian faith. One of the artful evasions of the Word to be heard and the Vision to be seen in this Book is to use it for purposes for which it is not designed. This is the error of "Bible-believing" fundamentalism. The Gospel is not to be confused with the multifarious and changing accounts of the processes and patterns of cosmic and human life. For information about these we turn to the natural and human sciences and not to the book of the Story. On the other hand, no modernity adept at making this point about the Bible as earthen vessel with its transient thought forms should cause us to fall into the other trap of relativizing all the perceptions of the Bible and replacing them with the categories of contemporary experience. Thus we are faced with the delicate task of identifying the abiding and distinguishing it from the transient.

The perennial truth to be found in the Scriptures has to do with the Storyline to be found within the Storybook, the chapters from creation to consummation that provide the framework for theology. This is the "apostolic teaching" set forth by the first generations in the Christian community in their debate with competing ideologies. Within the various rules of faith that emerged as baptismal formulae in the early congregations, there is a discernible body of belief which gave identity to this community. While the particular listing of the elements of that teaching is influenced by the perspective of those times, these formulae do trace the outlines of the Christian saga. It is along this biblical Storyline that Christian theology does its work.

Apostolicity was the criterion of the New Testament canon. Critical scholarship has demonstrated that these writings cannot be thought of as the simple report of one or another apostle. But the rationale for the inclusion of this book rather than that one is its reliable transmission of original apostolic testimony. The layers of subsequent tradition have not obscured the proclamation of salvation, and its apostolic authority therefore remains.

The apostolic testimony to the central acts in the Christian drama, the deliverance wrought in the life, ministry, death, and resurrection of Christ, is the prism through which the light of biblical revelation is to be seen and understood. Thus the seventy-seven percent of the Book that is the Hebrew Bible, our Old Testament, is to be understood within its New Testament context. How the law and the prophets are appropriated in the Christian faith is determined by how their promise is illumined and fulfilled in the New Testament. The full depth of the Fall and the full width and length of the Covenant are measured from a future vantage point. The Word of God, enfleshed in Jesus Christ and interpreted by the eye and ear witnesses to the Incarnation, is the center from which the whole range of biblical data, the whole work of the eternal Logos from creation through covenant to consummation is perceived.

To describe the Bible as the source of the Story could mean that Christian thought starts with this material, or does its work with an eye on its origin, or uses it to provide the symbols of this tradition, but then takes off on the wings of human experience to spin out more adventurous themes. Our conception of the source, however, is more encompassing. Faith is grounded in and *returns to* this orientation. The source of faith is also the *norm* of faith. The Scriptures of the Old and New Testaments, apostolically understood, are the guardian of faith, the checkpoint, the place of adjudication of theological assertions. Although the Christian Story must be constantly retranslated into new categories, implicit themes rendered explicit, all claims made to the telling of the Christian Story must finally be shown to be consonant with, and a faithful interpretation of, the biblical source and norm.

A commitment to the Bible as norm can be misleading if it is not understood in the context of earlier remarks about the apostolic teaching. The Bible is the norm touching the fundamentals of faith, the Christian Story. These basic affirmations within the Scriptures—those having to do with the being and doing of the God who purposes and achieves in Jesus Christ the liberation and reconciliation of all things—constitute the apostolic norm within the great variety of materials that make up the Bible. This set of perceptions, these defining characteristics, constitute the "canon within the canon." Hence, in our diagrams of the rings of authority there is a dark line that represents the inmost edge of the biblical circle, the Storyline within the Storybook, "the faith" within the Bible. In order to tell the Christian Story responsibly, our translations must be judged by this definitive expression of the biblical norm. Here, as we shall indicate in the discussion of revelation, is the reliable testimony of the eyewitnesses to the deeds of God, those who by the eye of sight view the decisive events and by the eye of faith perceive their inner meaning.

The Church as Resource

"How are they to hear without a preacher?" asks Paul (Rom. 10:14). How can the Vision be seen without a seer? Preachers and seers are not only the ordained and gifted, but the whole Christian community wherever it helps to unstop our deaf ears and open our blind eyes. The improvement of our hearing and the sharpening of our sight come from the people of God, past and present. The fathers and mothers of faith bequeath us the result of their own struggle to hear and see, and the brothers and sisters, our present companions in the Church, also make for clearer hearing and seeing. This gift of the Christian community comes to us in creed and council, catechism and confession, dialogue and proclamation. It meets us in the ancient lore of the Church and the present learnings of the Christian community. This common life and its wisdom, brought to us by the constant activity of the Holy Spirit, is a fundamental resource in our engagement with the biblical source.

By identifying the Church as resource and by placing it within the second ring of authority, we recognize its accountability to the Bible. The Church precedes the Scriptures, chronologically. But by its own choice, in creating the canon to which it is responsible, the Church itself has given the Scriptures theological precedence. The formulations of the Church do their work when they elaborate and translate the Story found in the Storybook in the thought forms of the day, thus building a tradition invaluable for understanding the fullness of that primal Tale. One can think of how the tradition is built by using the metaphor of a face perceived from different angles. The Christian community views its Gospel from a different perspective in each age and thus adds a new angle of vision enriching our perception of the physiognomy of faith. Whatever the fresh perspective discerns of the features must always be tested against the core narrative it finds in the Scriptures. But without the response to the Holy Spirit's fresh movement in history by the living Church, the truth that is ever breaking forth from the Holy Word is not heard.

The World as Setting

From the original perception and transmission of the Christian Story by the biblical authors to the present communication of the Gospel in our own time, the ideas, feelings, and attitudes of the world make their presence felt. The very texture of the language we use to preach and teach influences what we say. And the Gospel itself is formulated in the thought patterns of the day and age in which it is articulated—from its understanding of the stars and stones to its view of the soul and society. The world in which we work and play, think and feel, suffer and struggle, live and die, is the setting in which our own theology is done. Its language, its frameworks of thought (scientific to philosophical), its living issues (economic to ecological), and its moral and religious experiences all make their contribution to the translation process of Storytelling. If we vainly repeat the Christian themes of another age, we are not faithful to the Holy Spirit's work of bringing new awareness of need and new expressions of truth to our own day. So the world is the *context* for understanding and interpreting the *text* of the Tale.

The position of the world on the circumference of authority means two things. First, all translations of the Story cannot help being that—*translations* in the idiom of the particular time. We cannot jump out of our skins. It is simple honesty to recognize the influence of the contemporary language and thought which we use. Second, we must use the best tools available, not disdaining the instruments the Spirit puts in our hands: the best of our moral, spiritual, intellectual, and aesthetic capabilities and experiences cannot be scorned by the Storyteller; the living issues into which God plunges us in our time cannot be isolated from the Story that continues to unfold in this history moving under God toward its End. In this double sense, therefore, the world is a presence in our authority structure.

The world is the most distant ring from the Story. This fact is disclosed by the Tale itself, for the state of the world is the occasion for the deeds of God. A stumbling and fallen world fails to see and pursue the Vision of God. In that blindness a new Light has shined to which Scripture and tradition attest. Yet even in the Fall the power of natural light is not altogether destroyed, and in a world now redeemed the flashes of the Spirit can light up even a darkened landscape. Open to these possibilities, the structure of Christian authority makes room by the role of *setting* for the experiences and ideas of the contemporary world.

Reductionism

We cannot leave the subject of authority without passing reference to the vulnerability of each of these rings. The power of each has exercised a fascination in Christian history which has lent itself to inordinate claims. The preeminence of the biblical ring has given rise to *biblicism* which severs it from the other rings and claims it to be the sole route to the Gospel. Thus the lively presence of the Spirit in the Church and the world is denied. Correspondingly there emerge among those impressed by the deliverances or vitalities of creed or council, bishop or preacher, charismatic or community, some who insist that the Church alone is to be heard on ultimate matters. So appears *ecclesiasticism* which either denies partnership with source and setting or calls into question the fundamental charter of the community. And finally, the worldly matrix in which Christians find themselves—the opinions, current sensibilities, regnant philosophies, moral and spiritual experiences—becomes so alluring that the world defines the faith, and the Bible and Church become marginal. Thus *secularism* both disdains its companions in the quest for the truth, the Christian community and its Book, and replaces the biography of God with its own autobiography.

The elements of authority do their work in getting the Story straight when they are bound together, and when each is honored for the gift it brings to the rest—a source, resource, and setting.

Perspective

The final element in the design of authority is its *perspective*. In diverse times and places in Christian history there emerges one or another way of looking at the Christian Story which affects what is seen. That perspective is shaped by the questions being struggled with in a particular setting, its unique sensibilities, values, and philosophies. At worst, a perspective tends to impose on the Christian Story those contemporary agendas and perceptions, and thus widely misses its target. At best, it seeks to respond to the real questions and understandings of an era, passing them through the disciplines of the Church's life and traditions, and ultimately bringing them under the scrutiny of Scripture itself. In this process the questions posed by an era are themselves transmuted, and the answers will be those that rise out of the Story, rather than the voice of the world hearing itself return unchanged except for the preacher's holy tone.

The form a perspective takes can vary. It can be the modest use of a term from the world which has resonance in the faith community—"Logos" in the early Fathers' dialogue with ancient culture, or "homoousios" to interpret the unity of Jesus with God in Nicea's statement about the meaning of Christ. Or it may be represented by a fighting word which the Church writes on its banners in the struggle with the errors and oppressions of its time—"justification by faith" in sixteenth-century Europe, "liberation" in Third World countries today. Sometimes a slogan, at other times a carefully worked out set of commitments to the meaning of the Gospel for that time—these kinds of visions attempt to relate and even restate the Christian faith, seeking in the process to be faithful to the Christian Story. On yet a more ambitious scale, the Christian faith will be reformulated wholesale in terms of either a dominant cultural premise or a powerful philosophy or political ideology. In the former case, an Enlightenment Christianity seeks accommodation with modernity, or a secular Christianity seeks to redo the Christian Story in essentially this-worldly terms. In the latter case, the philosophy of Aristotle in the high Middle Ages or existentialism and process thought in our own day have been offered as frameworks for reinterpreting the whole of Christian faith.

One of the lessons in this variety of experimentation in perspective seems to be that the more exuberant and encompassing efforts in restatement—by either cultural premise or philosophical reformulation—carry with them a tendency to domesticate the Christian faith in the categories of the time, rendering it incapable of doing the critical work it must do vis-à-vis that time, and eroding the Story's own distinguishing features. The art of perspective therefore is to learn to *relate* but not to *capitulate* to the culture out of which that perspective grows.

Uneasiness about the tendency toward captivity to the world in the history of perspectives has prompted some to reject the need for this kind of principle of interpretation, putting in its place the assertion that all that is required is the simple setting forth of the Story from the Storybook. This is an understandable reaction to the manifest dangers of skewing faith in the interests of being understood and acceptable. However, there is a hollow ring to such formal declarations of independence from cultural influence. The feeling tones, premises, and even philosophical themes of the worldly matrix in which all theology takes place still exercise an influence on those would-be escapees from the facts of theological finitude. To ignore the context simply means the importing of many unexamined assumptions from the world into theology without benefit of close scrutiny and critique. Better an examined perspective than an unexamined one. Better, too, modest relationships to cultural creativity than wholesale adaptation to the culture's fevers and philosophies, with its attendant captivity of faith.

What we are calling *perspective* functions as a principle of selection and organization of biblical material, formed from these materials and relating them to the tradition and contemporary experience. While it gives contemporaneity to the Bible, it is, however, *not* a canon in the sense of passing judgment on the biblical materials, being ultimately answerable to this source and norm. Perspective suggests not only the formative nature of a point of view, but also its relativity.

We turn now to our own perspective for this particular translation of the Christian Story, seeking to identify modest but meaningful cultural awarenesses to which our theology must be alert. In identifying these, we make an attempt to formulate them with sensitivity to our cultural setting and in responsibility to the biblical source and churchly resource. A viable principle of interpretation will open up the Story to be found in Scripture and tradition, but in such a way that it may be seen by and speak to the people of this time and place.

Vision

Out of the Christian community's experience in the contemporary world rise some motifs and metaphors that enable us to communicate the Christian Story with special power. These ideas and words must be tested in dialogue with Scripture and Christian tradition. The themes that follow have gone through that kind of three-way conversation. The fact that the language of the culture and the Christian community converge in these images gives them special viability. But translation is not a simple phonetic crossover, for usage in the Christian Story enlarges, enriches, and transfigures the meaning of the metaphors.

Several modern developments provide the background for the choice of our idiom. One is the dramatic appearance and universal impact of the new *visual* media of our era. We do not have to accept all the exuberant claims made by the prophets of our electronic environment to recognize the phenomenal spread and influence of just one of those new forms of communication, television. Across the globe, and especially in technologically developed countries, a generation has grown up with its psyche shaped by the images and messages received through this medium. And to this can be added a range of other potent visual forces from film, art, and architectural form, to the political, social, and personal deed. Without succumbing to a nonverbal ideology, it is possible to honor the formative power of things visual in this epoch.

Alongside of, and in some way probably shaped by the visual, are the *visionary* phenomena. The second half of the twentieth century has been characterized by the emergence of persons and movements driven by vast hopes and dreams. For the array of new nations it has been the time of rising expectations. For those of oppressed class, race, sex, age, and condition it has been a period of striding toward freedom. And together, weighed down by the perils of war and the threat of world cataclysm, many and varied peoples have raised a cry for peace. Even nature seems to have joined in the dream of a ceasefire against its rhythms and patterns with a nascent ecological revolution. This new kind of hoping received poignant expression when Martin Luther King, Jr., declared in the 1963 March on Washington, "I have a dream!" While the frustration of these hopes has turned some of these dreams and dreamers away from the historical horizon and inward and underground in the direction of mystical or spiritual visions—the effect of the resisting reality which confronts the vision of fulfillment—the lure of the horizon ahead has marked our era.

The visual and the visionary, the sight of the outer and inner eye, combine to make *vision* an image and idea available for interpreting Christian faith.[1] It is an apt one for such use not only

1. H. Richard Niebuhr associates the vision of God with the contemplative-rational-Greek tradition in Christian thought, in contrast to the prophetic–Hebrew theme of "the Kingdom of God" (*The Kingdom of God in America*, New York: Harper & Bros., 1937, pp. 20–21). While our interpretation of vision and dream here is taken from a decidedly historical usage—the vision of God *is* the Kingdom of God—and does not depend on the *visio Dei* tradition in theology and spirituality, it is interesting to note the case made by A. H. Curtis for the biblical meaning of the term *vision* (A. H. Curtis, *The Vision and Mission of Jesus*, Edinburgh: T. & T. Clark, 1954). He shows that in the Old and New Testaments the presence of vision is always conjoined to a summons and commission to action.

because it suggests a deep modern sensibility, but because it is a refrain within the Christian tradition itself. Its power as a bridge theme is related to its explicit appearance in the dreams and prophecies of the Old Testament—particularly the projections of future hope in the prophetic tradition—and in the New Testament—particularly the future-oriented visions in Jesus' teaching about the Kingdom of God and in John's Apocalypse. And the visual motif receives just as strong an accent as the visionary in the central events of the Christian Story, the historical acts of God from Exodus to Easter and Pentecost. It is the motif-metaphor of vision, therefore, that provides the form into which affirmations about Christian faith are poured. As such it is the *formal principle* of interpreting the Christian Story in our time.

Vision takes its meaning in these pages from both the cultural usage and the prophetic and eschatological traditions of the Bible. Vision is picturing with the eye of the mind a desirable future state of affairs. It projects on the screen of the future the day when the wolf and the lamb will lie down together. A vision is an imaginative leap into the Not Yet, an internal perception of a scene of fulfillment often portrayed in rich metaphor. Thus the yearnings of the culture and the hopes of biblical faith can be expressed in the language of vision. It must be noted that on the borders of both spheres is the association of vision with the uncanny and even necromantic. It is not the preternatural that controls our usage here, but the prophetic. The seer points toward the *hoped-for* tomorrow and calls the people to it. That this kind of portrayal of the future by the biblical seer is indeed a discernment of the promise as well as the purpose of God is intrinsic to our Story, and therefore vision in its profoundest sense is *foresight*.

Vision happens in the light that makes seeing possible. As vision and light are inseparable, so these are actively related metaphors in Christian thought. In fact, light is a pervasive image in the Bible, theology, liturgy, hymnody, and devotion. In our translation of the Christian Story, we shall therefore make use of *light* as a secondary metaphor.[2]

2. Its association with the theme of vision, its importance as a Christian image ("God is light"—I John 1:5), its prominence in the history of religion, and its wide presence in contemporary culture prompt us to use light as a secondary metaphor. However, it must be scrutinized and

The employment of vision does not preclude the use and power of another metaphor-motif which has been so important to Christian communication: word. "Hearing the Word" does not conflict with "seeing the Vision." It is no accident that in the Gutenberg epoch the print-verbal-auditory configuration should become the most important way the Christian faith is both presented and interpreted. The Reformation with its commitment to the written and spoken Word and its affirmation that "faith comes by hearing" was a natural correlate to deep and wide cultural forces and technological capabilities. These forces are still with us, much more so than the clichés of nonverbalism are willing to grant. More important, word and hearing aspects of the Christian Story are integral to its statement to human beings for whom intellect and audition are defining characteristics.

But for this epoch informed by the visual and visionary, the companion biblical image of vision must come into its own. As Christian consciousness expands to give recognition to the riches in its own tradition of vision, it will also be better equipped to tell its Story, to share its vision with its contemporaries.

Part of enlarging our awareness includes the reinterpretation of key resources in the Christian tradition. One that is related to the question of vision and audition is "Logos." As appropriated by recent Christian thought, and in the Reformation tradition as a whole, it comes to us meaning "word." As such it has performed and continues to perform a valuable role interpreting the meaning of Christ, the significance of the Bible, and even the character of theology as *theou logos.* There are, however, other nuances to this ancient term (Philo uses over 1300 variations). And more important, as the meaning of it must come in Christian thought from Christ himself, there is another way of translating it in a contemporary rendition of the Christian Story. Alongside of the traditional reading of Logos as eternal Word of God, we shall interpret this classic term, thought of originally as the architect's plan of the

---

employed with a sensitivity to racist abuse. Racism has made the simple equation: light=white and dark=black. We do not accept this equation any more than the preaching and praying of black churches do, for there and here darkness and light are distinguished from black which is beautiful and white which is ambiguous. Light is not white, but the full spectrum of color, and darkness is not black but the absence of light.

universe, as the eternal *Vision of God*. The exploration of this will be done in our Prologue to the Christian Story, as we try to understand the Trinity. Here we simply note it as an example of mutually supportive rather than mutually exclusive perceptions of the Christian tradition. Thus a change in perspective complements and enriches earlier statements of Christian faith made from other angles of vision.

Liberation and Reconciliation

We have a vision. But what do we see? The form of Christian faith must be filled with content. To the formal principle of vision must be added the material principle of *liberation and reconciliation*. It is this twin theme of liberation and reconciliation that supplies our translation key to the classic teachings of Christian faith. And what is true of the form is true of the content: translation means that the experiences and ideas that give substance to liberation and reconciliation in the modern world provide the beginning but not the end of our perspective. The world's interpretation of freedom and peace, liberty and solidarity, are transformed by the understanding of them in Scripture and Christian tradition.

But why *this* vision and not another? In accord with the concept of authority developed earlier, a perspective is viable when by the power of the Holy Spirit it rises out of contemporary experience, is tested by the traditions and life of the Church, and is legitimated by Scripture. In this process, indeed, the motif undergoes change, as in this case the meaning of liberation and reconciliation is deepened in its dialogue with the source and resource of the Christian faith. The emergence of a perspective is not the use of current ideology or popular jargon for Christian purposes, as when the "leader principle" was offered as a way of communicating Christianity in a Nazi setting. The cultural idiom must have some inner connection to the commitments of the Christian Story. From Exodus to Easter the themes of freedom and solidarity make contact with events in the biblical epic, as they do also with specific interpretations of the meaning of its central chapter (Luke 4:18; Rom. 5:8–11; Gal. 5:1; Eph. 2:16; Col. 1:20), even as they are enlarged in these encounters.

The worldwide struggle against economic, political, and social tyranny has brought the idea of liberation forcefully to the consciousness of our time. The Third World thrust to establish its identity free from the domination of both the First and Second Worlds has given greatest currency to the word, and in Christian thought has given rise to "liberation theology." In this demand for liberation the quest for bread, justice, and deliverance from class oppression comes forcefully to the center. But there are places where the freedom from want has been won and the liberation from political tyranny is a battle yet to be undertaken. And in countries that boast of political freedom, the struggle against racial injustice discloses another dimension of the liberation mandate. To this has been added the reach for freedom by women long submerged by masculine hegemonies. The vision of "release to the captives" (Luke 4:18 RSV), however, has in our time been stretched beyond the horizons of class, race, and sex to include the maltreated prisoner, the disinherited aged, and the forgotten handicapped, all of whom suffer their own form of economic, political, and social exploitation. Liberation in its fullest sense is the work of the Lord which, as Mary celebrated it, "put down the mighty from their thrones, and exalted those of low degree" (Luke 1:52 RSV). Liberation has the eyes to see *"all* sorts and conditions" of invisible human beings, those whose low degree puts them beneath the threshold of conventional sight. Liberation is the deliverance of all these captives, a vision that cannot be foreshortened to partisanship for only one or another victim of dehumanization. It is this inclusive understanding that we draw upon here as a working tool of translation.

The struggle for liberation extends also into the psychological and biological arenas. Thus there is a dream that we can be free of age-old personal anxieties and physical debilities with dramatic new therapies and medical and biomedical resources. Further, freedom of the natural environment from the tyranny of pollution and the anarchy in its own processes is a compelling vision of the day. Environmentalists warn us of the disastrous ruin of our air, water, and soil and the wastage of our irreplaceable natural resources. Technologists, meanwhile, offer paradisaical promises of the harnessing of nature's powers and the restraint of its tumultuous tendencies. While the interests of these two groups often clash, they are at one in the envisioning of possibilities of the liberation of nature's power and glory.

Sometimes bashful while liberation is bold, at other times in reversed prominence, the theme of reconciliation keeps it company. The two intertwined commitments can, in fact, on occasion be made to mean the same thing. Thus the "freedom revolution" of the 1960's in the United States was understood to mean the reconciliation of white and black as well as the liberation of black citizens. "Life together" is part of the vision that moves many in this generation. Disavowing a premature integration in which the strong attempt to absorb the yet-to-be-free, liberation movements have made it clear that any reconciliation worthy of the name will be the coming together of equals. Reconciliation must, therefore, presuppose liberation. But liberation movements in their advanced stages also know that freedom is freedom *for* as well as freedom *from.* Freedom for the other means that we are called to be *free to be together.* Those who have thrown off their shackles and established their identity have the power to *reach out.* That stretching toward the other in freedom is the reach to overcome estrangement, the reconciliation of the alienated.

The quest for reconciliation is most visible in the struggle to end war, whether it be the fires that rage in a nation, turmoil between religions or races, or the threat of international nuclear conflagration. But it is present as well in the search for internal wholeness and the overcoming of the divided self in the multifarious movements of spiritual healing. And the crusade for ecological wholeness is yet another sign of the universal longing for the unity of all creation that is deep in the modern psyche.

Reconciliation takes its place alongside of liberation as part of the vision that emerges in contemporary experience. As a point of contact for Christian faith it connects with the biblical vision which is decisive for our translation of the Christian Story. The word we shall use for the biblical vision is *Shalom* (Ezek. 34:25–29). While its meaning must appear in the actual recounting of the narrative of the deeds of God, we identify it here by our key terms. Shalom is the liberation (Luke 4:18; Gal. 5:1) and reconciliation (Rom. 5:8–11; II Cor. 5:18–21) of all things. It is *freedom from sin, evil, and death* and *the reconciliation of God, humanity, and nature.* Found originally in the prophetic pictures of a liberated and reconciled world, and climactically in the eschatological hopes of the New Testament, Shalom envisages the end of every bondage and the overcoming of each alienation. As such, Shalom begins with the personal, societal, and natural perceptions of liberation and reconciliation which mark our culture and transfigures them by both a deepening of perception regarding the source of these slaveries and estrangements and a lengthening of the vision of their resolution toward the future of God. To this end our Story presses.

Reality

While the seeing of visions and the dreaming of dreams has characterized this generation, so also has the experience of living with these hopes in the midst of intractable realities. As the expectation of "freedom now!" has grown, so also has the peril to it. A case can be made for the picture of our times as a succession of the hopeful 1960's by the hopeless 1970's. Many of those who believed they saw a blazing light at the end of the corridor, an open door to the future, and rushed toward it in excited anticipation have crashed into its hard resisting wood and now sit stunned at the threshold believing that there is no way out. They crouch looking for the light in the neomysticisms and neopietisms of the hour. And not a few in the culture follow them in their own way, preoccupied with the facts of evil and the presence of the demonic, or hypnotized by the issues of death and dying. Many in the late twentieth century seem to have taken Edith Wharton's advice: "Look not at visions but realities."[3]

The grounds for this surge of realism lie in the frustration of the hopes and hopers of a visionary period by the very real assaults upon them. Sign and symbol of the collision of vision and reality are the murders of the visionaries themselves. Among those felled by the assassin's bullet were the one who had a summer dream and

---

3. The term *reality* is to be understood here in its relationship to the word *vision,* and therefore in its simplest dictionary meaning. *Webster's New Collegiate Dictionary* (Springfield, Massachusetts: G. C. Merriam Company, 1973, p. 1308) itself cites the Edith Wharton quotation with this understanding of reality in its definition of vision. Similarly, the word may be understood in the tradition of biblical realism (Reinhold Niebuhr). The term *reality* refers to the empirical givens. Thus its usage here is to be distinguished from a philosophical or religious usage in which its reference is ontological, or the "really real," or "unseen reality," or ultimate Reality. In this latter sense it is the Vision which is itself Reality located as it is in the Godhead.

another who declared, "I dream of things that never were and say, why not?" And falling alongside of them were the too sanguine expectations for peace and freedom.

Both the hopes and the frustrations extend far beyond the more visible political and social struggles of the hour. For as time wore on and the measure of utopianism in all its expressions was taken—from personal and interpersonal salvation promised by encounter group or commune and biological or technological utopia forecast by technocrats or futurists—a hard realism appeared regarding the ambiguities and impossibilities that plague all human ventures. Suspicion too has set in about the claims of politician and priest, a zeal to discover their Achilles' heel and thus confirm the skeptic's disdain for visions and accredit the paralysis of will.

Any interpretation of the Christian Story that connects with the sensibilities of this age will have to come to terms with the fact of frustrated hopes and the widespread perception that the future is at worst disastrous and at best ambiguous. Thus its talk of vision must be joined to its profoundest understanding of reality, and its fullest perspective must be vision *and* reality. As with envisioning so with realism—its own translation will be also a transmutation. The Christian understanding of the reality that contests the vision, and the outcome of that polarization, will be different from that of the culture.

The Story's material principle opposite to liberation and reconciliation—*bondage and alienation*—will have an equivalent depth and range. For the reality perceived by the eyes of faith includes slavery to the alliance of foes ranged against the Vision of God: sin, evil, and death. And the effects of their assault include a fundamental rupture of the internal and external relationships of humanity, nature, and God. Our examination of the chapter of the Story about the Fall will come to grips with this understanding of reality. Therefore, joined to the Vision toward which the narrative itself thrusts, the translation key of Christian Storytelling today becomes *vision and reality.*

Perspective and Authority

What is the effect of this perspective on the authority structure here described? With respect to the circle of the world, it means that the contemporary experiences of liberation and reconciliation on the one hand, and of bondage and alienation on the other, are the most important worldly context for understanding and translating the Gospel. Christian theology is done in the setting of *praxis,* solidarity with the people and places of slavery and estrangement, and participation in the movements of freedom and unity. Where the struggle for deliverance from all kinds of enslavement—physical, social, intellectual, spiritual—goes on, there the Storyteller and theologian must be found. The dimensions of that Shalom or anti-Shalom, however, are not finally defined by the world's criteria. The locus of sin, evil, and death and the focus of freedom and peace with neighbor, nature, and God, as these are understood from within the Story, determine where that praxis happens.

The perspective also influences how the Church past and present provides resources for the statement of Christian faith. It seeks to draw from the ancient wisdom and from the current life of the Christian community whatever insight it offers on the visionary and realistic aspects of Christian faith. How liberation and reconciliation, bondage and estrangement, were and are conceived and portrayed in the multifarious environments in which the Church makes its life and does its work is drawn upon to form the Story told. That churchly resource includes hymnody and liturgy, ministry and mission, as well as the more formal concepts of theology.

While the ultimate authority for definition of the perspective itself is the Bible, the perspective influences the way we relate to the Scriptures. Commitment to liberation means deliverance from darkness of mind (and therefore the use of the best light of scholarship) and from the shadowy powers of injustice (and therefore a Bible read from within the struggles for freedom and peace and in identification with the poor and the oppressed). The perspective is also the working principle of selection within the texts and in the interpretation of them. The vision and reality take shape from what the Old and New Testaments perceive them to be, and that insight in turn works to illuminate the Storyline which makes its way in the Scriptures from prologue and creation, through fall and covenant, to the Person and Work of Jesus Christ, the nature and mission of the Church, salvation and consummation.

The perspective contributes to the work of integration as well as selection and interpretation. The authenticity and timeliness of the Story told is not only related to the inclusiveness of and priorities within the authority structure, but also to the degree to which the source, resource, and setting are gathered around the perspective. Thus it is as the Bible is read within the Church that in turn is plunged into the places and issues of bondage and alienation, liberation and reconciliation in the world, that both the Story and its translation become valid and compelling. Reflection goes on with the Bible in one hand and the arm of the Christian brother or sister in the other, as the Christian company moves on its journey in the world and toward the future.

Authoritative Translation

A statement of Christian faith, a translation of the Christian Story, is authoritative if it has passed the tests we have set forth. To summarize, it must be 1) rooted in the biblical source and accountable to its Storyline norm, 2) continuous with the traditions of the Church, past and present, 3) intelligible to those to whom it is addressed, connected to the realities of their time and place, and illuminative of their lived experience. If a perspective leads us through the circles of authority in this fashion, its outcome will be a responsible and compelling recounting of Christian narrative. Our goal in the pages that follow is to follow this method in the exposition and interpretation of the Christian faith.

REVELATION

By understanding our authority for telling the Christian Story, we have also a way of establishing the *identity* of our faith. Implicit in this but as yet unresolved in our discussion is the question of the Story's *veracity.* The Christian Story is not just a statement of who we are, but an affirmation about the way things really are. It makes truth claims. The search for authority in Christian faith leads therefore to the allied question of revelation: how the truth about the ultimate nature of things is disclosed to us.

Any exploration of this aspect of the "how" of Christian faith inevitably touches upon some of the "what" of the matter. Form is inseparable from the content. So our talk about revelation anticipates what is believed about the agent of revelation, the Holy Spirit. The work of the Holy Spirit in classical Christian thought includes "illumination." (Martin Luther says that the Holy Spirit "calls, gathers, enlightens and sanctifies"; the ancients speak of the Spirit as giving "life and light.") Therefore when we examine the meaning of revelation as the bringing of truth about God, we are assuming that the power that furnishes this light is the Holy Spirit. Revelation is "seeing the light," the truth of the Christian Story, by the gracious action of the divine Spirit.

The subject of revelation has been hotly disputed in recent Christian thought. The word and concept were used as a key to much neoorthodox interpretation of Christian teaching in its effort to establish the validity of faith in a way other than that of either the literalist or fundamentalist. These latter tended either to associate revelation with the words of the Bible understood as dictated by the Spirit in their original form to the writers (the "plenary verbal inspiration of the Scriptures"), or with propositions about God revealed in the tradition of the Church preserved by its ecclesiastical teaching authorities. The neoorthodox conception of revelation sought to disengage the idea of revelation from words and propositions, allowing for the freedom of inquiry into the ancient documents and traditions, and the freedom of God from the captivity to human forms. In attempting this, it pressed revelation back of forms to the deeds of God in human history, and forward to the moments of immediate encounter and disclosure in the life of the believer. Revelation was understood to be the Word of God, acting in history, incarnate in Jesus Christ, reported by the eyewitnesses to these events in the Bible, and heard by us as we came with the ear of faith in personal engagement with the Word as we hear it through the words of the Bible.

While this way of understanding revelation does avoid the rigidities of an earlier interpretation, one that both imprisons God and constricts honest human inquiry, it has been subject to increasing criticism. Does it reflect the way the Bible thinks of revelation? Is it too intellectual a way of conceiving revelation? Is it too spiritual a notion that in fact is not propositional enough? Does the talk about encounter with God and the Word bear any resemblance to our actual modern experience? While these questions and criticisms do not undercut the real insights of the "revelation theology" of another day, they do press us to look for some other way of understanding the disclosure of truth.

In line with our use of vision as a contemporary perspective on faith, and from strong warrants within the biblical tradition itself (revelation *is* a visual metaphor in much of the biblical usage), we shall examine revelation by way of this metaphor and meaning. In doing it, we shall restate and enlarge some of the themes on revelation from the neoorthodox perspective.

The origin and purpose of revelation are in the Godhead. Whatever is disclosed to us has its source in the eternal Vision of God. This Vision is the *intention and goal* of God, Shalom. We shall explore it more carefully in our discussion of the Trinity, and in the specific acts of God that thrust toward its fulfillment. For the present we may say that the revelation of the Vision of God unfolds in these very acts. From creation to consummation the deeds of God are the objective events which make possible whatever perception we have of that Vision. The process of revelation unfolds in the enactment of the purpose of God in the history of the world. The center point of enactment is the enfleshment of the Vision of God in Jesus Christ.

Through Jesus Christ shines the eternal Sun of God. In him we come to know that the ultimate source of revelation is the everlasting Light, the Vision of God which was with him from the beginning, the Son of the Father. Revelation is the manifestation of this eternal Logos, the Word speaking to us, the Vision unveiled. In this process, therefore, it is *Jesus Christ* who says and shows who he is.

The revealing of the intention of God takes another step toward us in the raising up of "seers" of that Vision which is at work in revelatory events. These visionaries live in the midst of those decisive events in human history on which the purposes of God turn. From Exodus to Easter the prophet and apostle who witness these key happenings are graced with eyes of faith that perceive their inner meaning. While the ordinary eye of sight does not see their significance, the miracle of new vision is given by the Spirit to see the unseen. This is the meaning of the "inspiration" of the Bible. By the power of the Holy Spirit the scales fall from the eyes of prophet and apostle; the blind see the Light of the Vision of God. Inspiration is a vehicle of revelation as it opens an inner eye that perceives the Vision of God in the deeds of God.

The vision granted to the visionary includes not only the grasp of the meaning of visible events in their history, but also vision of actions of God "fore and aft." *Fore-vision* is included in the seeing of the inner eye as prophet and apostle sketch pictures of the fulfillment of the Vision of God at the end of history. And *after-vision* is part of the seer's gift too as the meaning of creation is captured in the images of the visionary.

The perception of the Vision of God, past, present, and future, is shared by the seer in the language of visual metaphor, the poetic idiom most appropriate to the experience of inner vision: the prophets' portraiture of vine and fig tree, sword and plowshare, and the apostles' descriptions of the Lamb of God who takes away the sins of the world. The Bible is the report in rich symbol of the inner eyewitnesses of the Vision of God that came, and comes, and will come to us in the actions of God. These images, taken from the world of the seer, bear all the marks of their time and place—the pastoral world of vine, fig tree, plowshare, and lamb—and as such are not replicas of the eternal Vision. These human images and their meanings must be sifted and studied by the best of human learning, and translated into comparable symbols and meanings that communicate the Vision to us today.

It is this act of appropriation, this seeing today, which is the capstone of the revelatory process. Revealing becomes revelation when the Vision, projected in events and perceived and communicated by seer, is received through the power of the Spirit by our own eye of faith. Revelation is the gift of seeing the Light that shines through the events and their visionary interpreters. It is *sight into* the meaning of these events, hence *insight*. Revelation is the Spirit's illumination of the horizons of God's action perceived by the eye of faith. It is the time of connection between the objectivity of the divine deeds and the subjectivity of our inner vision. Revelation is *illumination*, a view of the Vision of God through the lens of faith. And this sight is made possible by the same Spirit that brought the Vision into history and enabled the biblical seer to see and share it with us.

Our description of the Vision of God will be in our language, just as that of the biblical seers of the original acts of God is in theirs. And we shall seek for metaphors and meanings commensurate with theirs that are true to our time and place. The portrayal of what we see of Vision in each generation builds a lore of visionary wisdom, a dictionary of metaphors, a body of theological meanings which constitute the tradition of the Church. Here is to be found a harvest of perspectives that represent each new angle of vision. They are not new revelations, but new perceptions of the one revelation, enriching its meaning for all, and providing a viewpoint illuminative of and illuminated by a given place and time.

ORIGINAL VISION

The need for the Light of revelation granted to us in the unique acts of God rises out of the dimming of the "light which enlightens every man" (John 1:9). "Original righteousness," as it is called in classical theology, has been severely compromised. In our translation, the original vision has been obscured. The image of God in us is no longer recognizable, a theme to be explored further in our chapter on the Fall. Its significance here bears on the question of "general revelation."

Some interpreters of the Fall conclude that the image of God has been altogether erased by sin, the Vision lost completely from view. As such there is no clue to its purpose in a debased human nature, and no power to pursue it. This view tends to appear in reaction to notions of human capacity which are confident about what can be known about God by the natural light of reason and what can be done by humans in the pursuit of the moral and spiritual life by natural grace.

The position taken here is that the original light granted to each human being is indeed so darkened by our "shutupness" (Kierkegaard) that its illumination is not sufficient either to demonstrate to us the goal of our journey or to give us the power to stride toward it. Into this wandering come the acts and disclosures of God that constitute the Christian Story. But even in our original stumble and fall and failure to see the horizon, the rays of the vision still seek us out. And in our prone position we can still see its reflections on the terrain of the world. The Light of God still shines on creation, and our turned face and dimmed sight can yet catch glimpses of it in nature and history (Rom. 1:19–20).

This reflected radiance provides enough illumination to see our way in the world. That is, the human race can grasp enough of the law of life—liberation and reconciliation—by its own lights to know something of what makes life livable. And this natural light graces us with the achievements of the arts and sciences that make and keep this precarious life more human. The good, the true, and the beautiful are sights to be seen even by our dimmed vision. And this very perception makes us aware of an unseen Source of that Light not visible to the natural eye. On the edges of our awareness there is a Presence. Yet it is an elusive one suggested by the reflections we do see, disturbing to us the more we realize how we are shown by the reflected radiance as living in the shadows. For the vision we do have comes as a conscience that judges us even as it seeks to lead us out of shadows.

While theories of moral law and natural theology have tended to conceive rather abstractly and individualistically these possibilities of the norms of life together and the existence of God, and do thereby witness to universal apprehensions, the reflected radiance also comes in special flashes and in disparate places. Thus a deeper grasp of justice will emerge in movements of liberation in a given time out of the particularities of its history, or a perception of the Presence will appear in the birth of a new religion with its prophet or sage. And there will be epochs in which new powers seek to understand the world, take responsibility for its future, and ennoble human and natural life. These too are grace, the historical acts of the God who preserves the world from the abyss and adds gift upon gift in a seeking Love. The breakthroughs of Light, whether they be in the high religions of the world or its creative times and places, are the work of Providence yielding to us a "general revelation," never leaving the world without some trace of its source, meaning, and goal (Acts 14:17). The world lives under this Light and its rebellion cannot put it out (John 1:5).

To the extent that the dimmed sight of the natural eye perceives the little reflected lights to be found in the world, there is this universal disclosure. It is the remnant of the original vision, maintained by the natural grace of God in order to make life livable in its fallen state. At its brightest points it sheds rational, moral, and aesthetic light and gives clues to its source. But for the world to rise and turn to that horizon from which these rays come, there is needed the enabling power of "special revelation," and a renewed Vision that brings "us out of darkness into his marvelous light" (I Pet. 2:9 RSV).

Why so? When that quality of spirit in human beings which is Providence's organ of enlightenment approaches the sensitive area of divine beckoning toward the Vision, then all these riches of human freedom—its moral, aesthetic, intellectual, and even religious powers—wilt in fear or react in arrogance. The divine claim is too much for the race to bear, its Word too insistent to hear, its Light too blinding to see. The powers of the human spirit are harnessed to its rebellion, for it does not finally want to know who God is, who we are, and for what the world is destined. This is the bondage of the will of which we must speak in our chapter on the Fall. Here we anticipate its effects in our struggle with the question of revelation. Our "reason," so in thrall to our self-serving flight from God, cannot discern the witness that God has left for it to see. Its blindness must be healed by a more ultimate revelation (Rom. 1:21–23).

THE WAY TO INSIGHT

Special revelation is a process, not a product. Its origins lie in Deity, and its issue is constituted by the acts of God in pursuit of the Vision, and the perception and transmission of them by visionaries. Its end point is insight, sight into the primal Vision by the eye of faith. Like its analogue from the aesthetic or intellectual sphere, the special insight of the Spirit is marked by a eureka experience. This connection, this Yes! that erupts in the encounter with any profound truth cannot be programmed, arranged, manipulated. In wider human experience it is recognized as an event that mysteriously happens when circumstances are right. Indeed, one may arrange the conditions, but the insight takes place "out of the blue." Either you see it or you don't. In the insight of revelation the comparable affirmation is couched in the language of grace. Insight comes as an unearned gift, "by the grace of God." Put another way, insight as truth in the sense of illumination, the Christian eureka experience, is self-authenticating. The Spirit brings the Vision, not we. The grace of insight is prevenient: it is not manufacturable or manipulable by us, but goes before us. The Holy Spirit blows where it will (John 3:8).

But there is an environment in which the process of revelation is known regularly to take place. While insight cannot be forced, there are preparations that can be made for its arrival. There is terrain on which the Holy Spirit has promised to be present. When we ask what that is, we are called back to the orbs of authority: the Bible, the Church, the world. It is in the Bible, within the Church, immersed in the world, that the Holy Spirit pours out light and power. It is when we position ourselves by the power of the Spirit in these channels that the sight of the Vision may be given to us by grace. To use the familiar pilgrim image: when we are on the road (in the world) traveling in the pilgrim band of the Christian community (in the Church), consulting the map (searching the Scriptures), we are in the right position to see the Light of our destination on the horizon.

We have been discussing the truth of Christian revelation as insight into the Vision of God, the illumination that comes by grace as the end-point of the process of God's disclosure of the divine Vision. As yet we have not spoken of the product of the process. That issue of the dynamics of revelation is the specific belief pattern that constitutes our reading of the Christian Story. What emerges from the believing community's view of the Vision are the reports of its perception. It is this aspect of the revelation process, the formation of statements of belief, which we are about in Christian Storytelling. We shall use another visual aid related to our target image to explore this by turning that figure to its profile position, seeing it now as a cone.

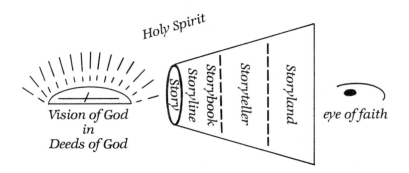

The Light at the opening of the cone is the Vision of God as it shines toward us. The scope that directs us to the Light is made up of the material of authority—those experiences of the world, traditions of the Church, and words of the Bible, shaped by the perspective of our time and place and aimed toward the Light. While it is our perspective that forms this vehicle, the Holy Spirit in turn shapes the shaper. The heat of the Light of God melts and molds the materials that direct our gaze toward the Light. It is the power of the Holy Spirit, its "tongues of fire," that crafts our viewing piece.

What then is the position and meaning of the network of Christian belief we are calling the Christian Story? It is the glass at the mouth that is designed and honed to admit the Light from beyond. Its purpose is to be transparent to the Light. Its fate in a fallen world is to be at best translucent, and at worst a thickness impervious to the rays of truth. "We see through a glass darkly" (I Cor. 13:12 KJV). Christian beliefs are the lens looked through by the eye of faith.

A transmitter of the divine Light, the belief structure of Christian faith must be aimed at the Truth and must take its shape from the cone. A good statement of belief—a sound translation of the Christian Story—will take its form from the biblical aperture. What we have called the source of the Story in our inquiry into the authorities of faith we identify here as the inner shape of the cone, the definitive contours of the opening to the Light. Whatever Story we tell must be faithful to the Storyline found therein. And beyond that inner core is the next set of materials from the traditions and perceptions of the Christian community, past and present. These lead toward and connect with the biblical center. On the outer edges of the cone is the contemporary world.

How these ingredients are fashioned so as to direct the gaze of the seer to the Light is determined, humanly speaking, by the perspective. When authentic, it will so shape the experiences of the world, the wisdom of the Church, and data of the Bible as to be accurately aimed at the Light and finally contribute to a clear "glass of vision" (Austin Farrer). Let us see what this means.

Beginning from the outer edges of the cone, an authentic perspective will attempt two things. It will so form its angle of vision from this point as to be *coherent* with the genuine learnings of human experience. Whatever it says will not violate what is known and honored in the best of rational, moral, and aesthetic experience. As the Holy Spirit is active in this ring of reality creating the true, good, and beautiful, this presence and its gifts are to be honored in the formulation of Christian faith. For example, any reading of the Christian Story that sets its face against the empirical data of science does not honor the work of the Holy Spirit in the world and will be off target in its aim toward the Light. Indeed the Spirit's work in the world may play a direct as well as an indirect role in shaping the faith perspective as the moral experience of the age makes explicit themes in the Christian Story that were in other translations at best implicit. The raised consciousness about the imperialism of masculine language in the formulation of Christian faith and the need to revise it in the light of fresh moral sensibilities that have emerged in this era is one example.[4]

Statements of faith will be coherent and yield insight to the extent that they rise out of engagement with the processes of liberation and reconciliation that are at work in contemporary experience. The Spirit of Shalom is a living presence in the world as well as it is in Book and Church. The incognito Christ to whom we relate in the feeding of the hungry, the doing of justice, and the making of peace (Matt. 25:31–46) is our companion in revelation as well as redemption. To see the Liberator and Reconciler in Book and Community requires a positioning within the world where the present work of liberation and reconciliation goes on. Christ opens the eyes of faith when the believer walks alongside of him in the ministries of deliverance and hope. The God who is at work in the world, the Holy Spirit, enables ever new light to break forth from the holy Word and the divine Vision.

The other aspect of worldly perspective, conjoined to coher-

---

4. The masculine domination of the traditional language of theology is undergoing telling criticism. Letty Russell (editor, *The Liberating Word*, Philadelphia: Westminster Press, 1976) and Hugh T. Kerr (*Theology Today*, Fall 1975) offer good guidelines for responsible theological discourse in writing. The practice followed here is the use of inclusive concepts and terms wherever the writer is in charge of the text. Where quotation is made, including biblical quotation from specific versions, the text is cited as it is. Indications are that forthcoming translations of the Bible will reflect a struggle with this problem and therefore new terminology in the text itself. See Bruce Metzger, "Trials of the Translator," *Theology Today*, XXXIII (April, 1976), 96–100.

ence with contemporary experience, has to do with the *intelligibility* of the Christian Story. Whether a particular rendition of the Story lets light in depends on the communicability of its images and thought structures. The Spirit works to bring to the fore those metaphors and meanings of an age which can direct the eye of faith clearly to its goal. How the glass of vision is shaped will be determined by what angle comes from this outer rim, what words and themes provide the way to faith.

Coherence with and *intelligibility* to the world in which God places us and where the Spirit works are decisive shaping forces in the formation of the lens of faith. A sound perspective will make use of the best materials in the shaping of the cone's circumference.

To coherence with and intelligibility to the world is to be added *continuity* with the life and witness of the Christian Church. Here again there are positive and negative aspects to be taken into account. The long experience of the Church has established certain zones of danger in interpreting Christian faith. "No trespassing" signs have been posted. Conceived in our telescopic terms, there are potential flaws in this ring, jagged edges that can obstruct the view. These must be eliminated in order to facilitate seeing. The Nicene and Chalcedonian learnings, for example, function in this way. To take the Church seriously, good perspective means honoring that ancient or contemporary wisdom about bad construction.

The positive work of the Church in shaping the glass of vision is the contribution of the common life and lore of the Church, past and present, by way of the themes and images which are tested and tried. No formulation of faith that fails to make use of the treasures of Christian wisdom and perception will find the way in to shape an opening that gives light.

The final and decisive mold is the testimony of the seers of the Light found on the pages of the Bible. It is toward this inner circle that the perspective must thrust in the shaping of the Story. It is from the fundamental material of the Bible that the most formative ring is made. From it the final shape of the faith statement is derived. The Story that does not grow out of this environment cannot be aimed in the right direction and will not transmit light.

Derivation means finally that the lens of belief takes its form from the biblical orb, the mouth of the cone itself. Our translation of the Christian Story is ultimately responsible to this Storyline which traces the shape of faith from creation to consummation. We have spoken of this in other contexts so the point does not have to be labored here. The Bible is the source of our Story. In the context of our discussion of the revelation process, it is the basic arena in which the encounter with the divine Light is to take place.

The glass of vision which is our translation of the Christian Story is authentic to the extent that it transmits the Light of revelation. Whether it does or not is determined by the shape of the cone of revelation composed of world, Church, and Bible. When the beliefs are *coherent* with and *intelligible* to the world, in *continuity* with the Church and its tradition, and *derived* from the Scriptures, then the beliefs can be revelatory of the Truth, and insight is possible. Possible—but only God makes it happen, as revelation is a gift of grace. Whether such a telling of the Story is a vehicle for revelation rests with the work of the Spirit that brings the nurturing elements together in such a way as to issue in insight. The most we can do to validate a particular set of affirmations about the deeds of God is to determine whether they are coherent with and intelligible to our contemporary experience, in continuity with the tradition of the Church, and derived from the Bible. As such, they are candidates for the revelation process. They are true to the shape of the cone.

To describe statements of faith as "candidates for the revelation process" and "true to the shape of the cone" means that there is another dimension to the truth question under discussion here. This preparatory status of theological assertions is established by their "fit" to the cone of authority and disclosure. A statement that meets the tests of derivation, continuity, intelligibility, and coherence is *objectively* true. That is, it corresponds to the objective reference points of the authority structure (determined to be such by the work of the Holy Spirit). Whether or not doctrinal statements are true in this sense of being *fitting* must be arrived at by analysis and public scrutiny of the conformity of these statements to the points of adjudication. While objective truth is the condition of *subjective* truth, the latter is finally a gift of grace and not a work of intellect, revelation not discovery. Truth in the ultimate sense of that which opens the eyes of faith, convicts, converts, and illuminates, gives sight into the Vision of God, happens only by the "internal testimony of the Holy Spirit."

When this kind of disclosure happens, statements of faith become *revealing* truths. When they serve the purpose for which they are designed, they do not claim to be *revealed* truths; they are not of a piece with the Light itself! They cannot claim to *be* the Light. That Light is distanced from the cone which we shape and use. What we hope for in our finitude is that our beliefs, shaped from materials the Spirit has given to us, will admit the Light and give us *insight.* This disclosure which comes as the gift of God is the use the Spirit makes of these human formulas to let in that Light. We aspire so to be led by the Spirit to shape a glass that will be diaphanous to the glory of God. The work of theology is the formation of that kind of a lens—the telling in the language of our time of that kind of Story that God will use to bring insight into who God is and what God dreams and does.

What then, in summary, is the revelation process here traced? It rises out of the eternal Vision in the Godhead making its first impact in the events of the Christian Story. Disclosure of the purpose of God as it takes shape in the deeds of God is perceived by interpreters of these events who by the empowerment of the Spirit become seers of the Vision at work in them, and whose testimony is recorded in the rich images and history of the Book of the Vision. That Book is taken up into the life of the Church, again by the work of the Spirit, each generation of the Christian community confronting the issues and idiom of its world and translating the Vision seen into the language of preaching, teaching, liturgy, and mission. As the believer searches these Scriptures from within the Church, engaged with both its ancient traditions and its contemporary glass of vision, the eye of faith is opened to see the shapes and colors of the eternal Vision through this translucency. This insight is revelation, the gift of sight into the purpose of God, given by the Holy Spirit who opens the eyes of the blind. Paul's hope for the church at Ephesus is ours also: "I pray that the God of our Lord Jesus Christ, the all-glorious Father, may give you the spiritual powers of wisdom and vision, by which there comes the knowledge of him. I pray that your inward eyes may be illumined, so that you may know what is the hope to which he calls you . . ." (Eph. 1:17–18).

God

"In the beginning was the Word, and the Word was with God, and the Word was God. . ." (John 1:1 RSV). This declaration is more than the opening sentence of the prologue of the Gospel of John. It is the prologue—literally the *word before*—"the foreword" of the Christian Story. This daring affirmation thrusts the origins of the tale into eternity itself.

The Greek term which John uses to set the stage for the unfolding drama, *Logos,* comes to us in translation as *Word.* Common to its usage in many philosophies and religions of the ancient Mediterranean world is the theme of an architect's plan for the universe, a design which holds together all that is. And it was believed that something of this design disclosed itself to the rational or spiritual capacity of each human being. Christian theologians in the early centuries made use of the Logos to express the unity of God with Christ, interpreting it as the eternal purpose of God; the divine "reason" on the one hand, or "word" on the other. Alongside these connections made with Greek and Oriental thought was a tradition within Judaism which spoke of a Wisdom and Word in some sense connected with God. Some biblical scholars believe this Hebrew idea may well have been as forcefully present in the background of John's use of Logos as the wider philosophical and religious understandings of the term.

FOREVISION

Is there a way of expressing this key theme in John in contemporary language? Building on our earlier translation of Logos, we interpret its Johannine usage against the background of the themes of design and wisdom as follows: "In the beginning was the Vision, and the Vision was with God, and the Vision was God. . . ." The prologue of the Christian story is the *forevision* as well as the foreword of God. God is the Envisioner of a plan, a hope, a purpose. God "had a dream." From all eternity God projects a vision of the divine intention, "God's hidden wisdom, his secret purpose framed from the very beginning to bring us to our full glory" (I Cor. 2:7). The Christian Story is the narrative of God's pursuit of that divine Vision from creation to consummation.

The Vision of God is "the hope of glory" (Col. 1:27). The inner eye of God is focussed on the future, the *doxa,* the "glory of God," or as we shall be describing this fulfillment of all things, *Shalom.* As the "secret purpose" and "depths of God's own nature" (I Cor. 2:10) this hope, this "glory of the Father," is the eternal Son of God. The biblical seer reports the vision of the future as the divine progeny because he has discerned "the glory of God in the face of Jesus Christ" (II Cor. 4:6). In the Nazarene is the radiance of eternal splendor, "God of God, Light of Light, very God of very God" (Nicene Creed). According to the Christian Story our own chief end is to glorify God by living toward and moving in that lucent reality.

Earlier traditions within the Church found it meaningful to think of Jesus Christ as the Word of God. So it is in the Reformation stream. Here the verbal setting for the Gospel is stressed in preaching and teaching. Allied with it has been a Gutenberg society in which print, reading, and writing were decisive. The Good News, as a Word spoken to and read by the believer, became a compelling way of understanding the Christian faith. And it continues to be so. But if we are right about the formative power and proper significance of the visual and the visionary, then the image of Vision should join, not replace, Word as a way of understanding the eternal purpose and historical enfleshment of God. Jesus Christ, the "Wisdom from on high," is also the "image of the invisible God," the "brightness of his glory" (Heb. 1:3 KJV), the eternal Light. He is the Word of God and the Vision of God.

EMPOWERED HOPES

But there are visions and there are visions. There are fanciful visions just as there are empty words. There are fantasies which are out of touch with reality, dreams with no hope of becoming fact. The God of the Christian Story has a dream, but is no "dreamer," no unrealistic visionary able to fantasize but not facilitate. As God keeps the divine Word, so God has the *power* to fulfill the divine Vision. As the Son is the Wisdom of God, so the Holy Spirit is the Power of God. Christian teaching about the Holy Spirit is rooted in the conviction that the Maker of the promises and the Creator of the visions has the capacity to keep the promises and fulfill the visions. The Holy Spirit is that busy active presence that connects dream to reality and finally brings them to a point of convergence. The Holy Spirit of God is the Power of God to achieve the eternal Hope.

To speak of the power of God in our prologue is to be reminded that many of the discussions of the nature of God begin with an abstract analysis of the perfections and attributes of God: omnipotence, omniscience, omnipresence, etc. Not infrequently the exciting story of the history of God gets tuned out by those who cannot get past these abstruse descriptions. But also a fundamental error can be made. Whatever we say about God, the central character of the Christian story, must be drawn first and foremost from the central event in that epic, Jesus Christ. We do not know the depths of God from general experience, whatever intimations of the divine are to be found there. That stream is too clouded by our own sin and finitude to see the bottom. We know the purpose of God because it discloses itself to us in key happenings. And from that same revelation we learn as well the meaning of the power of God. Indeed, the notion of omnipotence itself, which we get from our general experience outside of that disclosure, contributes to the tendency to interpret the divine power as the ultimate extension of constraint as we know it. God is indeed all-powerful. But the *what* and *how* of that power is redefined by the death and resurrection of Christ. We shall return to this when examining "theodicy," the question of how we hold together a belief in the power of God, the love of God, and the reality of evil. Here we must say that God's power is indeed all-sufficient. It is not power in the abstract, however, but power to fulfill the vision of God. God has all the power needed to achieve the divine purpose.

THE TRINITY

Envisioner, Vision, Power: Father, Son, and Spirit. We employ a contemporary figure to express the classical Christian doctrine of the *Trinity* as the prologue of the Christian Story (II Cor. 13:14; Matt. 28:18–20). But not so contemporary after all, since it continues the pattern of "psychological analogy" developed in one of the profoundest treatises in Christian thought on this subject, Augustine's *De Trinitate.* Augustine grounded his use of psychological images in John's own psychological metaphor of Logos, conceiving the eternal Trinity as Memory, Understanding, and Will. One of the strengths of the Augustinian tradition is its determination to preserve the oneness of God. That is a value in the use of the psychological metaphor of inner relationships to suggest the meaning of the "immanent Trinity."

Impossible as it is to penetrate the final mystery of the Trinity—Augustine declares after all his reasoning that what we say is so because we cannot simply settle for silence—there are some obvious traps to be avoided in any discussion of the threeness of God. One is the temptation to treat Deity as if "they" were some sort of club made up of three selves, Father, Son, and Spirit. The psychological figure is helpful at this point, for it asserts the unity in the one "personality" of Memory, Understanding, and Will, or Envisioner, Vision, and Power. While the classical doctrine of the Trinity did in fact use "person" as a term to describe each of the relationships within the Godhead, the meaning of that word originally was not what we think of today as a self—a conscious ego—but rather a "subsistence," or "mode of being." Perhaps some of the traditional symbols for the Trinity make that clearer than our words do. For example: the triangle △ or the trefoil ♣. And, of course, in the life of worship, we instinctively relate to God as One with whom we have to do, rather than addressing our prayers to a plurality or referring to God as They.

For all that, there has arisen another image of the Trinity which is *social* rather than *psychological,* stressing the threefoldness rather than the oneness. The translation of the term *hypostasis,* subsistence, as *person,* and the association of modern notions of self-conscious ego with the modes of God's being, has given impetus to a community understanding of the Trinity, as well as the biblical usage that suggests the individual agency of each Person.

Indeed, sociality is the presupposition of the Incarnation, the coming of a Son, united with yet distinguishable from the Father, very personal familial imagery describing the eternal being of God. The personal action of the Spirit also reinforces the social metaphor (I Pet. 1:12; John 16:13–15; Rom. 8:27). And from the patristic period to some contemporary exegesis the appearance of the pronoun "us" (as in Gen. 1:26 and 11:7) is cited as an argument for the divine society. Alongside the triangle and trefoil, therefore, is to be placed the triquerta ⚛ .

Yet the social analogy and this symbol of linkage and partial overlap must be called to accountability before the oneness of God, which is so important to the Christian Story. This is captured in the long-standing teaching of "perichoresis" or mutual interpenetration of the Persons, and the ancient "law of the Trinity" in which all the works of the Trinity are one.

Although each has its foreground and background position in its respective roles—Father to the fore in creation, Son in Incarnation, Spirit in the continuing and culminating acts of the drama—yet the Son is also present in creation, Father also in Incarnation, Spirit in creation and Incarnation, and so on. Thus our controlling metaphor here is the psychological one, and the social metaphor is secondary. The latter secures the integrity and personal agency of each of the subsistences in Deity. But it is finally the one God who is personally active as Father, Son, and Spirit.

In Christian tradition a distinction is made between the "immanent Trinity" and the "economic Trinity." The former has to do with the inner-trinitarian life of Father, Son, and Spirit, and the latter with the missions of God that express this inner reality, the Father as Creator, the Son as Reconciler, the Spirit as Redeemer (a building up of the meaning of God by way of the acts of God). We would not know what the Prologue of the Story is unless it were for the creative, reconciling, and redeeming actions which constitute our saga. Yet as these faces of God (*persona* is the Latin word for the mask worn in the ancient theater by an actor playing different parts, and is one source of the idea of the three persons of the Trinity) are not serial roles of God as taught by Modalism, but are three concurrent and coinherent realities within the being of God, they require us to struggle with the meaning of the immanent

Trinity, as we do here in reflecting on the eternal Envisioner, Vision, and Power.

What then do we make of all of this? With Athanasius who declared at the Council of Nicea that there never was a time when the Word was not, we also affirm that there never was a time when the Vision was not. God the eternal Envisioner cannot be conceived without an eternal Vision anymore than an Eternal Father can be thought of without an eternal offspring. And a divine Vision cannot be thought apart from the divine power, hence the eternal work of the Holy Spirit.

To know Jesus Christ is to know what the eternal Vision is! That is what it signifies to say the Son was always with the Father (I Pet. 1:20). The latter does not mean that another divine ego was always there with God in eternity, plotting and planning what was to come. Such an association would be polytheism. Nor does it mean a supernatural man who existed before all time, a notion declared heretical by the ancient Church because it denies the singular enfleshment of the Incarnation.

The Christian Story does speak about a Father and a Son who during and after the Incarnation are both united and distinct. In fact there is the belief in the "glorified humanity of Christ," risen and ascended to be with the Father. About this we shall have more to say when treating the middle and end of that Story. For now our attention is drawn to the eternal beginnings shrouded in mystery, yet a mystery at the core of which there is meaning. A Light does shine in the face of Jesus Christ. That Light has its origins in the eternal Light of the triune God. Jesus Christ, God of God, Light of Light, Vision of Envisioner.

THE MASCULINE IMAGERY OF THE TRINITY

As each generation makes the Gospel its own Good News by finding images that connect faith with the culture of the day, so it may be that the metaphor of Vision helps us at another point. With our growing awareness about how language forms reality, and our sensitivity to the dominance of masculine language not only in the wider society but in liturgy and theology, we have some clear responsibilities for fresh translation. This is a task that the whole

Church must undertake and which it will finally resolve in that catholicity, with leadership given by those most deeply affected by it. But it is incumbent upon each teller of the Christian Story to attempt the task of language reconstruction. What then of the masculine social imagery used to describe two of the Persons of the Trinity? What of the "he" pronouns for God "himself," a gender carried over traditionally also to all the Persons?

Christian faith takes its understanding of God from the acts of God with their center point in Jesus Christ. On this question the picture that emerges from this center point, gained from how Jesus relates to human beings and what he envisions for the world's fulfillment, is one that transcends the patterns of dominance and submission which mark this fallen world. The eschatological vision embodied in Christ is one in which "there is no such thing as male or female" (Gal. 3:28). This is our clue to the nature of the eternal Vision in the Godhead. The everlasting Purpose transcends our divisions and imperialisms. The Vision of God is inclusive of our particularities and finally beyond our gender distinctions. Something of this is captured in our Advent hymnody as it seeks to go beyond the masculine qualities usually imputed to the second Person of the Trinity and draws upon the Wisdom tradition of the Old Testament (Prov. 9:1–6) with its female associations ("daughter of God" in rabbinical texts). Thus, "O come thou Wisdom from on high, And order all things, far and nigh; To us the path of knowledge show, and cause us in her ways to go" ("O Come, O Come, Emmanuel"). Inclusiveness is again reflected in the strand of piety in the Middle Ages in which prayer to Christ made use of both feminine and masculine ascriptions. Integral to the image and meaning of Vision is its androgynous character.

An inclusive Vision cannot rise from a less-than-inclusive Envisioner. As all the Persons coinhere, the eternal Envisioner is not limited to masculine characterizations. The One who eternally begets the Vision is ultimately the fullness of divine *Parenthood.*

There is an important distinction between theological definition and liturgical usage. The latter takes into account the conditions of communication. While God is ultimately Parent, we no more address Deity that way than we do our own father or mother. Both the honor and the intimacy of the relationship is expressed in terms of those particularities. Whether God can be addressed meaningfully in both of these ways, as is appropriate to the inclusive nature of Deity, depends upon whether one or both of these terms do in fact communicate to the worshipper. Perhaps the time will come when both images can be used alternatively in Christian liturgy and the inclusive nature of the eternal Vision can be seen. Until that advance is possible, we must use personal address that communicates with those with whom we speak or lead in worship, yet always pressing beyond limited visions to a theologically holistic view of the Godhead.

A model for this principle of communication is the act of Incarnation itself. The eternal purpose of God came into a real humanity as a male figure in a patriarchal society. (In fact it is argued by some Christian feminists that the Incarnation had to be in a male figure in order to challenge the machismo view of Deity, for this male, Jesus of Nazareth, is the embodiment of a vulnerable and compassionate love that calls radically into question traditional and worldly conceptions of both true Deity and true humanity.) Thus the Vision does its work through all the limitations and ambiguities of a less-than-visionary world. God accommodates to our condition (Irenaeus, Calvin). Yet even as this Vision works within the frailties and sins of our history, it does so in order to expand and finally explode its parochialism. Accommodation thrusts toward transformation, in God's communication and ours.

Father, Son . . . and Spirit. Letty Russell notes that the Hebrew word for Spirit, *ruach,* is feminine, and the Greek word, *pneuma,* is neuter. Further she observes that the work of the Holy Spirit tends to be associated with the empowerment that brings life, and hence the nurturing function. Why not then refer to the Holy Spirit as She? This way of questioning the masculine dominance of our thoughts and words about God appears to fit our own developing themes about the Trinity. It provides a certain symmetry within the Godhead with its suggested reconceptualization as Parent, Son, and Spirit: an inclusive first Person, a masculine embodiment of the second Person, and a feminine third Person. Connections might even be seen here to Jung on the one hand (selfhood being constituted by both masculine and feminine principles) and Barth on the other (the image of God—and thus, by implication, God—being both male and female), although these two kinds of assertions can also be related to other ways of conceiving God. As inviting as this line of thought is, it does ignore the coinherence of the Persons, and thus the impossibility of assigning some attributes to one and not to others. Further, it accedes too quickly to certain culture-bound assumptions, on the one hand defining women in terms of the nurturing role and on the other precluding the nurturing functions of the male. For all that, it represents the concern to enlarge our vision of the nature of God and points to the importance of understanding the Holy Spirit, as other modes of God's being, in an inclusive fashion.

The discussion of male and female terms for God brings the inevitable protest that God cannot be adequately conceived by anthropomorphisms, let alone by gender distinctions. That is surely true. Yet if we are to speak to or about God, if prayer or positive theology is legitimate, as well as a holy silence or negative theology (saying what God is not), then we must borrow metaphors from our world of common experience, allowing them to be opened up by the Christian Story. It is personal terms that best express and address the God with whom we have to do in this drama. As there is no such thing as a person in the abstract, but only one with role and gender, so these come into prominence in talk about God. Especially is this so where familial images play such an important part, as they do in biblical faith. And in particular, in trinitarian usage each Person is addressed as a You in prayer, and personally referred to in the third person by pronouns. (This liturgical practice does not mean the belief in three separate self-conscious egos, but, in our conceptuality here, the personal Envisioner meeting us as *personal* Vision and *personal* Power.) The problem of "aggiornamento" with regard to our inherited language about God here is its male bias. This is not adequately dealt with by reminders that all our language is anthropomorphic, or by substituting impersonal language which, whatever the disclaimer, suggests the sub-personal, but by enlarging the gender perception and description. A general consensus on how best this may be done is yet to be found in an inquiry that must engage the whole Body of Christ, including the too-long submerged presence and leadership of women believers.

FREE TO BE TOGETHER

The metaphors of faith, classic and contemporary, help us to capture the trinitarian roots of the Christian Story—Father, Son, and

Spirit; Memory, Understanding, and Will; Envisioner, Vision, and Power. But they do not tell us what kind of Parent it is with whom we have to do, or what the Will or Vision of God are. Familial, psychological, and visionary images suggest the form but not the content of the divine life.

As with the form of trinitarian belief, so too with its content we must move to the middle of the Story. Because Christian faith is a narrative, we can only know who God is by what God does. It is in the events of that biography that we come to know the character of God. And it is in the definitive event of Jesus Christ that the fundamental identity of God is disclosed. As Bethlehem and its Johannine interpretation enable us to view Deity as Vision and Envisioner, so Galilee, Calvary, and Easter provide a horizon for understanding the nature of that Vision and Envisioner.

Manifest in Jesus Christ is a holy Love active in liberating the world from the tyranny of sin, evil, and death, and reconciling humanity, nature, and God. Coming at the center of the Story, after the offense has been mounted against the purposes of God, the revelation of who God is takes place as *liberation from* an enemy and *for* the *reconciliation* of estranged friends. Liberation and reconciliation are therefore post-resistance ways of describing the pre-Story purpose of God we are reaching for in the Prologue of this narrative. In their primal meanings the Word and Will of God are Freedom and Peace. We shall describe this eternal Vision in the Godhead as *Shalom,* the freedom and unity of all things portrayed so vividly in the prophetic writings. As in the divine Life God is free and together, so the Dream of God is for a world that is *free to be together.* This is the nature of the holy Love that fills the divine heart and pours content into the divine Vision.

The heights and depths of this Vision of liberation and reconciliation can only be charted as we follow the divine purpose from beginning to end. Our preliminary reflection on the doctrine of God in the Prologue therefore presses us immediately forward to the opening act of the drama, Creation.

CHAPTER I

Creation

"In the beginning God created the heavens and the earth" (Gen. 1:1 RSV). The opening words of the prologue are matched by those of this first chapter. One speaks of the Source from which all comes, the other about the first expression of that primal being. Creation is the opening chapter of a plot conceived in eternity.

Why did creation happen? There are clues in the Christian Story but no firm conclusions. If God is *free* and *together*, then how natural it is for there to be the creation of a world which enacts "out there" the coming to be of that Vision. The long reflection of the Church on this question has prompted the judgment that creation is not necessary to God. God does not depend on the world for divine fulfillment. The Spirit fulfills the Vision within the plenitude of the divine life itself. Modesty is therefore appropriate to the question of the ultimate why of creation. But there is no doubt in the Christian drama that this creation is the overflow of freely choosing Love ready to enact outside the divine life the reality so central to the inner depths of God. God does not will to be God without the world (Barth).

What then is done in creation to express this inner freedom and peace of God? It is the bringing to be of another, who, in freedom, can enter into a life together with God. God's love begets that other who is invited to choose to be with God, and in so doing embody the dream of Shalom. The creation of the world makes possible the circumstances through which that Vision can take on historical reality. Thus is born the covenant partner of God.

FREEDOM IN CREATION

The light of the purpose of God shines back on the way toward the goal. "The end pre-exists in the means" (Emerson). If freedom and peace compose the intention of God, then we may expect that the pursuit of it will manifest these things. There is no clearly readable blueprint of this in Scripture or tradition. But there are some indications, and they prompt some deductions, however tentative they may be, and however constantly subjected to scrutiny and alteration.

The intention of God requires in the covenant partner a real freedom to respond to the invitation. Mutuality cannot be programmed. Genuine life together can rise only out of a love born in freedom. So it is with God, and so it must be with us. The freedom that God confers on us as participants in eternal covenant is the condition for that reach. Freely we have received, freely we are to give. Thus the freedom intrinsic to the Vision is a gift given at the beginning of the pilgrimage toward it.

Partnership includes humanity but does not exclude others. The whole cosmos is part of the Christian Story. Stones and stars enter into the design of God and the heavens are to declare his glory. The Genesis account spends considerable time on what are viewed as preparatory stages for the coming of humanity (Gen. 1:1–25). We can so understand them still, transposed out of the scientific forms of ancient time into our own cosmological key. Thus the history of the world from its inception to this stage of humanity is the birth and nurture of spontaneity—freedom fulfilled in mutuality. The emergence of the universe is the slow cultivation by a gracious God of that tiny grain of sensibility, at the first and even now at the most elemental level of finite being, in the direction of fullness of freedom. And in the structures of nature from lowest to highest there is the guide and goal of life together (Ps. 19:1). The Vision of Shalom is at work in the rhythms and patterns which form and enable natural existence. On the margins of the Christian Story the notations of process and panpsychic philosophies suggest interpretations of the meaning of growth and response in the cosmos.

Why this long and torturous stretch of time in which the world passes through stages of evolving freedom? Again, the end preexists in the means. For the goal to be embodied in the way, the growth toward the goal cannot be forced, or freedom would be a mockery and love would have no reality as a means to the end of Shalom. While we can only speculate that this is so, it would seem that the process of time itself is intrinsic to the Vision, a span in which freedom to choose can grow, and Love can do its nurturing work. What is true of the emergence of nature is even truer for the ways of humanity where a developed freedom requires a longer, more arduous pilgrimage, and finally the radical suffering of God, in order to evoke that response to the divine intention.

UNITIES IN NATURE

The Light of God that shines upon the world is reflected in the unities as well as the spontaneities of creation. The divine Vision is mirrored in the multifarious harmonies of nature: "The firmament ... the waters under the heavens ... the dry land Earth ... vegetation, plants yielding seed, and fruit trees bearing fruit ... lights in the firmaments of the heavens ... swarms of living creatures ... and every winged bird according to its kind ..." (Gen. 1:6ff.).

The probes of modern science have opened to us the unending horizon of these rhythms and patterns. Microcosm and macrocosm yield a limitless view of their intricacy and grandeur. But we do not need the electron microscope or the Palomar telescope to see for ourselves the awesome beauty and order perceived by the Genesis writer. The same blue vault above, the mysteries and symmetries of the ocean below, the bounty of the good earth and the fecund life that covers it, the radiance of a spring morning, the eagle's flight and the sandpiper's trail, all are signs to us of the Vision through Whom and by Whom all things are made (John 1:3).

The biblical seer describes the primal scene in its perfections, and that is how it is viewed from the angle of ultimate Vision. But the world of nature as we know it now is short of this divine purpose and one in which misery is inseparable from grandeur. Yet even a groaning creation reflects the glory of its conception. Thus the writer concludes his chronicle of cosmic birth by the judgment,

"And God saw that it was good" (Gen. 1:25 RSV). Its goodness lies in its derivation from the divine Goodness. It comes from and still bears the marks of the trinitarian Life together with its animating Vision. The heavens do declare the glory of God and the earth does proclaim the divine handiwork (Ps. 19:1). We are not left without a witness to the glory God is and wills.

HUMAN NATURE

The freedom to say yes to God comes to full flower in the arrival of the creature with a human face. The creation of humanity brings into the history of God that other whose capacity to choose and therefore to enter with deepest intimacy into communion with God is maximal. And with that comes the sharpest imprint of the goal toward which that history moves, the Vision of Shalom. At the birth of humanity comes the commission to enter the partnership, and a capacity to see what that means.

In what does the uniqueness and special dignity of humanity consist? The traditional expression is the *imago Dei:* human beings are made in "the image of God" (Gen. 1:26; I Cor. 12:7). Many are the opinions as to what this means. Here we interpret it in the context of our developing Story and its major motifs. Thus the Light of God was directed with intensity to one point in creation—it shone on us and we see its Source; the Vision of God was opened to humanity—the gift of clarity of sight and the eminent ability to respond were given to this creature. In humanity is mirrored the Vision of God. Here is reflected the inner Light of Deity. This unique status includes both a special *relationship* and a special *capacity.*

This creature with the human face is drawn into a singular relationship with God. With this segment of creation there is to be a history of claim and response. Humanity thereby represents creation before its Maker. On this race the Light shines and to it the eye of God turns. The relationship we individually have, a being-be-fore-God, is our *soul.* Out of this divine communion with humanity is born a capacity to see the Intention of God and to choose to obey its imperatives (Gen. 2:17). Thus the power to perceive the freedom and unity in the Vision of God is granted to the being made in the image of that Vision. The sight of Shalom gives us understanding of who God is, who we are, and the community for which we are destined (Gen. 2:15–18). This capacity includes our *reason,* but rises above it in its perception of the purpose of God and freedom to choose it. Such self-transcendence is *spirit.* As God is Spirit, so humanity made in the divine image is spirit (Job 27:3; 33:4).

What is granted to humanity in creation is subject to the Fall, a theme yet to be examined. Therefore what we have and are as humans in *existence* is not the same as the humanity we share in *essence.* The image of God in us becomes distorted and the Vision perceivable by the essential eye of the soul fades from the horizon of our existential eye under the impact of our rebellion. Whether the essence be thought of as given in a period of literal paradisaical life before Adam and Eve ate the apple—a cosmology not here assumed—or whether the essence of humanity be understood as the intention of God at the creation of the first emergent humans and even now as the Light shines on each of us calling us to responsible use of freedom in decisions yet to be made—the view here presupposed—it suffers the obfuscation of our sin, and therefore meets us as a shadowed image. How serious this defect is we shall presently inquire. Here we describe "original righteousness" as that relationship and capacity as it is formed for the return of God's overture of love. In its essential nature humanity is shown the Vision and given the power to respond to it.

While we are made in the image of God we are not gods. The image of God is conjoined to and inseparable from the physical and social roots that mark all creation. A human being is characterized by *creatureliness* as well as by the image of God. Creatureliness also entails relationship and capacitation. As creature, humanity is finite not infinite, brought to be by the Infinite and dependent upon the Creator of all things. The relationship of finitude and derivation is manifest in the spatiality and temporality of human creatureliness (Gen. 2:7). The limitations of living "at the juncture of nature and spirit" (Reinhold Niebuhr), the dependence on the network of social and natural processes, formation by institutional as well as biological forces, all register the finitude of capacity that reflects the finitude of relationship. Our contingency extends to the powers of the image of God itself: humanity's reason and spirit are shaped, although not exhaustively determined, by the physical and social factors that are partners in the psychosomatic and psychosocial unity of human selfhood. Our dependency and inter-dependency, our genes and our environment, remind us of our derived existence (Ps. 90:3–12).

CREATION OUT OF NOTHING

While creation is not God, it is *good*. The material and historical world is not cut from the cloth of divinity, but it is brought to be out of the divine Dream. Therefore it is a reality to be affirmed and celebrated. The ancient teaching of "creation out of nothing" steers a course for the Christian Story between two tempting and finally disastrous alternatives. On the one hand, there are those who seek to ennoble either nature or humanity by elevating them to divinity however conceived, from nature worship to giddy claims of human virtue. In so doing they invite either naturalistic worship of tree and star or the modern demonic expression of the same, the worship of blood and soil. Or they can fall prey to illusions about human nature that follow the predictable route from fanaticism and self-righteous fury to disillusionment and retreat from the human venture. While there are no utopian expectations in the Story about nature and humanity, there is the affirmation of their fundamental dignity as creatures that come to be out of God's intention and execution. ("God invented matter, therefore he must like it"—William Temple.) But this creation is "ex nihilo." It does not ooze out of divinity itself and therefore cannot be confused with its Source nor give grounds for the idolatries that follow from that divinization. Also, because it is "out of nothing," the world was not formed from pre-existing matter whose dualistic status makes it, by definition, of dubious parentage, or somehow out of the range of divine concern and even control. "Being, as such, is good" (Augustine). Therefore, no matter how created being may stubbornly resist its purpose and fall away from the Vision of God, it is, in its most essential character, a good gift of God.

SCIENCE AND STORY

An interlude in our narration is appropriate here in order to under-score an assumption. We have dealt with creation without defensive sorties against, or hat-in-hand collapse before, the scientific under-standings and related philosophical interpretations of the origin of the world. The reason is twofold. On the one hand, the painful debates of the nineteenth century have helped us to see that the fundamental intention of the Christian Story is not to detail the way the world came to be; the Bible is not a book on astrophysics. The Storybook tells the tale of its meaning and destiny. On the other hand, when science performs its task, it reports on how it was and is with this world, as discerned by the most rigorous study of its patterns and rhythms. Indeed as the Storytellers have a way of making use of the current wisdom on the question of the "hows" in dealing with its own "whys" and "whats," so the Genesis account of creation uses the science of its day to make its point.

When we see the use so made by the biblical narrator of the culture's intellectual frameworks, we must take them for what they are: cosmologies of that time and place. Scientists do the same kind of borrowing when they step out of their laboratories and speculate about what it all means and where it is headed. But we must also take that for what it is: scientists wearing the hat of philosopher or believer. If the Bible is read not for encyclopedic wisdom that can be better gotten from encyclopedias, then the telling and hearing of the Tale will go on without diversions which lead nowhere.

But there is another reason for discussing the partnership possible between science and faith. It has to do with learnings that some believers once felt were threatening, but now in fact are supportive. Research and interpretations of the origin and devel-opment of the universe and the human race do, by the very nature of their growth metaphor, posit both a beginning point and a pilgrim-age. In each instance the best thought of the scientific community and its attendant philosophies converge with themes integral to the Christian Story: that there *was* a creation (in contrast to notions of the eternity of the world), and that there *is* a history, a movement with direction. The fact that there is a beginning to the Story is integral to its meaning, and so is the affirmation of movement, however crude the cosmology used to describe its earlier phases, or however dubious some of its accounts about events at its culmina-tion point. The science of a particular age may choose to argue otherwise, but right now the conventional wisdom seems to accord with faith's perceptions of a real beginning and a real movement.

Because of this convergence, as well as the recognition of the particularities of each area of inquiry and belief, there is no noise of battle here between the affirmations of faith and the discoveries of the laboratory.

CREATION AND TRINITY

The work of creation we have been exploring is the labor of the trinitarian God. In ancient thought about the Trinity, especially in its early phases, the Trinity emerged as a way of expressing the chapters in the Christian Story, or the fundamental divisions of them, sometimes described as *creation, reconciliation,* and *redemption.* And the modes of the triune God's being were seen to be manifest in and through those movements: God as Father and Creator, Son as Reconciler, Spirit as Redeemer. Therefore when we speak of the work of the Trinity in creation, it is God's parenting action that is to the fore, as in the Apostles' Creed: "I believe in God the Father Almighty, Maker of heaven and earth." The first person of the Trinity is God the Creator.

Yet all the actions of the Trinity interpenetrate in the oneness of Godhead. From the beginning of Christian reflection about the creation it has been insisted that the Son and the Spirit were also present and active in creation. Our own idiom accents this partnership, for the world is made according to the design of the Vision of Shalom. It bears the mark in its freedom pilgrimage and guidance toward solidarity of the work of the Son. Jesus Christ is the Alpha of creation. The Logos Vision gives the world shape and direction from the beginning. "He was in the beginning with God; all things were made through him, and without him was not anything made that was made" (John 1:2–3 RSV).

The same partnership is true of the Holy Spirit. The power of the Spirit etches the Vision indelibly on the universe and in humanity. It is the Holy Spirit that brings the world to be in accord with the dream of Shalom. And that same Son and Spirit persist with the Father, continuing the creativity that bestows freedom and moves toward unity. Creation is a making, done by the Envisioner according to the Vision and enabled by the Power of God.

CONTINUING CREATION

"God calls the worlds into being, creates humankind in the divine image. . . ." These words of a contemporary confession (The United Church Statement of Faith, revised) put the doctrine of creation in the present tense. The divine creativity is not limited to the beginnings of the world. The continued existence of the world depends on the freedom of God to re-create, to perpetuate this great experiment in Shalom (Lam. 3:23). But more, the newness that marked inception persists. The process of "creative transformation" that has claimed the attention of contemporary science and philosophy is the continuing work of the God who "makes all things new" (Rev. 21:5). The freedom thrusting toward togetherness at the center of the Vision of God is empowered by the Spirit to bring to be the things that were not in the patterns of universal growth. So the trinitarian Life leaves its mark in the processes of creativity and mutuality in the world (cf. Augustine).

The chapter on Creation, original and continuing, sets forth the Christian belief that God did not will to be God without the world, that it was not fit that none behold the Light (Gregory of Nyssa). As brought to be by God, creation's existence and fulfillment is God's intention. Therefore the goal toward which this Story presses is one that includes the glorification of nature and humanity, the cosmos in all its heights and depths. This chapter tells of a Dream born to be. Creation is the great invitation. We turn now to the response to that invitation.

CHAPTER II
Fall

<hr/>

While we can grasp some of the meaning of the creation from the continuing divine creativity, it is another chapter of the Christian story whose effects mark our life today more profoundly. Because of this act in the drama, the full possibilities of creation go unrealized and largely unnoticed. Here is recounted a stumble, and finally a Fall that cripples our pilgrimage toward the goal and obscures the Vision set before us.

Hearing the Story's report of what happened connects so forcefully with the fact of our present fall, that what was said to be an event then could and does pass for an account of what takes place right now. Adam, after all, means "humankind." His saga is ours. However, what is with us is what always has been. The first creature with a human face to emerge from the womb of the world participates in that Fall as surely as we do, and thus marks its beginning (Gen. 3; Rom. 3:10,12).

How that drama of perverted vision is enacted we express with the categories at hand. In this case it means an ancient writer in the Storybook, populating the scenery with talking snake, holy tree, and modest couple. But again the *that* and *what,* rather than the *how* of the happening, are the heart of the matter.

Our curiosity, and perhaps our ambition also to eat of the tree of absolute knowledge of good and evil, prompt us to theorize that some biological inheritance of our progenitor's self-serving tendencies may explain our own. This indeed is a convenient theory, even reaching orthodox status in some eras of Christian thought. But the theory itself is a nice bit of evidence of the very sin it seeks to explain. For it places the blame back there somewhere on "the first man," thus relieving us of responsibility. And it has introduced into the bloodstream of Christianity a foreign body that has done untold damage—the denigration of the flesh and the sexuality which are presumed to be the conduits of this inherited capacity. Zealous attempts to penetrate what we must finally admit is the "mystery of iniquity" are best left to others less impressed with the infinite capacity of a self-deception that attends the Fall. It is enough for us to know that the human race has fallen, that the intention of Shalom has met the deepest resistance in ourselves. And to know *what* that means, to understand its dynamics, is a companion insight from this chapter of the Christian Story.

SIN

The Fall of humanity means that *sin* is our response to the invitation of God. Sin is the code word in the Christian Story for the turning inward of the self, and thus the turning away from God, neighbor, and nature. It is the use of our freedom to serve ourselves, rather than the employment of that freedom in the service of God and the divine purpose. Sin is an "ego trip" inward, rather than a pilgrimage outward and ahead toward the horizon of Shalom (Rom. 8:7).

The self-serving life is more than just a moral lapse. As militancy against the Envisioner of freedom and peace, sin is an assault on God. It is the preference of one's own vision to God's Vision, a perception of the world as circling about the self, rather than a Shalom in which God is the center around which we orient our lives. As a strategy to preempt the place of God, sin is idolatry. To reject the divine Vision and to substitute for it another dream is to live in a world in which the place of God is usurped by our megalomania (Rom. 1:18–23).

As with Prologue and Creation, so the fundamental meaning of the Fall is to be traced to the center of the Story. The lethal reaches of human sin are revealed in our dealing with the God who comes into our midst in Jesus Christ. As the purity of the Vision is disclosed in him, so also is exposed the animosity to the Vision in the human heart. The depths of the resistance to Shalom manifest here and in our subsequent struggle with the Incarnate Vision give us the framework in which the teller of the Christian Story views the universal human plight and the specific biblical account of it in this chapter.

One of the searching perceptions of the human situation found in the Christian understanding of the Fall is its grasp of how we actually seek to use the primal Vision for our own purposes. In our sin we never completely escape an awareness of our destiny as both the support and screening of our own self-seeking. We pretend that what we do is in fact *for* God! Self-serving is cloaked in the garments of righteousness. We claim that the things we do, things which are calculated to puff our ego and promote our reputation, are in fact for the benefit of God, humanity, and even nature. Those who know the Christian Story will therefore always have a sharp eye for the hypocrisy which shrouds itself in piety. Christ opens our eyes to the pretentious who declare, "Thank God I am not as others!" And surely among the pretentious Christ includes our own self-righteous fury that uses virtue as a veil to its self-seeking and does not understand its own lethal possibilities. Thus it is the good people and the wise people and the religious people who come in for sharpest criticism in the biblical narrative. And most of all, those who read the Story aright know that it is we, in our own presumed piety and morality, who must come under the most penetrating searchlight of this exposure of phariseeism (Luke 18:9–14).

What are the effects of the turnaround to the self and turnaway from the Vision of God? The most obvious is the rift it creates among the intended friends of God. The greatest harm is done to the relationship between humanity and Deity. Our rebellion separates us from God. By turning from the Light we put ourselves in the Night. We are out of touch with what we are called to be; we are not in that communion for which we are made. By rejecting the friendship of God we make an enemy. To turn from the Light is to reject Life and choose death. The wages of sin are death, a death that in its profoundest meaning is separation from Life, and therefore from God (Rom. 6:23).

The death grip of alienation affects all the intended relationships to which we are called. We become estranged from our neighbor as well as God. We set ourselves against the intended human partner; swords are raised and spears are sharpened. Into the world comes a disharmony that issues from the competing claims of a self-serving humanity. And that same incurving impulse extends to nature as well as to our fellow humans. Rather than enter into community with the birds of the air, the beasts of the wood, and the flowers of the field, we pollute the atmosphere, rape the land, and convulse the animal world with our unfeeling attacks on the environment. Humanity sets itself against itself and nature, as well as against God.

The effects of sin seep into the self as well as into its relationship with others. The very Light given in creation, the sight of Shalom as our destiny, loses its brilliance. As we turn to the darkness, we lose sight of the Light. We can no longer perceive it with clarity, surrounded as it is with our self-made shadows. Our turning inward puts in the shadows the divine spark. Thus the original image of God in the depths of each human no longer has the power of attraction it had in the original purpose of God (Rom. 1:21). Our conscience is no longer clear or compelling.

But that image continues to disturb and entice us. God's original claim upon us never departs. God does not "leave himself without witness" in the depths of the self (Acts 14:17 RSV), and in the lengths and breadths of nature and history. We are always aware of something of our destiny, a dim reflection of the primal Light, a persistent clue to the Dream. We have discussed the import of this in our exploration of "general revelation." That inner eye made to see the Light always is aware of the terrible breach of the covenant. Thus we are divided within ourself as well as separated from God, neighbor, and nature. We know what we should do but cannot do it. "The good which I want to do, I fail to do, but what I do is the wrong which is against my will . . ." (Rom. 7:19).

We cannot do as we ought, as Paul testifies, because our state has become a slavery. The mystery of iniquity includes the bondage of our will. We have given ourselves over to sin and cannot by our best efforts break out of this self-imprisonment. We are captives of our megalomania, our idolatry. "I see in my members another law at war with the law of my mind and making me captor to the law of sin that dwells in my members. Miserable creature that I am. Who is then to rescue me out of this body doomed to death?" (Rom. 7:23–24). We are enslaved and alienated. Who will bring liberation and reconciliation?

EVIL

"Deliver us from evil" our Lord prayed. Evil has been painted in many colors and drawn in many shapes by the Christian tradition. It has been thought of as the Evil One, Satan, the Devil, the personification of all that opposes the Vision of God. Evil may be described also as the demonic forces that account for a range of disruption running from sick bodies and deranged minds to natural disasters and historical cataclysms. In the Old Testament's picture of the origin of sin through the blandishment of the snake, and the New Testament's record of the temptation of Jesus by Satan, the powers of evil play a role as the occasion for sin, including the very predisposition to the Fall. How can we translate these themes and images into the language and thought of our own time and place?

Evil comes to us today less in the guise of anthropomorphic figures of major or minor proportions, and more in terms of forces ranged against Shalom, at work in the self, in history, and in nature. We have different words for them—psychological, sociological, political, geological, medical—but they are no less real today than when another cosmology identified them in its own categories. When these powers of darkness confront us in high technology warfare, oppressive political structures, enslaving economic systems, raging impulses in personal and mass psychology, horrifying disease, and natural disaster, they do the same kind of damage as that perceived by Luther as the Satan at whom he threw his ink well. While we may not be prone to think of them personified in a Devil, they are at the very least Evil. Many are the efforts to exorcise these forces, from the levitation of the Pentagon by the countercultural protester to the strange readiness of a multitude in our presumed secular society to believe in, supplicate, or arrange their lives around, the movements of the stars and the ids.

That there are evil forces at work in our midst which keep company with our sin is part and parcel of the Story, confirmed by contemporary experience. This experience sensitizes us to the reality of "principalities and powers" as Paul calls them (Eph. 6:12), ranged against the visions of freedom and peace. How they are to be described depends on the framework of thought that is meaningful to a given time and place. Here we identify them as the forces of evil.

The Story tells us about some aspects of the *what* and the *that.* In the Genesis account we learn that evil, symbolized by the snake, poses the temptation that occasions the Fall. The character of the temptation of the serpent and the fact of the predisposing force give us a clue to contemporary meaning. The temptations of Adam and Eve were to eat of the tree of the knowledge of good and evil. This was an offer of power, a power which was the snake's to give. What characterizes the "thrones and authorities" is *power,* be they power structures or inner drives, the power to form the future. In ancient thought, angels have the power that humanity does not have. And now the offer comes to a dependent creature of God's, a humanity "lower than the angels," the temptation to seize power that belongs to God alone. Knowledge is immense power when we consider the strength to shape the future that our present knowledge has given to us. And so the acquisition of power for self-serving ends is the temptation that precipitates the Fall. Power corrupts, and the kind of absolute power offered by the authorities of this world—the power to be like God—corrupts absolutely. These structures and drives in self and society, in nature and history have never ceased to work their wiles upon us. We can understand the Story's report of the first drama of sin because it conforms to the power-hungry self-seeking found in our own private theater of action.

Is it possible that this corruption of freedom by the lust for power sheds some light on the existence of evil itself? How do these forces of evil come to be, forces that the Storybook indicate preexist the Fall of humanity itself? There is no clear answer given in Christian tradition, although there are some scenarios that have exercised great influence, and not infrequently have been confused with the more modest affirmations of the Story itself. Again, this is a case where cultural motifs are harnessed to the work of making faith intelligible. The occupational hazard of this type of translation is that the clever themes of the current world view have a way of intruding themselves into the Story, finally distorting it. Our borrowings can help or hurt. Modesty is the best policy, an unobtrusive sortie in philosophical and social exploration that stops short of explanation.

We have suggested that there is in the growth of the universe a spontaneity thrusting toward unity. The philosophical theories that project these images and interpretations are characteristically reticent about such themes as "sin" and "evil." There is little indication of skepticism or sobriety about the signs of indeterminacy in nature. Where there is philosophical curiosity about freedom in the cosmos, its possibilities are viewed as conforming to the vision of unity. A less sanguine view of that sensibility might speculate about its abuse as well as its use, a perversion similar in kind to the corruption of human freedom. Can *powers* as well as *persons* pervert freedom? Does the refrain of fallen angels suggest the possibility of a pre-human distortion of the growth God intends toward Shalom? Is there a continuing tendency to turn away from the purposes of creativity and mutuality in the world of nature and the structures of the power around us? Is the report of the snake tempting Adam and Eve a biblical witness to a perversity within nature corrupting the good creation of God?

One does not have to deal in the kind of imagining that comes easier to earlier epochs to speculate in philosophical terms about wrong directions in the cosmos itself. Such speculation is not part of the Christian Story, but it sheds some light on an aspect of the Story: that all creation, humanity as well as the powers, is *as such* good. Power and persons come from God, with the stamp of Shalom upon them. No metaphysical dualism that sees evil as an eternal No alongside of God (and not ultimately related to the divine sovereignty or dealt with finally by the same regency) is compatible with the Christian Story. The powers in the universe come from God even as we do. Power structures and drives, authorities and principalities were made to serve a function in the divine economy. But powers as well as persons may have gone through the cycle of temptation and Fall. Indeed the source of the Fall may be the same, the temptation to abuse power. Why both they and we fall, why that power proves too much for our freedom and theirs we cannot answer, as it is veiled in the "mystery of iniquity." But *that* there are powers which manifest themselves in nature and history at work against Shalom we do know. And *what* we do know also is how they are the occasion of human sin, Adam's and ours.

DEATH

In common parlance death means biological termination. In Christian faith the meaning of death reaches further. It includes the culmination of history itself, a subject we shall deal with in the last chapter of the Christian Story. And in its profoundest meaning death is separation from God. It is in this final sense that we deal with it here, for the wages of sin and evil are this kind of demise. The result of bondage is alienation.

Separation from God in our translation of the Story is estrangement from the Vision of the Envisioner. It is death to the Dream of God. As such it is severing of all the ties that bind us. If life is the unity of humanity, nature, and God, then death is their fracture.

Death is the alienation of the self from God. It is turning away from the Light in pursuit of one's self-serving ends. Sin is the about-face from the Vision which brings upon itself the stumble and fall into the darkness. What we choose is what we get: "sin pays a wage, and the wage is death" (Rom. 6:23).

Death is alienation *within* humanity as well as *between* humanity and God. As in Donald Baillie's suggestive figure of the circle of joyful dancers who choose to turn away from the Light and therefore must break their handclasps with companions, so our alienation from God brings in its wake separation from the neighbor. The effect of our self-exaltation is the sundering of the bonds with fellow-humanity. And the unity within the self as well as the community among humans is destroyed as we experience inner discord together with outer strife.

Death is also alienation between humanity and nature. The arrogance of human sin is such that it carries out its designs against its neighbor, nature. Its attacks on the environment poison the atmosphere, contaminate the soil and waters, relentlessly consume its riches, and ravage the creatures with whom it shares this home.

Sin finds an ally in its destructive work in the powers of evil. These mysterious forces in both history and nature add their lethal impact. The fallen systems and structures of this world and the skewed processes of nature fashion pruning hooks into spears, make nature red in tooth and claw, and bring fire and flood, plague and pestilence (Rom. 8:22).

Inseparable from this larger death of the Vision of God is mortality itself. Captive to the powers of sin and evil, our destiny in this world is not life but death, God projected a larger future for us in the divine Vision, but we chose another path. The reminder of our wanderings in a far country is mortality and the sorrow that attends this end short of the Kingdom for which we have been made

(Isa. 40:6–8). But the close of our odyssey on earth is not the End of the Tale.

PROVIDENCE

The Maker of heaven and earth is also its ever-present Sustainer. And that sustenance in a fallen world means support for the things that make for Shalom and defense against the enemies of God. This belief in Providence is integral to the Christian Story. In the most elementary terms, it is the conviction that "God takes care of his own." God's own is first and foremost God's Son, the Vision of liberation and reconciliation. God takes care of Shalom, protecting it from its enemies and encouraging it in its friends. Thus Providence is the *power* of the Purpose that runs through the world, the Spirit that "in everything . . . works for good" (Rom. 8:28 RSV).

As the conviction that history is the workshop for "perfectly wise and loving ends" (General Assembly, Church of Scotland), the belief in Providence is a way of viewing the entirety of the Christian narrative. Time is in holy keeping. Neither fate nor chance, neither the stars nor the cycles of nature and history, determine what shall be, but the implacable love of God moving toward its goal. Providence is not puppetry; we are free to be for that goal. But we are not free from its call and claim. As with Creation and Fall, so Providence rises out of the defining deeds of God from the deliverance of Israel to the resurrection of Christ. Our understanding of divine governance comes out of Israel's history with God, our Covenant chapter, and its fulfillment in the person and work of Jesus Christ. While we leap ahead of our Story for the fact and character of this direction, we discuss Providence at this point after the Fall as witness to the commitment and power of God in the face of the most malignant of opposition. For the way in which a patient Providence establishes final dominion we wait upon the climactic events of Easter and Eschaton.

Providence can be seen in the processes of self and society, history and nature. It works to heal over the scars of the destructive bolt of lightning that slashes a tree, effects the same Shalom in the wounded body whose cells repair at the tender urging of this secular grace, and its power is manifest in the mind cloven by hate that makes its way to health again. Providence can show a sterner face when a nature ravished by pollutants strikes back through the inversion layer over the city, the chemically eroded food and water sources, the infertile fields, and the desolated timber ranges. The work of judgment comes to the self that has failed to learn the lesson "love or perish," and to the society that has not listened to the prophetic call to let justice and righteousness reign, and which therefore suffers from the "rod of my anger" (Isa. 10:5 RSV). In the history of nature and humanity there is a law of Shalom at work. It cannot be violated with impunity or the consequences are dire. When the structures meet us in judgment or buoy us up in grace it is the Providence of God being confronted, one that "has brought down the monarchs from their thrones, but the humble have been lifted high" (Luke 1:52).

It is not only in the macrocosm of nature and history, and in the boundaries set to the rebellion of the world, that Providence does its work. There is also a tender and individuating care that numbers the hairs of our heads and marks the sparrow's fall (Matt. 10:29–31). The eye of faith sees the hand of God laboring to shape our personal lives toward "wise and loving ends." Indeed the meanings to be found in this microcosm do not come easily. Providence struggles with "thrones and authorities" only too eager to fell the sparrow and bruise the head. Yet the light that comes from the central chapter of this Story, the knowledge that the powers of this fallen world do not have final charge of our destinies, illumines even those events whose darkness seems most impenetrable.

Toward the decisive act in this drama which gives us perspective on Prologue, Creation, and Fall, we continue to move.

CHAPTER III

Covenant

The Vision of God has been lost from view in the fall of the world. A wandering humanity stumbles on its journey towards the horizon and wanders into darkness. In the gloom the Light cannot be seen and therefore holds no attraction. Somehow the goal must be brought to visibility again so it may exercise its compelling power, and the world may be turned toward its destination.

For the sights to be seen by humanity, this horizon must reappear in history. To be in history is to be at a specific place and point and therefore to risk the "scandal of particularity." That presence in one strand of the human community assumes the role of *pars pro toto,* the part on behalf of the whole. The next chapter of the Story tells of a persistent God unthwarted by the resistance of the race who moves toward the world to make the Vision known. A particular people is chosen to *see the Light.* God makes a covenant: the Vision will shine before Israel as a pillar of Fire, and the people will follow it.

We have already drawn upon some insights from this chapter for our understanding of the form and content of the foundational covenant of God with the world. As with Easter so with Exodus, the central events in the narrative are clues to the meanings found throughout the Story. From the history of Israel we learn that God does not will to be God without a life together with the world in freedom and peace. That is the primal covenant. We now examine this particular covenant that sheds light on the all-embracing one.

A covenant, *berith,* is the solemn promise to fulfill a declared purpose. As a chapter in the epic of God's dealings with the world, Covenant has to do with the divine promise to keep the divine purpose: it is God's word to fulfill the Vision. Set as it is in the midst of the history of the world's rebellion against God's intention, its initiatory and in-spite-of character comes clear. Covenant in biblical perspective is the stubborn, unswerving commitment to the Shalom God wills for the world. But more than a general faithfulness to that purpose, it is a pledge to execute this intention through a particular people. It is by way of Israel that the Dream will come to reality. We shall explore the living out of this compact in the deeds done, the Word shared, and the Vision disclosed in the life of this people and its chief prophet, priest, and king.

Covenant is demand as well as gift. To whom much is given from them much is required. In God's covenanting action the partner is beckoned to follow the pursuit of the Vision. While no human act of obedience or disobedience can make or break the covenant, judgment attends our disdain of it and faithlessness to it. Neither the rebellion of a particular people nor the assault of the world on the Vision can turn God aside from the promise made. But imperatives do keep company with the indicatives of election, and our accounting shall be made in the penultimate judgments of history and the ultimate reckonings of eternity.

Why this people in this time and this place? We confront an enigma, the mystery of divine election. This scenario will be the sternest testing of the sturdiest stuff. The fertile crescent is such a place to carry on an experiment in faithfulness, located in a Mediterranean land bridge for marching armies, a prey of imperialisms and the pawn of political machinations. If an act of loyal seeing and serving is to be authentic, it must weather the worst of the world's turmoil. And more than that, it must face the hatred evoked by that people seeing and saying what the world is made for.

For this mission God needs the sturdiest and the most stubborn. Why Israel as the chosen people? Finally our speculations fade into silence, replaced by our thanksgiving that God also is a stubborn God who will not give up on us, and therefore enters this covenant to keep the Vision before us.

EXODUS AND LAW

An event takes place that gives high visibility to the divine purpose. God does a deed among his people that enacts the Dream of liberation and reconciliation. The chosen people are freed from slavery. God leads Israel out of Egypt and into a land flowing with milk and honey, a homeland of Shalom (Exod. 12:37–14:31). The people of God taste the fruit of the promised land of freedom and togetherness. The Exodus becomes the pivot on which their history turns, and the event that makes them a visionary people.

The deliverance from Egypt is followed by a rhythm of promise and fulfillment in the history of Israel. The God of the Exodus displays a "mighty arm" in preserving the vision of this people, goading them into loyalty to it, protecting them from the assaults of enemies, and giving portents and signs of Shalom. In these events, Israel perceives and records the divine initiative and steadfast loyalty of this God to the purpose and people of the covenant.

This covenant cannot be understood without real hope for its embodiment of Shalom in time and space, and belief in the God whose presence in history makes these promises possible. But this action of God comes in judgment as well as promise, for the One who liberates also rebukes (Exod. 32:30–35). Time after time God calls the people to account for breach of the covenant. Yet, especially in the early layers of covenant tradition, there is the assurance that the deliverance from Egypt represents a kind of relationship that the people of God can always expect from the One who has chosen them, thus assuring vindication of Israel's hopes. Moreover, the covenant sealed by the Exodus action of God points not only forward to fulfillment but also back in due time to the covenant of creation itself in which it is demonstrated that God does not will to be God without this world, and that this Deity confirms the originating bond with humanity in the covenants with Noah and Abraham, and now at Exodus by the call of Israel to be the light that enlightens the nations. Exodus and its antecedents and derivations, therefore, announce the action of God to pursue determinately the vision on the very terrain of its resistance, by way of enactment, disclosure, and support of that Purpose and those people called to respond to it by an electing, prevenient grace.

As part of this covenanting action God sets forth the laws of the New Land, the precepts of Shalom: a *decalogue* of imperatives of the love of God and the love of the neighbor (Exod. 20:1–12). The patriarch is given the eye to see clearly what our failed human vision only dimly perceives. And it is shared with the people, these commandments of turning to the Light, and the seeing and serving of God and neighbor. This Law is a realistic one which presupposes the already present fallenness of the world, couched as it is in its "thou shalt not's." And that Law is kept alive by priests who celebrate it and make atonement for those who break it, and sages who meditate on and expound it. Hence the ritual life of the temple that environs the Law, and the wisdom traditions of the people of God.

THE PROPHETS

Most of all, the vision of the intended future, of which the Promised Land, its laws, rituals, and lore are at best foretastes, is given to certain *seers* of the ultimate Light. These *prophets* are forthtellers of the claims of God on the people. But they tell what they see. Therefore they are fore*seers* as well, those who perceive the vision of this intended future of God with their inner eye, and declare its meaning to the chosen people in both word and deed. The prophet portrays in the most vivid colors and sharpest outline the goal of God—a world in which nature, humanity, and God dwell in peace and freedom.

The life together to which the seer points reaches into the animal world. "The wolf shall live with the sheep, and the leopard lie down with the kid; the calf and the young lion shall grow up together . . . and the cow and the bear shall be friends, and their young shall lie down together" (Isa. 11:6, 7). From there it spreads throughout the realm of nature. "The wilderness will become grassland, and grassland will be cheap as scrub. Then justice shall make its home in the wilderness, and righteousness dwell in the grassland; when righteousness shall yield peace and its fruit be quietness and confidence forever" (Isa. 32:15–17). And this healed nature itself shall reunite with its Maker. "Mountains and hills shall break into cries of joy, and all the trees of the wild shall clap their hands, pine-trees shall shoot up in place of camel-thorn, myrtles instead of briars, all this shall win the Lord a great name, imperishable, a sign for all time" (Isa. 55:12–13). Thus the restoration of nature from its tyrannies and alienations means that God shall "create new heavens and a new earth" (Isa. 65:17).

The new harmony reaches up to encompass humanity, reknitting the torn fabric of relationship between humanity and nature. "The infant shall play over the hole of the cobra, and the young child dance over the viper's nest" (Isa. 11:8). "Then my people shall live in a tranquil country. . . . it will be cool on the slopes of the forest then, and cities shall lie peaceful on the plain. Happy shall you be, sowing every man by the waterside and letting ox and ass run free" (Isa. 32:18–20). "I will rid the land of wild beasts, and men shall live in peace of mind on the open pastures and sleep in the woods. I will settle them in the neighborhood of my hill and send them rain in due season, blessed rain. Trees in the countryside shall bear their fruit, and the land shall yield its produce, and men shall live in peace of mind on their own soil" (Ezek. 34:24–27).

To the healing of nature and the relationships between nature and humanity is added the healing of the nations. "They shall beat their swords into mattocks and their spears into pruning-knives; nation shall not lift sword against nation nor ever again be trained for war" (Isa. 2:4). And conjoined to this harmony will be freedom for the oppressed and justice for the downtrodden. "Listen to this, you cows of Bashan . . . you who oppress the poor, and crush the destitute" (Amos 4:1). "Shame on those who lie in bed planning evil and wicked deeds and then at daybreak they do them. . . . they covet the land and take it by force; if they want a house they seize it; they rob a man of his home and steal every man's inheritance" (Mic. 2:1–2).

The freedom and peace among people and nations becomes freedom and peace within persons as well. "Each man shall dwell under his own vine, under his own fig-tree, undisturbed" (Mic. 4:4).

And it is the prophets that pull the various images of the future together under the embracing theme of Shalom: "I will make with them a covenant of *shalom* . . . and they shall know that I am the Lord, when I break the bars of their yoke, and deliver them from the hand of those who enslave them. They shall no more be prey to the nations, nor shall the beasts of the land devour them; they shall dwell securely, and none shall make them afraid. And I will provide them plantations of *shalom* . . ." (Ezek. 34:25, 27–29). "Then justice and righteousness will dwell in the wilderness, and righteousness abide in the fruitful field. And the effect of righteousness will be *shalom,* and the result of righteousness, quietness and trust for ever" (Isa. 32:16–17 RSV). The pressures of this Vision come to this people and they have been its stewards ever since. As representatives of all of us they have seen the light and felt the heat of the rays of the Not Yet, and in turn share that pressure and pain with humanity. Through them we see what we were made for.

Being what we are, the response to that Presence in our midst has been one of hostility. We do not like to be reminded of the purpose for which we are made. The Vision of Shalom is an embarrassment to us. So the message is identified with a messenger. This people of the vision have had humanity's hate of its destiny heaped upon them. The roots of anti-Semitism go deep into the soil of the sin in each human being. The resistance to the original Light finds yet another target in the history of the chosen people as the world directs its holocaust hate against those who steward the Vision of God.

WHERE DOES THE COVENANT LEAD?

The clarity of Israel's vision of the purposes of God early posed certain enigmas to its people. If the Lord of history wills shalom, then why do those who pursue it suffer and those who scorn it appear to prosper? The entreaties of the psalmist and the protests of Job combined with assurances and hopes of the same that this will not finally be so. Interlaced with the struggle over the disparity between the claims of Deity and deeds of the wicked, there was a sense that for those who breached the covenant there were ways of making amends. At first conceived more in ceremonial fashion, but later in fundamentally moral terms, were the priestly tradition's rituals of atonement. Joined by penitence to the offering, the sinner made a sacrifice to God. Repentance so executed reestablished the broken bond.

As the prophet lived with the vision and read the calamities of Israel in the light of it, the earlier questions of the suffering of innocents and the sins of the wicked were seen in a deeper dimension. Now it was perceived that "the heart is the most deceitful of all things, desperately sick; who can fathom it?" (Jer. 17:9). The division between the righteous and the wicked is transcended by the division between God and humanity as such. Why are the good in fact sinful? And how can the Shalom of God exist when the chosen are faithless and the day of the Lord promises to be "darkness, not light" (Amos 5:20)? How will the steadfast God who calls all wickedness to accountability fulfill the promise to bring the Kingdom when all its hoped-for citizenry set their faces so resolutely against that purpose and deserve a rebuke commensurate with their rebellion?

Answers to those questions are advanced in various late traditions of the Old Testament. Their common features are: 1) God can be counted on to keep the divine promise. Wickedness will be punished, righteousness will prevail, and the purpose of God shall be fulfilled. 2) The future will be the time of fulfillment. 3) It will be universal in scope, covering all history and nature.

Within the agreement that God shall vindicate the divine purposes exists a diversity of expectation. The late prophetic tradition suggests an intra-historical consummation in which the poor and oppressed will be vindicated and justice and peace shall prevail. Yet the character of this fulfillment is so different from the way things now are, as for example in the transformation of nature ("the leopard shall lie down with the kid"), that it appears to entail a qualitative rather than a quantitative leap, and thus a radical alternation of our world rather than a simple extension and perfection of what it now is. Another strand of belief is much more stark in its declaration of discontinuity. For the apocalyptic tradition the world culminates in a catastrophe, and a cleansed and transcended Kingdom of righteousness replaces the old world.

In both the historical-transhistorical and the transcendent completions anticipated in the prophetic and apocalyptic traditions, there are the outlines for a figure who in some way facilitates the transformation. In the former case, this person takes the shape of a great prophet like Moses who will lead the people out of slavery. In the latter, the hoped-for vindicator appears more as the Son of Man who will descend from heaven to settle accounts. Thus a Messiah of mundane or supra-mundane qualities is associated with the fulfillment scenarios.

In the characterizations of the fulfillment and the facilitator of it, there is yet another thread of Old Testament thought: that the universal redemption to be wrought must deal with the deeper problem of rebellion posed by the thwarting of God's intention by the "righteous" as well as the wicked. Here portrayed is a universal fulfillment that takes into account the universal rebellion, and which therefore assumes that some fundamental acts of atonement must be part of any consummation. In this context, the messianic figure emerges as a "suffering servant." A rebellion so deep-going that the righteous and chosen also fall under judgment means that any fulfillment to come must bear away the radical sin of the covenant breach. "On himself, he bore our suffering, our torments he carried, while we counted him smitten by God, struck down by disease and misery; but he was pierced for our transgressions, tortured for our iniquities; the chastisement he bore is health for us, and by his scourging we are healed. We are all strayed like sheep, each of us had his own way; but the Lord laid upon him the guilt of us all" (Isa. 53:4–6).

The dynamics within this chapter in the history of God's hope thrust beyond the chapter itself. This doctrine of the covenant portrays the Vision of God as Shalom displaying the steadfast will of God to bind the world to that purpose through historical action. It exposes the conflict between the divine purpose and the world's response, poses the dilemma implicit in this fact, and reaches for the elements that seem to be necessary in any resolution of that dilemma: a real redemption that includes history but is not exhausted by it, a figure that enables fulfillment, a costly act of suffering that is commensurate with the sin of the world. It is within this people of the Covenant who have been called to "be a light to lighten the Gentiles" that the Vision has been given. And it is they who experience God's pursuit of it, who measure the degree of resistance to it, and who point toward the promise of fulfillment and some of the conditions necessary for that fulfillment. So the stage is set for the central act of the drama.

CHAPTER IV

Jesus Christ: Person and Work

What and who will it take to turn the world from darkness to Light? How and where shall liberation and reconciliation be accomplished? This narrative is the *Christian* Story because of the answer it gives to these questions. Its central affirmation is that the *Person* of Jesus Christ is who and what it takes, and the *Work* of Jesus Christ is how and where this deed is accomplished. Here in this decisive chapter is an act of involvement with us which shows the *depths* and *lengths* to which God will go in the struggle with sin, evil, and death. The depth is seen in the enfleshment of the Vision— the *Incarnation.* The length is seen in the life, suffering, death, and victory of the Vision—the *Atonement.*

Although the Person and Work of Jesus Christ in the narrative itself are inseparable, for the purposes of clear analysis it is necessary to treat them individually. As we examine the meaning of the Person of Christ, there will take shape the doctrine of the Incarnation. And as we investigate the Work of Christ, the doctrine of the Atonement will emerge.

THE PERSON OF CHRIST: INCARNATION

Who then is this Jesus Christ? The clamor to answer this question is deafening. Who is he? He is Jesus Christ Superstar, antihero of the counterculture. Not at all! He is the One who walks in the lush garden of Jesus People piety. By no means; Christ is no sentimental Savior of the lost soul, but the aggressive Liberator of the oppressed society . . . or sex . . . or class . . . or race. The air is filled with the claims and counterclaims of those who are quite sure they know him and walk with him—in the garden alone, or with the freedom fighters at the barricades.

In the current wave of interest in the figure of Jesus are two kinds of answers to the question of who he is, not unlike those that have recurred time and again in Christian history. One views him as someone much like us. He is the embodiment of our highest *values*. Jesus is what we are or aspire to be, writ large. On the other hand, there is a view that seeks to separate him from the ordinary lot and likes of humanity. He is what we are not and does what we cannot do, and thus is a fulfillment of our deepest *needs*. In the first case, Jesus is continuous with the world, in the second he is discontinuous; in one he is of a piece with us, albeit the brightest and best, in the other he is no part of us but comes from beyond. Which is he, Superstar or Superman?

This question also vexed the early centuries of Christian thought. Thus it was that the issue of the Person of Christ came to receive the greatest attention in this formative era. Just as in childhood we begin our own identity quest, so Christian theology was preoccupied with this quandary, Who is Jesus Christ? And as the maturation process in humans involves experimenting with different identities borrowed from others (playing the roles of a "significant other"—George Herbert Mead), so the history of the Church's identity quest is marked by a testing process in which some of its members tried on the hats, shoes, and clothing of contemporaries. Experimentation went on with a variety of options that reflected the same duality about Jesus we note today. Hence the "spiritualized" emphasis of such points of view as Docetism, Apollinarianism, and Monophysitism. Beginning with the earlier forms and growing into increasingly sophisticated variations on the same theme, each called into question the earthly reality and humanity of Christ. On the other hand, partisans of Christ's humanity reduced him to that single dimension, or so stressed it as to call into question its relationship to his unity with God. Hence, Ebionism, Adoptionism, Arianism, and Nestorianism. As it happened, each of these particular options was finally deemed a "heresy," a partial truth that passed itself off as a full account of the Person of Christ. But that is to anticipate our own struggle. What we might observe at this point is the common shortcoming of these heresies. Because their versions of Jesus' identity were controlled by the values or needs of the interpreter, they did not do justice to either the record of Jesus in the Book of the Story, or to the experience of and reflection about him in the life of the Christian community. Their account turned out to be more autobiography than the biography of God.

As it matured, the Church developed some guidelines on what that identity does and does not look like. The particular heresies were found to be clothing that had to be discarded, shoes that didn't fit, hats too garish, coats unsuitable for the job and the climate. In the process the Christian community discovered some modest but basic things about who it really was as well as who it was not, having to do with the Person of its Lord. These affirmations, which have achieved universal recognition within the Church, are related to the refrains we have seen expressed in both the current and ancient debates about the meaning of Christ. And as forceful as they are in both what they affirm and what they deny, the Church's theses are minimal, serving more as "no trespassing" signs, warnings of dangerous terrain, and as signposts in the direction of promising exploration. Formulated in different stages at the councils of Nicea (325) and Chalcedon (451), these declarations still enjoy an ecumenical consensus. Who is Jesus Christ? He is *truly God, truly human, truly one.* This fundamental doctrine of the Incarnation—the Deity, humanity, and unity of Jesus Christ—is the Church's effort to be faithful to the figure it met and meets in the pages of the Bible and in its own life with him. As we seek to say what these assertions mean to us today, we must go through that same discipline of understanding the biblical testimony and relating it to the Christian community's experience, past and present.

The Biblical Witness

There is a strong movement today in theology to begin all thinking about the Person of Christ "from below." This means the determination to root whatever is said about Jesus in the earliest layers of Christian tradition, and therefore in those New Testament texts that can be established by critical scholarship to be closest to the words, deeds, and destiny of the Nazarene. This christological method draws heavily upon the research of scholars engaged in "the new quest of the historical Jesus." Those engaged in this inquiry believe that the outlines of Jesus' teaching, behavior, self-understanding, and fate can be discerned in and through the proclamation and editorializing which another generation of biblical studies had deemed too thick to penetrate. Interest in this approach is also related to two other convictions. One is that the Church will only receive a hearing from this secular generation on the basis of well-founded historical claims. The other is that as a religion rooted squarely in history, Christianity should be prepared to deal actively with the Jesus of history.

The quest from below is juxtaposed to Christology "from above." In its traditional form, this method takes the New Testament texts at their face value, without the analysis of historical scholarship, and amasses them as evidence for demonstrating Christ's Deity (for example, John 17:5; 12:45; 14:9–16; Matt. 16:16; 3:17; Mark 1:11; Luke 3:22; 22:69; Heb. 7:3; 1:3; Rev. 22:13) and humanity (for example, Matt. 1:1; 26:37–38; John 4:6; Luke 1:31; 4:2; I Tim. 2:5; 3:16; Gal. 4:4–5; Phil. 2:8; Rom. 8:3; Heb. 2:14; I John 4:2). In its critical form, the quest from above harnesses the results of historical scholarship (the study of the titles ascribed to Jesus, events in his career, homilies, liturgies, catechetical fragments, etc.), accepts the New Testament data as essentially the Church's proclamation, and develops its conception of the Person of Jesus from this testimony, disengaging it from ancient cosmology and sometimes reinterpreting it in existentialist categories.

The approach to Christology from below is a corrective to both the proof-text method of the tradition and the abstract tendencies of "kerygmatic" theology. However, in its present critical mode it gives imperial authority for interpreting the meaning of the central chapter of the Christian Story to a tiny segment of the Christian community, those with technical skills in historical scholarship. This expertise is a genuine gift to the Body of Christ and must be honored as a valuable perspective on the meaning of the Person of Christ. But it must also be demythologized, especially so when it reaches establishment status with power commensurate thereto, for its offerings are themselves conditioned by the sin and finitude common to all. The statement of Christian doctrine is contoured by its learnings (the glass of vision shaped by the rings of Church and world), and the perception of the Gospel is influenced by its findings (the eye of faith peers through the rings of Church and world), but the light of Truth is finally given by the Holy Spirit and passes through the biblical aperture open to all who choose to look through it. We shall make use of the findings "from below" as part, but only as part, of the larger effort to take into account the witness of the biblical seer to the meaning of the Person of Christ.

Our use here of key New Testament data about the Person of Christ is related to our narrative method of expounding Christian belief. As such it might be characterized as Christology "from before" rather than "from below" or "from above." We seek the meaning of Christ from within the unfolding Story. That plot is grounded in the primal Vision of God and proceeds through the events of invitation, resistance, and overture: Creation, Fall, Covenant. Our understanding of who Christ is must have an intrinsic relationship to the thrust of this saga. We shall seek to interpret the doctrine of the Incarnation—the Deity, humanity, and unity of Christ—against this background. And we shall draw upon the resources of Christian tradition and the setting of our contemporary world as well as the biblical source in recounting this central chapter of the Story.

The Deity of Christ

If the answer to who Jesus Christ is grows out of the history of God—as the next chapter in an unfolding narrative—then are there any clues within our Storybook that connect the chapter on Incarnation with its antecedents? Wherever the fulfillment of messianic expectations is cited, it constitutes one set of such clues. Christ's own self-interpretation, messianic or unitive with God in some way, is yet another, leaving aside the exegetical question of whether these passages are in fact the actual words of Christ or those of a later interpreter (for example, Christ's parable of the vinedressers who refused the messengers, then killed the vineyard owner's emissary son, Luke 20:9–16). However, there is a commentary on the meaning of Jesus Christ which puts his coming into the longest possible perspective and makes daring connections between its ultimate origins and their sequel. The manifest insight of this passage has made it a classical locus of christological thought. We refer again to the prologue of John.

The author of this prologue sets the stage for the Incarnation in eternity. The beginnings of Jesus Christ lie in the Godhead. We have called this Logos the eternal Vision of God. Whatever Jesus is to the natural eye reviewing the events in Galilee, the eye of faith sees him in unity with the history of God's pursuit of his eternal purpose. And so John traces the Vision's pilgrimage from the source—"In the beginning was the Vision, and the Vision was with God, and the Vision was God" (John 1:1)—into the maelstrom of claim and rebuff. Thus comes creation in which the Vision marks all that is: "The Vision, then, was with God at the beginning, and through him all things came to be; no single thing was created without him" (John 1:2–3). Also comes that crown of creation, humanity, called to answer for the world God's invitation to Shalom: "All that came to be was alive with life, and that life was the light of men" (John 1:4). But darkness descended, the "No" said by the world to the offer of life and light. "But the darkness never mastered it" (John 1:5). The beckoning of God continues as the "law was given through Moses" (John 1:17). This new vision of the divine claim still does not turn the race away from its pursuit of darkness. Yet the last of the line of this people's visionaries, the prophet John, points to another horizon. For now what was far away signalling to the world from a distance has drawn near. This seer discerns in our midst the Light of the world. "This is the man I meant when I said, 'He came after me, but takes rank before me, for before I was born, he already was'" (John 1:15). In Jesus Christ "the Vision became flesh; he came to dwell among us, and we saw his glory, such glory as befits the Father's only Son, full of grace and truth" (John 1:14).

The Incarnation is the arrival of the One whose previous invitations and entreaties have gone unheeded. Enfleshment means "Emmanuel," *God* with us. The coming of Jesus is the approach of God to the scene of rebellion. No more will messages and messengers do, the inner light of conscience, the outer lights blinking in nature, the pillar of fire that moves in history, or the future light portrayed by the seer. These flashes have been obscured and avoided by the darkness of sin, evil, and death. Now no hiding is possible, for Light comes into our very midst (Luke 2:32; John 8:12; 9:5). "God was *in* Christ . . ." (II Cor. 5:19).

The Journey of the Logos

The way the author of the prologue expresses the coming of God gives unusual insight into the nature of Deity and the relationship between God and the world in Christ. He uses the primarily personal or psychological metaphor of Logos which allows distinctions to be made within Deity, ones that are carried through in such a way as to take account of the narrative of God's action culminating in the unique event of Christ.

Following the Logos distinctions made by Theophilus of Antioch, we might say that the narrative begins with the *Logos endiathetos,* the indwelling Logos, as the inner plan, purpose, reason, and vision of God. Thus God is conceived as *One with Logos,* in both senses of the phrase. There is no God without a purpose, no designless, purposeless, planless, visionless God. Yet there is in this unity a distinction between Purpose and Purposer, Reason and Reasoner, Plan and Planner, Vision and Envisioner. Thus unity and duality are both honored by the metaphor: "The Vision was with God and the Vision was God."

Since the attention of the writer is fixed on the relation of God to Christ, there is no mention in the text of the third aspect of the Godhead, the Holy Spirit. But the narrative implies that the Holy Spirit is the Power to fulfill the Vision, an idea later made explicit in the thinking of the Church as the Story in its fullness was developed.

The focus of the continuing narrative is on the Logos. This is the organ of divine activity, the way God reaches out. John switches to a secondary metaphor regularly associated with Logos, namely light. Reading it against its background meaning, the activity of the divine Light in creation is that of the *Logos prophorikos,* the outgoing of the indwelling Logos. Now inner reason becomes outer expression or word. In ancient thought, a word does what it says; it has effectual power. Hence, the word is creative of the world. Brought to be is the covenant partner of God, the intended friend of God. By using this concept of Logos, the writer and his patristic interpreters were able to link their affirmations about Jesus and the God of Jesus with the cultural sensibilities. In this case it meant that he is of a piece with that design that shapes creation. And more: he is the key to knowing what it is.

At the peak of creation is humanity. Made in the image of God, granted the little light of reason and vision, human beings received the *Logos spermatikos.* This characterization from another ancient father, Justin Martyr, interprets John's references to the "light which enlightens" each person who comes into the world. Joining the metaphor of sowing to that of reasoning, Justin speaks of the seeds of divine wisdom scattered among all people and found in the rational capacity of humans. As we attempt to restate the kernel theme of the tradition in our own idiom, we identify the light granted to humans as the possibilities of vision, and we find John's own references to this capacity as light very hospitable to such an image.

The climax of John's account (in fact a prelude to action yet to come, for this is a prologue which deals with the Person who is about to engage in the Work) takes us from an indwelling Logos through an outgoing and enlightening Logos enacted in the history of Israel to an *enfleshed* Logos. *Logos ensarkos* is the final thrust toward the recalcitrant world, this time one that enters the arena of God's long-time reach and the world's constant rebellion. Incarnation is the enfleshment of the seeking Vision of God, of the God with Shalom on his mind, with the intention of liberation and reconciliation in the divine heart. Incarnation is God with us, God in the Person of the divine Vision, the second Person of the eternal Trinity. In the familial imagery which grows out of the New Testament picture of Jesus' own intimacy with God, what took place at Bethlehem was the coming of the eternal Son of the Father. The trinitarian language of God as Father and Son is a return to the beginning of the metaphor of sonship as a way of expressing the duality in unity of enfleshed Logos. The point being driven home in both incarnational and trinitarian images is that we encounter in Jesus Christ a singular and real Presence of God, a reach into history of that aspect of the Godhead that has been already in lively and agonizing engagement with the world. And this intersection of Vision with reality is one that expresses what God most essentially is, the Envisioner of an eternal Vision.

Two wrongheaded conclusions can be drawn both from the kind of metaphor used to express the finally inexpressible mystery of the Incarnation and from our frail human attempts at clarification. The images of Vision (or Word) and Son both suggest that Incarnation might involve only a side or part of God, that the Envisioner or the Father is once removed from the encounter.

Classical theology evolved the earlier-mentioned notion of "coinherence" of the Persons (mutual interpenetration) to fend off such misunderstanding. Incarnation means the enfleshment *of God as such,* not a feature or phase of Deity. The work to be accomplished in the Incarnation can only be efficacious if it is God in the fullness of Deity that enters the arena of rebellion. The interpenetration of the Persons of the Trinity means that all are present in the functions of each. Thus the Father and Spirit are present in the Person and Work of the Son. Or in Logos terms, there is no Son without Father: the Logos is the "knowledge by which God knows himself" (Augustine); or the Vision by which God sees himself; Christ is the "effulgence of God's splendor, and the stamp of God's very being" (Heb. 1:3); God of God, Light of Light. While it is the Vision of God with which we have to do, it is the Envisioner who shines that Light in the face of Christ. The Father and the Spirit are both present through the Son, Jesus Christ.

Another false path is travelled by popular understandings of Christ, led astray by the language of paternity. Thus some think of the Incarnation as the coming of either a supernatural man who lived with God from all eternity, or as the enfleshment of a second God called the Son who sat in eternal council with Spirit and Father and left this region to be with us. The first idea is a denial of the Incarnation, postulating the preexistence of an eternal man and thus calling into question the uniqueness of the joining of Deity with real humanity in Christ. The second is an exercise in tritheism which fractures the unity of God. The eternal Sonship of God is best read in the light of the personal metaphor of Logos which honors the unity of God, rather than the other way around.

The Spirit is to be understood not as yet another member of a divine club but as the nurturing power of God that brings Bethlehem to be. Jesus Christ is "conceived by the Holy Spirit" and as such is the enfleshment of God. The eternal Son of the Father enters our history by the Spirit. By his power the Vision of the Envisioner appears in our midst.

The Miracle of Shalom

"Conceived by the Holy Spirit, and born of the virgin Mary." The ancient creed celebrates the historical reality of God's power. The descent of the Spirit, divine grace, is characterized always by

97

both favor and power. Grace is *favor toward* and *power in.* The traditional debates about God's personal grace toward us have revolved around whether it is the declaration of pardon toward us or the activity of spiritual power in us. Exclusive emphasis on grace as power has fallen prey to the error of "salvation by works." An exclusive emphasis upon grace as pardon has neglected the fact that we shall know the presence of grace by its fruits, its seeds springing up in good works. The foundation for the duality of favor and power is the Incarnation itself: "The girl's name was Mary. The angel went in and said to her, 'Greetings, most favored one! The Lord is with you'" (Luke 1:27–28). In the ancient world the conviction that the special favor of God had made its entrance into history at this point came to expression in the way divine intrusions were marked, by astounding nature miracles. Favor toward Jesus Christ meant power, and therefore power to make the ordinary extraordinary.

How can this authentic perception that grace is divine favor that manifests itself in divine power be expressed today? In our time it is not the astounding feat of nature but the miracle of history that commands attention. Rendered blasé by both the wonders of science and the constraints of its empirical worldview, the Incarnational signal once given by the teaching of the Virgin Birth no longer is heard by the world. In our era the sign of power is a changed life, the conviction carried by things seen. It is who Jesus was and what Jesus did in his day-to-day relationships that will be scrutinized for evidences of the power that authenticates.

Here a picture emerges from the work of contemporary biblical scholarship on the historical Jesus. The Incarnation of the Vision of Shalom manifests itself in *miracles of shalom.* In what Jesus Christ did in his life and ministry to liberate from the powers of darkness is attested the presence of the Power (Spirit) of the Light (Son). Where the sinner is forgiven and renewed, the arrogant and apathetic turned around, the principality of evil challenged or exorcised, the sick healed, the downtrodden lifted up, the dead raised, and the Good News preached, there the power of Shalom breaks into our history. These things that Jesus did were grounded in who he was: a personal exemplar of Shalom. His life style of selfless love and servanthood embodied the love and servanthood of God. His behavior gave evidence of a freedom from the dark powers and an unswerving commitment to the Light which its ministry sought to extend to others. The Incarnation as a theological affirmation was attested by the signs and wonders of his historical *being* and *doing.* In that twofold sense he is our Peace, and he is our Liberator.

The signs of divine power spill out from the being and doing into the teaching and preaching of Jesus. To him was given the power to see the Vision. Jesus pointed to and prayed for the onrushing future. The reign of God was coming toward the world, the rule in which the pure in heart would see God, the peacemaker would be vindicated, the prisoner released, the lame walk, the dead be raised, and the Kingdom come. In political, personal, and natural idiom he portrayed Israel's ancient hope of Shalom. For him this New Age was at hand when humanity, nature, and God would be free and peaceful before and with each other.

This pointing was more than the future-orientation of the prophet. "At hand" meant *here,* as well as *near.* The power of evil was even now under attack and losing ground to the coming King. And this heavenly favor toward us manifests itself as the power of the Regent who even now casts out of the world the occupying armies of the Evil One. That is why the sick are healed, sins are forgiven, demons exorcised, temptation overcome, and faith empowered. And we are called to pray that this Kingdom finally come on earth in the power of its fulfillment and the glory of its light.

The work of biblical scholarship also gives us a clue to yet another evidence of the inroads of the Vision. It is Jesus' self-understanding. He views himself as the first wave of the inbreaking future. Through him the powers of the New Age find expression. He has authority over the demonic and makes the wounded whole. Through him others are put in touch with the portents of freedom and reconciliation, the firstfruits of the Kingdom that shall be. He is in unity with the new realm and on terms of intimacy with its King. While the debate over the meaning and self-application of the titles of Jesus continues to wax warm, there is an impressive body of scholarship which holds the view that Jesus saw himself to be of a piece with the divine initiative being taken in the Kingdom's arrival.

From Jesus' self-understanding, his embodiment of and teaching about the Kingdom of Shalom, it is a short step to the Church's declaration that in Christ "dwells all the fulness of the Godhead bodily" (Col. 2:9 KJV), and the varied expressions of this unity in the names and categories ascribed to him. He is the Son of the Father, the second Adam, Lord, Logos. Here is the one in whom Vision intersected reality, Light penetrated darkness.

The Humanity of Christ

The accent upon both the presence and power of God in Christ has sometimes been such as to call into question the real connection of the divine reach with the ordinary things of this life. It is possible so to celebrate with fervor this invasion and to insist with rigor upon its pervasiveness that the "*God* with us" erases the "God with *us.*" This happened early in the history of Christian thought and practice, as in the Docetism of the second century which turned the events in Jesus' life into phantom appearances. A highly spiritualized Jesus only *seemed* to have but did not in fact have a body which was born in the travail of childbirth, hungered when without food, and bled when pierced, or a spirit which doubted and suffered. And in subsequent times after this teaching had been discounted as heresy, the same impulse to make Jesus more divine than God intended took subtler forms: as in Apollinarianism which taught that the Logos preempted that all too fallible capacity in human beings called mind or spirit; or as in Monophysitism in which the passion for divinizing Jesus acknowledged before the Incarnation in only a formal way that the "two natures" of Christ exist—his full Deity and full humanity—but so fused them after Bethlehem as to let the former annihilate the latter.

In addition to these misleading options, declared to be such by the teaching arm of the ancient Church, there were subtler things in the practice and beliefs of the Church of the early centuries that pointed in the same direction and were never officially called to account. Thus a favorite image, one we have here found also to be of value, light, lent itself to the overdivinizing tendency by way of a popular Incarnation figure of Christian writers, the incandescent coal. The glowing coal ignited by the divine Fire suggests a transformation of the historical Jesus that does not comport with the formal declarations of these same writers of his real and persisting humanity. This view of Christ had its counterpart in both a portraiture of Jesus and a spirituality about him that was once removed from the moil and toil that God came to share and redeem. And the false spiritualizing of Christ continues as a tempting heresy to this day whenever the Christ who was born as we are, and suffered, struggled and died as we do, is censored from the Christian Story.

The reason Docetism and its heirs are a wrong reading of the Christian saga is twofold. First, the picture they paint of Christ does not bear any resemblance to the figure described in the Book of the Story. Second, as implied in that data and developed in the theology of the Church, the Incarnation of God, of the Vision of God, means divine *solidarity* with us. Why? The battle for Shalom must be fought out on this plane. If the enemy are to be met, they must be confronted in the arena in which they are to be found. It is in this world that sin, evil, and death do their business, and they must be met in a way commensurate with the divine nature itself. As Irenaeus put it, God plays fair, engaging the foe by the "persuasion" that befits the divine nature, not by the tyranny of brute force. Thus Incarnation means a solidarity with us in which the battle is waged in our own homeland, for this is the enemy's terrain, and such a locale is part and parcel of God's terms.

Not only must the war be *waged* in general here, but in a human being must it be *won*. However that victory is conceived in different versions of the Christian Story, it would not be the authentic Story if the triumph did not take place in a human being who was truly one of us. The victory may be viewed as one of obedience in life, obedience unto death, or variations thereof in a cascade of Atonement theories we shall presently explore. But what is important is that the central problem of sin in the self finds its resolution. And that resolution takes place in us, the chief rebels against the Vision of God. To this end God takes our flesh to redeem it. It is for the Work of salvation that Jesus Christ is truly human as well as truly God.

Sharing Our Common Lot

True humanity, in the sense that we mean it here (it can also mean truly human in a *normative* sense as well as in this *descriptive* sense—as what persons ought to be at their best, not only what they most essentially are in their common humanity), true humanity in Jesus covers each dimension of our ordinariness. In its most elemental aspect, Jesus' humanity is his *bodily* humanity. From the genuine pangs of his birth, through his suckling at Mary's breast and "diapering" at her hand, to the stomach hungers and aching arms at noonday in Joseph's carpenter shop, the dusty and dirty feet and sweaty limbs in his Galilean pilgrimages, and finally the hemorrhaging side and parched lips and agonizing physical pains of his death, he truly shared our common lot. Identification with us is participation in all the ills to which mortal flesh is heir.

Sharing our common lot also means having a truly human *mind*. (We are using the familiar tripartite distinction of body, mind, and spirit as a way of expressing the dimensions of our humanity, understanding that these are not separate segments of our being as in the older "faculty psychology" but inseparable activities within a psychosomatic unity.) Jesus thought the way we think. To take this affirmation of a truly human mind as seriously as we take the equivalent declaration about Jesus' truly human body does not come easily. Many of us draw back from its implications and at this point become practicing Docetists. For to believe that Jesus Christ is truly human in his intellectual powers means that he simply does not know everything. He is no creature whose X-ray eyes can penetrate objects and even know the thoughts of others, a superhuman view of Jesus that has had a long history in popular Christianity. His mind is formed by the times and teaching to which he was exposed, evolving as it does for everyone else in natural fashion: he "grew in wisdom and stature" (Luke 2:52). This means that Jesus thought in the categories provided for him by the period in which he lived, a time of late Jewish Messianism, a period of outward struggle with Rome and inward struggle marked by the religious and political factions of the day. His teaching took these contemporary thought-forms and molded them according to his unique vision. Marked as this teaching is by the transient movements and perceptions of time, it carries all their limitations, including the expectation of the end of the world in the years immediately ahead of him. When God chose solidarity with us, the divine self-limitation risked that kind of finitude.

He is "one who in every respect has been tempted as we are . . ." (Heb. 4:15 RSV). Participation in the depths of human existence means acceptance of *all* its vulnerability. As the writer of Hebrews is at pains to point out, this entails vulnerability of *spirit* as well as mind and body. Christ did not have cast-iron protection against the cares and allurements of this world any more than against the ills of this mortal flesh. He could hear the beguiling voices of temptation to arrogance at the beginning of his ministry and despair at its close, the invitations of sensual satisfaction and the easy out. Dare we imagine Christ was subject to the same onslaughts of spiritual incitement or malaise as we are? Yet how could we not believe this to be so if he is to be the One who rescues us? "He can help those who are tempted because he has been tempted and suffered" (Heb. 2:18). He speaks and acts with the authority of One who has been there too.

The more forthrightly we attend to the human qualities of Christ, the more insistently comes the question: If Jesus is the enfleshment of the Almighty God, how can this kind of frailty and finitude be ascribed to him? Must not the God-Man by definition be "above it all," sharing in the divine omnipotence? While this quandary belongs to our exploration of the unity of the Person to be discussed next, we examine it here at this special pressure point.

The uneasiness about a full-blooded affirmation of Christ's humanity is invariably associated with a false conception of divine presence and power with which we have to contend throughout the Christian narrative. It is a notion that conceives of God's almightiness according to our own norms of absolute power as instant control everywhere. But in the trinitarian origins of the Christian Story the power of God is the Holy Spirit, the Spirit of the Son of God, the Vision of God. The Spirit that brings freedom and peace acts in a fashion commensurate with that end, not by despotic overlordship but by a liberating and reconciling love. To forswear machismo means that in all the deeds of God from creation to consummation, we have to do not with "sultanic" power but with "He who lets us be" (Geddes MacGregor). In the Incarnation this vulnerable Love manifests its omnipotence precisely in its capacity to let Jesus be fully human, in withholding the impulse to dominate. Ultimately that omnipotence is exercised in both the Person and Work of Christ when the power of powerlessness, the lure of the Vision of suffering Love, brings to be in the Nazarene the "first of a new race" destined to live in unity with God. This is "the weakness of God . . . stronger than men" (I Cor. 1:25 RSV).

The Sinlessness of Jesus

He was "tempted as we are, yet without sinning" (Heb. 4:15 RSV). What is this? An intrusion upon the unfolding logic of Jesus' real humanity? A perverse change in the thrust of the text by forces bent upon defending Docetism at one last barricade? Modern humanizers of Jesus dismiss not only this text, but the long tradition declaring the sinlessness of Jesus as just that kind of timidity unwilling to acknowledge the radical identification with the human condition which is sin itself. And is there not a Pauline assertion that for us he was in fact "made sin" (II Cor. 5:21)? Out of such reasoning comes the lush growth of contemporary speculation on this or that sin to which Jesus gave either tacit assent or active expression.

Clarity on this aspect of the Person of Christ requires that we ask whether the insistence on the sinlessness of Christ in Christian tradition is accounted for only by a latent Docetism. Also, we must be clear about the meaning of the term as it applies to Jesus.

We interpret the sinlessness of Jesus in the Christian Story in terms of our translation key, vision. Sin is blindness to the Light, turning away from the Vision of God in pursuit of our own dreams. Sinlessness is the unswerving sight of the divine Light, undeviating obedience to the divine Vision. The sinlessness of Jesus is "unclouded vision" (Herbert Farmer) of the Kingdom of God and the "set of the will" (C. F. D. Moule) commensurate thereto. Here is the purity of heart that wills one thing: Shalom. When the Kingdom comes "the pure in heart shall see God" (Matt. 5:8 KJV). But the Kingdom has entered our history in Jesus, the sight of God has been given, and those who see God *are* pure in heart. The power of the divine Light has pierced the darkness of this world, capturing his attention and drawing him toward its Source. Christ as the seer and server of the Vision of God has unclouded sight; he is "of purer eyes than to behold iniquity" (Hab. 1:13 KJV). The firmness of this perceptual bond as it is attested to in the New Testament record is such as to prompt the traditional formulations of Christ as *non posse peccare:* Jesus was not able to sin. He so lived out of this Vision that he could not be other than what he was. In spite of the tempting bypaths, the attraction of the Light was too great, for it was impossible for him to be out of character.

Clarity of vision, steadiness of intent, and purity of heart do not exhaust the meaning of sinlessness. Implied in these things is the public expression of the Vision, the deeds of liberation and reconciliation. By whatever measure we have, be it the outlines of his behavior perceived through historical analysis of the most primitive layers of New Testament tradition, the testimony of the gospels, or the absence of any tradition outside the corpus of Christian writings that questions its character, a life emerges whose conduct conforms to the Vision of the compassionate love that frees and unites. Jesus of Nazareth liberated us from the bondages of sin, evil, and death and made possible a reconciliation between humanity, nature, and God.

The Church came to assert the sinlessness of Jesus not only from its confrontation with the New Testament portrait but also from what appeared to be the logic of the Atonement. If redemption of the world from sin, evil, and death happened here, then there had to be certain necessary features of the Person that did the Work. Satisfaction, substitutionary, and sacrificial theories required a guileless Jesus who deserved no punishment and therefore was free to offer his innocent life in propitiation for our sins. Even if these understandings of the Atonement are less than adequate, they do demonstrate the inseparability of Person and Work and illustrate the importance of the teaching of Jesus' sinlessness. Can we restate their intention in our own framework?

As we shall see in our subsequent examination of the Work of Christ, the role of Jesus as Prophet of Shalom, the seer and exemplar of the Vision of God, is one of the aspects of his liberating and reconciling Work. Here the Dream is displayed in human history, one that discloses who God is and exposes who we are. If this Work is to be done, then the life of Christ must be transparent to the divine Light. We must be able to see in and through him the unstinting Love that bears the world toward freedom and peace. What adds further to this role is the interpretation we have given here of the power of God that gives visibility to the favor of God declared to be present in the Incarnation. For the Work of Christ as Revealer of Shalom there must be a clear glass of vision, and for the reality of Christ as the Person of Shalom, there must be evidence of the miracles of Love. The declaration of the sinlessness of Christ is the assertion that in and through the attitude and action of Jesus of Nazareth we have an unobstructed view of ultimate Reality. This has nothing to do with speculations about the ambiguity of moral decisions of one who lived and worked in the real world of a carpenter's shop (that Jesus could have used products that might have been looted from some passing camel train), or legalistic observations (that the breaking of the alabaster vase and the cleansing of the temple, although intended to witness to his messianic role, were short of his own concern for the poor and his cheek-turning counsels), or theories that interpret temptation as itself already sin. The sinlessness of Jesus is not a pedantic tabulation of the perfect record of a moral and spiritual virtuoso, and one thereby destroyed by a flawed 99 percent grade. Rather, the sinlessness of Jesus is the capacity of this figure in its firmness of intent and constancy of character to direct the eye of faith to the Vision of God.

The atoning work is not exhausted by the Prophet of Galilee, but thrusts toward the suffering Priest of Calvary and the risen King of Easter morning. The earlier-mentioned theories of Atonement have rightly seen that the sinlessness of Christ is a necessary assumption of the priestly office of Christ. But its integral relation to the crucifixion does not consist of a need for an innocent sacrifice slaughtered in our place in order to appease an angry Deity. (An alternative understanding of the act of substitution will be explored in our subsequent inquiry concerning the work accomplished on Golgotha.) Rather, it is the necessity of finding in this human being the kind of undeviating commitment and radical obedience to the Vision that constitutes the requisite organ of Atonement. Jesus' sinlessness in passion and crucifixion consisted of that set of the will and unswerving pursuit of the Light that beckoned him forward to his destiny. His perfection consisted in his "obedience unto death" (Phil. 2:8). He was the fit instrument for the work of suffering that was to defeat sin and evil, a hard-won faithfulness that passed through the fires of temptation to deviate from the course, one that persisted to the very end. That is the consummate nobility of purpose and action that draws from the faith community the testimony that here is one who has conquered where we have experienced defeat: true humanity in the normative sense. Here is the one who is "tempted as we are, yet without sinning."

While it is important to understand why the Church has clung to some form of the sinlessness of Christ, there is no guarantee that in believing this to be so one will accord to the Incarnation all the meaning it is due. In fact those who have spoken most enthusiastically about the character of Jesus, as have his nineteenth-century biographers, may say nothing about the "*God* with us" aspect of this chapter of the Story. The same thing is true about the virgin birth teaching. It is no guarantee of a "high doctrine" of Christ, for among its most vigorous defenders were the second-century "Adoptionists" who asserted that Christ acquired divinity at his baptism, the point in his life when he became a member of the Trinity, a teaching declared to be unacceptable because it slighted the full enfleshment of God in Jesus Christ that began at conception.

As the first centuries of Church history were characterized by the overdivinizing tendencies noted earlier, so this same time of experimentation produced other kinds of overhumanization like the Adoptionists. The earliest wave was represented by Ebionites for whom Jesus was the greatest in the line of Israel's patriarchs and prophets. As the councils and creeds of the Church became more explicit in declaring off limits the cruder forms of overhumanizing, this anthropocentrism took subtler forms as in the famous Arian view that the Son was divine but created in time, falling short of participation in the eternal being of the Father. And in the still hotly debated position of Nestorianism, the humanity was so accented as to call into question its genuine unity with God in the Person of Jesus, the two natures being joined like glued pieces of wood.

It is this uneasy peace between affirmations of both the Deity and humanity of Christ that lead us to the climactic assertion in the early debates about the Person of Christ, and the third element of what has come to be an ecumenical consensus on some fundamental aspects of the Incarnation: the unity of Christ. To this we now turn.

The Unity of Christ

The formal declaration of the unity of Jesus Christ's Person was made by the ancient Church-in-council at Chalcedon in 451 A.D. In him is to be found *one Person,* in *two natures.* And these natures are "without confusion, without change, without division, without separation; the distinction of the natures being in no wise done away by the union. . . ."

The assertion of oneness of Person was made against the immediate background of the Nestorians' seeming inability to get the two natures together, ending up with what looked like a concept that turned Christ into two persons. On the other hand, the Monophysites, pressing for the Deity of Christ and pursuing relentlessly a simplistic unity, ended by turning the unity of the Person into oneness of nature, the divine nature. How are we to walk this tightrope, falling off neither on the side of two persons nor one nature?

Some things came clear in the early debates about what ought to be and ought not to be asserted in order to maintain this critical balance. We get a clue from the struggle with the Apollinarians mentioned earlier. In this exchange the right of Jesus to his own human ego was won. It is strange indeed that this had to be defended, but such is the imperialistic inclination of the partisans of Christ's divinity. The integrity of Jesus' self was reiterated in the sixth century in the Dyothelite controversy when Monothelitism was rejected, and the reality of Christ's own human *will* affirmed. Thus two natures means that two centers of choosing, two egos, have to be taken into account in any statement of the unity of Christ.

But does not this violate the oneness of Person? Is this not a schizophrenic Christ with double personality? To find a way of saying No to this while saying Yes to the two natures is difficult indeed. Another blind alley was marked out in the debates around the word *anhypostasia,* which is translated as impersonal human nature. The ancient Church opted for this in some of its formulas because it seems to guard the unity of Christ. It declares that there can be only one Person in Christ and that is the second Person of the Trinity, the Logos, the Son of the Father. Thus the unity of the Person of Christ is protected by the integrity given to the God-Man by the divine Person. What happens to the humanity of Jesus then? It must be asserted, but interpreted as *impersonal* humanity. Here we run into translation problems because the Greek word *hypostasis* which we translate person does not necessarily nor originally mean self-consciousness as it does in modern parlance, but *subsistence* or *continuing identity.* Hence what is being said in the notion of anhypostasia is that the fundamental defining identity of Christ is given by the "Godness" of Christ, that without it there would be no uniqueness. However, our translation of this as impersonal human nature is an awkward one, as it seems to suggest a cold, abstract and non-self-conscious quality. But the rejection of

Apollinarianism and Monothelitism argues otherwise; it does not mean non-personness in the sense of non-ego, or non-self-conscious willing. What we can learn from this debate is that 1) unity must be maintained whatever the duality of selves and 2) the unity is finally grounded in God.

Can we go beyond saying what this unity is not, avoiding the temptations to fall off on either side and having only the barest of guidelines (one Person, two natures)? Some say this is as far as we can go in making sense out of this classic teaching. Or as it is sometimes put, we have to do here with a "paradox." A paradox or antinomy is the bold assertion of mutually contradictory statements. Those who defend this characterization of the Incarnation are at pains to distinguish paradox from a straightforward contradiction. A paradox is something made necessary by our experience. The experience cited may be the commitment one has to the Scriptures or to the traditions of the Church. Here the belief in Jesus Christ as both God and human is assumed or asserted, and we bow before this authority. Or experience may be understood as our own personal religious experience in which we come to know Christ personally in this mysterious duality-in-unity. Or, as in Donald Baillie's famous discussion of paradox, our *experience of grace* as captured in Paul's declaration "I . . . yet not I" (I Cor. 15:10) may be used as an analogy for understanding the Incarnation. Yet again, we may demonstrate that paradoxes are necessary for the grasping of many general human experiences, as for example the complementarity of wave and particle theories of light. However used, the idea of paradox seeks to maintain the modesty that is appropriate to the mystery of the Incarnation.

The option of paradox seems particularly inviting when the efforts to go beyond it in the history of Christian thought are canvassed. Their zeal to explain the mystery drives them regularly off one side of the tightrope or the other. Here is the key, says a popular modern option: the unity lies in the fact that the humanity of Jesus maximized is what the Deity of Jesus means: human love reaching its zenith is God's Love. However elaborated (as for example by making Jesus' love light-years away from our puny efforts), this scenario ·cannot intrinsically recognize the radical newness, the overagainstness, the action of God toward us, that the Incarnation of Deity is meant to announce, for it is trapped in a distinction of degree. But *here* is the key, says another: the unity of Christ consists in the manifest power of God in the extraordinary not the ordinary, the superhuman not the human, the miraculous not the natural. But if Deity so construed is seen in the wonder-worker or in the moral and spiritual paragon, where then is the ordinary, the human, the natural which the doctrine of Incarnation honors? So Christ becomes God walking around in the disguise of a human being and once again Docetism beckons. The sacrifice of either true Deity in the first instance or true humanity in the second is too high a price to pay for a neatly drawn formula of unity.

A Shared Vision

The philosophical or religious reductionisms that erode the affirmation of One Person and two natures do not exhaust the options. The paradox cannot be *explained,* but it can be *explored.* While the final mystery of the Incarnation cannot be penetrated, we do not have to settle for a simple assertion of paradoxical unity-in-duality. The metaphor-motif we have been working with sheds a small glimmer of light on what the paradox might mean for us and our contemporaries.

The visionary movements and persons of our time have given us some experience of the process of envisioning. Whether it be a Martin Luther King, Jr., who holds up a brilliant dream of liberation from oppression, or a modern astrophysicist who dreams of the exploring of outer space, we know something about lifting the sights of vision to view what these seers project. It is *their* vision. If it were not for them our sight would be dimmed, but the fires of their perception kindle ours. And we come to see something of what they point to. In fact where this enabling of widespread dreaming does not happen, a culture is seriously impoverished. "Where there is no vision, the people perish" (Prov. 29:18 KJV). Visions are made to be shared.

The unity of Jesus with God is to be found in their common Vision. What God projects on the screen of the future, the man of Galilee sees. What the Envisioner emblazons before Jesus is the Light of the Vision. This is the eternal Logos, the Son of the Father. Jesus is one with the eternal Logos. His dream of the Kingdom is God's Dream. The nature of Jesus' seeing is his own, as is also the nature of the envisioning God. Yet they coalesce in the unity of the

Sight seen. The oneness of the Person of Christ is the subsisting identity of the action of an envisioning God and an envisioning Jesus. The seeing by the inner eye of the human Jesus is not possible except by the prevenient action of the Envisioner. The Vision of God goes before the vision of Jesus. Thus the identity of the Person of Christ is taken from Deity, as the awkward language of anhypostasia sought to say, but it in no way eliminates the genuine human process of envisioning in Jesus who "catches sight of" the Glory of God.

While this metaphor gives some meaning to the paradox of unity in Christ, it cannot be pushed to its limits without doing violence to that same unity. Thus it assumes a psychological setting, the development of Jesus to the place where he points to and announces the Kingdom of God, and does not cover that time from conception to the launching of this ministry. Driven to its logical extreme, it would express a form of Adoptionism and foreshorten the Incarnation. But the Light of Shalom is in unity with Jesus not only when he perceives it to be so, but throughout his life. He lives and moves and has his being in the Light, envisioned or otherwise. Thus it is but a modest metaphor that yields up some insight but does not give a God's-eye view of Incarnation. It is an explored but not an explained paradox, and therefore remains a paradox, meaningful but not metaphysically encompassed.

Jesus Christ, truly human, truly God, truly one, the Vision made flesh, the Light of God in the face of Jesus (II Cor. 4:6). "And we saw his glory, such glory as befits the Father's only Son, full of grace and truth" (John 1:14).

THE WORK OF CHRIST: ATONEMENT

We come now to the fundamental action of the Christian drama. The chief protagonist confronts the antagonists on their own ground. The incarnate Light meets the armies of night. Here, Christians believe, deliverance happens. Jesus Christ liberates from sin, evil, and death, and makes possible the reconciliation, the *at-one-ment* of humanity, nature, and God.

As this is the turning point in the epic of redemption, so its report and interpretation are central to the life of faith and theology.

Our understanding of the Work of Christ is our Christian faith in microcosm. What we have to say about this teaching is the key to how we read the whole Christian Story.

A strange irony attends this centrality. While there is an ecumenical consensus about the Person of Christ—Jesus Christ, truly God, truly human, truly one—there is no equivalent agreement in Christian history on the Work of Christ. We may have to qualify this by an "as yet," for as it took four hundred years in the childhood of the Christian community to establish its most elementary self-concept, the Person of Christ, so it may be that the search for an understanding of the Work is still an adolescent identity quest. Indeed some of the tumultuous struggles from the high middle ages through the Reformation and Enlightenment to the erratic pendulum swings of contemporary theology (from the death of God to the new surge of piety) seem to suggest just that kind of puberty. Be that as it may, there is no comparable framework for examining Christian belief about this crucial affirmation. And it may be because of its fundamental nature that the faith community must work that much harder and longer on its definition, and that such high passions and partisanships surround that search. No doubt clarity of conviction also waits upon the coming of a life together within the Christian community. Catholicity of belief rises out of universality of corporate existence, a common life we have not had since the first major cleavage of the eleventh century. Perhaps the growing informal unity of common mission and theological work portends that community of life and thought.

While there are no ecumenical assertions about the Atonement, there is a rich vein of material which is mined by various theological working parties. This ore is shared by all and suggests a unity of direction and vision which the specific differences of formula may conceal. Let us examine this common lode.

A. *Biblical Data*

1. *Old Testament Trajectories*

Included here are the sacrificial-priestly, visionary-prophetic, and political-kingly traditions in a messianic framework.

2. *Contemporary Jesus Research*

In the discussion of the Person of Christ, we traced the outlines of the figure of Jesus of Nazareth as these are discerned by contemporary historical scholarship. That material is important also for our understanding of the Atonement. The glimpse we have of the Galilean includes his proclamation of the coming Kingdom of God, its presence as well as its futurity, its powerful signs to be seen wherever liberation and reconciliation happen in our midst, Jesus' own profound sense of unity with this Kingdom and its God and the authority this unity gave him to call to accountability and to forgive sin, and his power to embody an extravagant freedom and love.

3. *Critical Events or Life Segments*

Birth, Galilean ministry, crucifixion, and resurrection are the focal points.

4. *Titles Ascribed to Jesus*

While these are often examined with a view to his Person, they also have strong implications for his Work. They include Messiah, Lord, Son of God, Son of Man, Master, Teacher, Servant, Logos, Shepherd, Lamb of God, Prophet, King.

5. *Metaphors of Work Accomplished*

The Work of Christ receives its earliest formulations by way of a cascade of rich images drawn from the world of the first century. Dominant metaphors are taken from (a) the Temple: atonement itself, purification, offering, cultic and priestly practice (John 1:29; I John 1:7; 3:5; Titus 2:14; Heb. 9:28; Rev. 7:14); (b) law court: judgment, punishment, forensic framework (Acts 10:42; 17:31; Rom. 3:20; 8:32–34; II Cor. 5:10; II Tim. 4:1; I Pet. 3:18); (c) the marketplace: debt, purchase, payment, redemption, commerce (Acts 20:28; Rom. 3:24; Gal. 3:13; 4:5; Titus 2:14; I Pet. 1:18); (d) pedagogy: teaching, learning, exemplifying, revealing (Matt. 20:26–28; Matt. 5–7; Mark 4:1–34; John 3:2); (e) battle: captivity, liberation, ransom, peace, victory (Mark 3:27; 10:45; Eph. 2:14–16; 6:14; Phil. 2:9–10; Col. 2:15); (f) presence: transfiguration, life, light (John 1:4; 5:26, 40; 8:12; 10:10; 11:25; 14:6).

B. *Tradition*

1. *Theories*

The complexity of the data and the need to bring the Christian vision to bear on the problems the Church faced as it confronted changing circumstances combined to generate a number of theories of Atonement. The process usually involved the elaboration of a particular metaphor. Thus the cultic imagery is developed into one or another form of sacrificial theory; the image of the law court is drawn out in terms of a penal substitutionary theory; a commercial theory emerges out of the marketplace metaphor; a conflict and victory or liberation theory extends the battlefield metaphor; a moral influence theory expands the pedagogical image; and beyond these constructs are theories that include exemplarist, incarnational, ransom, rectoral, satisfaction, penitential, representative, etc. In an attempt to do justice to other New Testament metaphors as well as to the richness of biblical data in general, each theory uses other imagery and themes as well. So in practice, the distinctions are never quite as sharp as the labels suggest. But one metaphor does tend to be the organizing center for the others and provide its dominant language.

2. *Issues*

Contributing to the choice of metaphor and the line of thought developed in connection with it is the question posed by the culture out of which the theory grows, or the issue felt to be most compelling by the theory-maker. Thus a principle of selection is introduced into the biblical data by the problem faced by the Church in a given time and place. If transiency and mortality press the Church for some word, then the interpretation of the Work of Christ is predisposed to think in terms of immortality made possible by the Eternal entering time, and hence a focus on the Incarnation. If ignorance is viewed as the issue, then the understanding of Christ as the revealer comes to be stressed. If the perils of nature or history are to the fore, then it is the liberating Work of Christ that takes on significance. And if sin and guilt grip a culture, or ought to, then judgment and mercy are decisive themes. In this way, questions and issues in a given milieu make their presence felt on a doctrine of the Atonement. And further, answers developed within the culture in the form of philosophical, social, or political systems and patterns also congregate around the question posed, influencing its understanding of the Work of Christ.

3. *Segments of Christ's Career*

Another factor that shapes Christian thinking about the Atonement, and specifically influences theory-making, is the attraction of the events in one or another leg of Christ's own journey. In fact there is a strong correlation between the issue felt to be decisive for the Work of Christ and the stage on Christ's way. Thus the problem of the passingness of things, as in ancient Greek culture and philosophy, draws from the Church its Incarnational themes in patristic thought, and therefore focuses on Bethlehem. And the question of knowledge and power have a way of fixing attention upon the life and ministry of Jesus, and thus Galilee is seen as the locus of Christ's Work. Sin and guilt as issues give rise to metaphors and meanings that gather around the cross, hence Calvary. And questions of evil and hopelessness about the future, penultimate and ultimate, prompt attention to the resurrection, and Easter becomes central.

C. *Role Models*

There is indication in the foregoing that there may be a way of organizing the mass of materials from Christian tradition into its critical elements. Discernable within the theories and the biblical data in general are the outlines of four ways of understanding the Work of Christ, four recurring "role models" of Jesus' atoning action. They tend to take shape around the issues and segments just discussed and are also influenced by one or another target. In our construction of these role models, we shall make use of the *issue* it addresses, identify the segment of Christ's life to which it gives attention, its *locus,* allude to the target of Jesus' work, its *focus,* describe the *action* involved in the Work, and suggest the *outcome* of the action. Looking toward our own attempt to express what is at the heart of this chapter of the Christian Story, both in the Church's historic teaching and in contemporary reformulation, we shall also make assessments of each model.

1. *Jesus as Example and Teacher*

The problem we face, the *issue* we confront in this first model, is our lack of knowledge of the truth and our absence of commitment to what little we do know. The bane of the race is its ignorance and apathy, our darkened minds and hearts.

Where do we go for salvation from blindness and torpor? Its *locus* is the Christ of Galilee. He is the Teacher of the truth and the inspiring Example of its practice. In his life and ministry we see the articulation and exemplification of a compelling way of life. The *action* to be seen there is that of the disclosure of who God is and what we must do. As it is frequently expressed in contemporary form, in Jesus' words and deeds we learn that God is love and that we are called to be loving. This gift and claim, expressed sometimes as the "Fatherhood of God and the brotherhood of man," is the sum and substance of Christian religion. And the *focus* of this Example and Teacher is you and me. Atonement means changing the hearts and minds of human beings so that they may love God and love their neighbors. The *outcome* of the action is the illumination of our darkened minds and the inspiration of our apathetic hearts so that human beings may be at one with God and with each other.

The strengths of this model are varied. It takes seriously the life and ministry of Jesus of Nazareth, a zeal that has given impetus to both the old and new quest for the historical Jesus. It understands a central feature of his ministry to be proclamation of the Kingdom of God. It gives forceful attention to the love of God, underscoring the Agape so central to the Christian faith. It is committed to an understanding of Christianity that expects the change of hearts and minds, especially reckoning with the ethical imperatives of biblical faith. We do need illumination and inspiration, insight and empowerment.

A fundamental weakness of this model, standing alone, was expressed in a comment by one who tried it: "We need more than good advice. We need Good News." The issue we confront is far more lethal than this model understands, and therefore the Work of Christ must be more radical than that of an Example and Teacher. At three points is this true: a) human sin is titanic. The apathy and arrogance of the human race is such that it does not yield to the counsel to love God and love the neighbor. "The good that I would I cannot . . . the evil that I would not, that I do." Paul's struggle with the incurved self, the bondage of the human will to its own self-serving agendas, is the classic expression of this Christian experience. b) The problem of evil is far more intractable than this model grasps. The historical holocausts and the vast natural disasters point to the presence of demonic principalities and powers in our midst. It is not enough to speak about the loving Father in heaven or the need to love others in the face of these horrors and our helplessness before them. There is no Good News if there is no word to be said about our struggle and destiny with the demonic. c) Inseparable from the problem of sin and evil is their result, death, both the mortality which we face individually and the larger meaning of death, the death of the Dream of God, the hopelessness that shatters the future of this great experiment in Shalom. When these perceptions about the depth and pervasiveness of sin, evil, in death are weak or absent, there is a commensurate neglect of the acts in the drama of Jesus which seek to speak to these problems— the cross and resurrection, Good Friday and Easter, and not infrequently the deepest meaning of Incarnation itself, Christmas. For when the depth of the world's plight is not adequately measured, the radical cure declared by the doctrine of the Incarnation—that liberation requires the enfleshment of God—is not understood.

Standing alone, the Work of the Example and Teacher leaves us with unanswered questions about the depth of our sin and the perils of evil and death. Indeed if Jesus of Nazareth is taken with absolute seriousness, just those questions are radicalized. As Luther found in his spiritual pilgrimage, the more he attempted to be obedient to the imperative which came out of the disclosure of what we are called to be and do, the more apparent the fact of human sin became. The kindly face of Christ the Example and Teacher becomes the stern face of Christ the Judge. We do not love God or our neighbor as we ought, and the revelation of the Law of this love drives the sensitive seer to despair, or to clever evasions which modify and deradicalize the claims of love. *Disclosure* becomes *exposure.* In the face of this exposure something more is needed for Atonement than illumination and inspiration. The ambiguities in the first model have given rise to a second one.

2. *Jesus as Substitute and Savior*

In this second model the meaning of the Work of Christ consists not in what Christ *shows to us,* but in what Christ *does for us.* And this model asserts how we need something done for us, for we are in deep trouble. Our sin is such that we have evoked the wrath and judgment of God. We stand guilty before the divine righteousness, deserving death and damnation. The *issue* therefore is sin and guilt. Because we are trapped in our sin, we cannot do what the Example and Teacher says we must do; we need a Savior. We need one who steps in to do what we cannot do, who represents us before the judgment bar, who stands in our place to deal with the well-deserved and terrible punishment. The *focus* of this model is not, first and foremost, the change of human attitudes and behavior, but the change of God's relationship to us, his severe judgment upon us.

The eye of faith that sees Christ as Substitute and Savior turns to the cross. Here is a *locus* with passion and depth that suggests the scale of agony and punishment appropriate to sin and guilt. And here, most essentially, is the *action* of the only One who can deal with their deadly consequences. The death of Christ on the cross meets the divine severity and turns aside the wrath of God. Just how judgment is transformed into mercy depends on the particular theory that expresses this model of Substitute and Savior. In one case, Anselm's "satisfaction" theory, couched in the language of medieval serf-lord relationships and the penance system of the Middle Ages, the death of Christ is a beyond-the-call-of-duty act, much like the extraordinary sacrifices of saint and monk whose consequent store of heavenly merits were thought to be transferable to sinners. Thus the favor won from the Father by the merits of Christ's supererogatory sacrifice on the cross satisfies the offended honor of the Lord. In another case, that of the penal substitutionary theory of Reformation orthodoxy, influenced by the judicial codes and penal practices of the emerging nation state (including a practice in which a friend could stand as surety for bail), the death of Christ was the endurance of the punishment for sin, now understood as the breach of divine law. By a passive receiving of the sentence rendered, in contrast to the active offering of death in the satisfaction theory, atonement is made. And in yet another instance of this model, the sacrificial theory, developed in conjunction with the Temple ritual metaphors of the Old Testament, the death of Christ is viewed as an offering well-pleasing to God. (In modern versions, the absence of ideas of legalistic equivalency of punishment are stressed, and also our own act of sorrowful and faithful co-participation.) In all forms of this model, the *outcome* of the action is the reconciliation of God and human beings. The obstruction is removed, whether it be offended honor, deserved punishment, or propitiatory condition. Jesus' intervention makes possible our acceptance.

Models characteristically attempt to include metaphors and meanings not directly related to their own construct. Thus this one seeks to do justice to the Galilean ministry of Jesus. The moral and spiritual perfections of example and teacher constitute the purity which gives efficacy to the death of Christ. In the satisfaction theory, only a perfect Jesus who did not have to die as punishment for sin could use his death as a merit transferable to sinners. In the penal theory, only a perfect Jesus who did not have to be punished by death for his own sin could offer his death as a substitute for others. And in the sacrificial theory, only the purity of an innocent Lamb would be pleasing to God.

We have spent longer on the exposition of this model because the idea of Atonement is associated in popular Christianity with one or another form of it. And indeed the notion of Atonement itself comes originally from the sacrificial metaphor expanded by one version of this model. In taking sin more seriously than the first model, it is profounder in its understanding of both human perversity and divine judgment. It sees more clearly the gravity of human sin and our accountability before the righteous God who does not lightly indulge our assault on the divine purposes. Its strength also includes the importance given to the cross, the central symbol of the Christian faith, and the sign of the agonizing cost, suffering and death, of any at-one-ment worth having. Further, its emphasis on the passion and crucifixion is faithful to the stress upon these in the Gospels, in the redemption scenarios of Paul, and in the proclamations of the early Church. Again, in this model the humanity of Jesus, the real choices and actions of one who faces toward God, is not lost from view.

The weakness of the second model lies in its reductionism. Its tunnel vision of the Work of Christ does not allow Galilee or Easter or finally Bethlehem to enlarge the significance of Atonement and even deepen the meaning of the cross itself.

A fundamental effect of a reductionism which eliminates a critical aspect of "Bethlehem"—the doctrine of the Incarnation which is the premise of any sound understanding of Atonement—has to do with the relation of Jesus to God on the cross. The logic of this model was expressed by the story of a convert won to the

Church by its preaching (as described by William Wolf). Seeing the picture painted of the sacrificial Jesus appeasing the wrath of God by his suffering and death, the convert declared, "I love Jesus, but I hate God." In the conventional forms of this model, God is portrayed as a distant figure calling us to account, over against the "Friend we have in Jesus." But the teaching of Incarnation is absolutely otherwise. "God was *in* Christ reconciling the world to himself. . ." (II Cor. 5:19 RSV). To believe in the Incarnation is to close the gap between God and Jesus, to see the Work of Jesus as the *Work of God,* not a Work simply done by God to Jesus.

A variation on this theme of cleavage is to be found in a modification which acknowledges the presence of God in Jesus, but describes the act of propitiation as done by the Second Person of the Trinity to the First Person, by the Son to the Father. Involved is a similar error, this time the flirtation with a polytheistic notion of Deity, the juxtaposing of God the Son and God the Father, violating the ancient teaching that the "works of the Trinity are one."

The rift between Jesus and God, or Father and Son, is the result also of a single motif model that gives no vital place to the Galilean ministry. In Jesus' life and teaching, God the Father is revealed as unconditional Love, an Agape which is poured out on all, regardless of payments or deserts. The Substitute and Savior model carries with it a conception of mercy that has not been transfigured by this disclosure of Unconditional Love. In common ideas of mercy, the notion of reciprocity is operative: what you give is what you get. Mercy is available when satisfaction is rendered. Acquittal is granted when the conditions for acquittal are met. As with all the metaphors that the New Testament uses to express the action of God, there is never a simple one-to-one correspondence between the usage from which it is taken and that for which it is appropriated. The continuity of the metaphor of judgment between its secular meaning and its description of the cross is that the crime of human sin cannot go unpunished in the Kingdom of a righteous God. The Judge shall execute the judgment. But the metaphor is transmuted by the New Testament vision of unconditional love and Incarnational action. The worldly assumption that the only way to avoid the penalty is to have the judgment evaded by its transfer to another, the Judge being "bought off" or his anger appeased by a satisfactory alternative, is transfigured into the affirmation that the Judge steps down before the bar and receives the very punishment that fits the crime. This is the kind of substitutionary action that must be seen by any model of Atonement that takes into account the whole picture of Incarnation and the revelation of the God incarnate in Christ whose righteousness is one with mercy.

The second model needs to be challenged and enlarged by the first on yet another count: the ethical mandate intrinsic to any full understanding of the Work of Christ. Preoccupation with cleansing of personal sin effected by the cross tends to eliminate the Vision of Shalom to which the Galilean Christ beckons us. The imperative of love of our human neighbor and of the care of our neighbor the earth disappears from view as we become either numbed by the sense of our own incapacity to respond to these mandates, or in the excitement of discovery of the expiation wrought on Calvary. But a full understanding of Atonement will make a place for the lure of the Shalom disclosed in the life, teaching, and ministry of Christ, as well as in his judgment upon us and restoration of us enacted at Golgotha.

As the Galilee before Calvary does not receive its fullest due in this model, neither does the Easter event after it. While resurrection is always affirmed in the expiatory view, it receives attention more as an appendage to its central idea—as the overcoming of our mortality—than as integral to its own understanding of the Work of Christ. This is because of the exclusive focus on the problem of personal sin, and thus the marginal interest in the world's bondage to the powers of evil and death in their profoundest sense. The foes which Jesus Christ engages in his atoning work include *all* the principalities ranged against the divine intent of Shalom: those in history and the cosmos as well as in the self. It is Easter which announces this victory, and with it is proclaimed the overcoming of that final death which is eternal separation of God, nature, and humanity. The conquest of the powers of evil and the call to participate in the present struggle against them, and the joining of hope for the future with faith in the forgiveness of sins, are aspects of the Atonement that must enrich the poverty of this reductionism. These latter perceptions lead us to examine a third model that seeks to do justice to them.

3. *Jesus as Conqueror and Lord*

In times marked by numbing historical crisis or natural cataclysm, the picture of Christ the Conqueror emerges with power in the Church. During the rise of totalitarian movements in the Europe of the 1930's, the Swedish theologian Gustaf Aulén sketched in *Christus Victor* the outlines of this model. He declared that a too-simple typology of subjective and objective theories of Atonement (corresponding to Example and Teacher and Substitute and Savior) ignored a third view, one which he asserted to be that of the New Testament itself and of such interpreters as Irenaeus and Luther. We shall not use the details of Aulén's picture of this model, although the contemporary Church is in his debt for lifting up the Conqueror motif in a forceful way.

In this model the *issue* is evil and death in their various expressions. In the ancient world the struggle took the form of conflict with demons attacking as sea monster, madness of mind, malady of body, the day-to-day perils of life, the whispers of temptation. In more secular times the enemy stalks in the random terror of natural disaster and the perennial sorrows and enigmas of disease, tragedy, old age, dying. To the groaning of creation is added the agonized cries of history, the poverty, hunger, and tyranny over body, mind, and spirit caused by political, economic, and social principalities and powers. And over all hangs the pall of death, both the fact of our mortality and the fear that evil will triumph, the suspicion that not only our life but the life of the world will end as "a tale told by an idiot, full of sound and fury, signifying nothing."

The *action* of Christ in this understanding of Atonement is to meet and defeat the foes of God. And it is not our behavior or God's relationship to us but the enemy powers that are the *focus* of the Work. The beginnings of the battle are traced to the Galilean ministry of Jesus. Here Christ confronts the Devil and the demonic hordes in the encounters of temptation, the infestation of the sick and troubled by the powers of darkness, and the resistance to his ministry. Christ is empowered to deal effectively with the enemy as the Kingdom he embodies and points to is at work healing torn bodies, minds, and spirits, and exorcising and fending off the armies of night. Yet a final assault is launched against the inbreaking Kingdom and its King and victory of the foe seems assured as death overwhelms this Pretender to the throne of the kingdoms of this world ruled by the powers of darkness.

What gives meaning to the life and death of Christ shadowed

by these powers of darkness is the light of Easter morning. In the resurrection of Jesus Christ from the dead, the *locus* of saving action, the question mark is removed. The defeat of the purposes of God in the death of Jesus is not what it appeared to be. Rather the cross was the weapon of suffering love, persuasion not coercion, that befits the God who will not act contrary to the divine nature. The sign that this weapon *does* defeat the dark powers is the resurrection. That God raised Jesus Christ from the dead signifies the victory over the powers of evil, and finally also victory over death in its deepest meaning, the death of hope for the world. Thus fear of the powers of this world and hopelessness about the future of the world are overcome by Christ the Conqueror of evil and death. Liberation from these powers, and life together with God, is the *outcome* of the atoning Work.

In this model there are assumptions about the nature of the powers and God that are integral to the affirmation of Christ as Conqueror. The belief in powers of evil is not the assertion of dualism, the notion that there are forces alongside of Deity in eternal conflict with God. The powers are themselves part of the good creation brought to be by God. But as humanity fell, so the powers too have become corrupted and now exist in opposition to the intention of God. The conquest of these authorities, viewed eschatologically as beginning at Easter and culminating at the Last Day, further underscores the non-dualistic character of the powers of evil. For all that, there is a genuine intermediate conflict and thus in Aulén's words a "provisional dualism."

The assumption about the nature of God has to do with the relation of Incarnation to Atonement. In an effort to affirm Bethlehem as the premise of Easter, and also its presence in Galilee and Calvary, the Conqueror model views the work of Jesus "through and through" as the work of God. It is Deity itself that wages war with the powers of evil and death in the Person of Jesus Christ. Hence this dramatic view of the Atonement is one that portrays salvation as the contest of God with the enemy forces carried out on earth in the life, death, and resurrection of the man Jesus Christ.

The manifest strengths of this view include the attention to, and integration of, the resurrection of Christ in a doctrine of Atonement. As in no other model, Easter is given a key role in the Work of Christ. Here the wretched of the earth, felled by the powers of evil and death, hear a Word that speaks to their condition. In our own time, it is the liberation theologies that strike this note, seeking to understand Christ against the background of the struggle against oppression. And as their strange ally, those less politically oriented interpretations of Christian faith which address themselves to the problem of evil and death, ones that may engage in exorcism and esoterica on the one hand, or view faith as a way of dealing with death and dying, on the other, represent a version of this model. Whatever their strategies and programs, their antennae are tuned to modern questions of theodicy and they offer in turn some understanding of Christ as Lord and Conqueror.

A further strength of this model is its recognition that the structures of nature and history are part and parcel of the arena in which the Atonement takes place. Christ is Lord over powers as well as persons, and his Kingdom is cosmic in scope. Tendencies to narrow the range of Atonement to the inner life or to personal and interpersonal relationships are here challenged. And not only are historical structures given their due, but also in this time of ecological sensibility the Lordship of Christ over the environment and ultimately over the heights and depths of the whole universe is affirmed and celebrated.

When the human problem is seen to consist of the evil and death "out there" in nature and history, then the corruption "in here," the self and its sin, can be overlooked in all its horror and depth. This is a basic weakness of the Conqueror model in both ancient and contemporary thought. The focus is so relentlessly upon the struggle with the powers external to the self that the internal quandary expressed by Paul—"I do not do the good I want, but the evil I do not want is what I do"—gets short shrift. Where attempts are made to include the presence of sin as a foe, the sin tends to be so objectified as a power that the aspect of personal culpability is not given its due. Paul's own use of the term sin gives it this role of overagainstness, one followed by Luther, but the way the word operates in both is as a relationship of the self to God, rather than simply as an objective power over against both humanity and God, as with evil and death. Thus wherever the model achieves prominence, as in patristic thought and in current versions of liberation theology, the struggle of the self with its own personal sin and guilt is marginal.

A related weakness has to do with expectations about history that accompany the Conqueror model particularly as its commitments are politicized. Where sin is not seen as a fundamental foe, then its corrupting effects, especially when they work upon the righteous (as is recognized in the realism of the New Testament about self-righteousness and in the classic Christian understanding of pride as the basic sin), are not assessed profoundly enough. This means that too sanguine hopes for history are cultivated by those who see Christ as the Conqueror of the powers of evil and Liberator of the oppressed. This utopianism, as Reinhold Niebuhr has helped us to see, eventuates in either despair at the frustration of inordinate historical expectations or fanaticism in the claims of those who believe they march in the legions of the conquering Lord. The fanatic fails to see the omnipresence of sin, especially as it grafts itself onto power, and most of all righteous power, and therefore has no principle of criticism by which to call to constant account, and expose the perversities of, the most just and virtuous movements. A fuller understanding of the Conqueror and Lord motif must include liberation from the sin of the self as well as from the powers and principalities of evil.

The use of the military metaphor which is integral to this model opens it up to yet another criticism. While the previous weaknesses are related to the missing expiation motif, this one is connected with the relative absence of the Galilean accent. The compassionate Christ who moves in selfless love throughout the pages of the New Testament does not come clearly into view in the characterizations of Christ as sword-wielding Conqueror. Indeed that sword is seen to be the cross, as the way of the Lord is that of persuasion and not force, but a formal acknowledgment that this is so does not carry the power of the war-like metaphor of conflict and victory which dominates the interpretation. The tenderness of the Galilean Christ and the suffering of the Savior need to take their place alongside the ringing commands and shouts of conquest of a Lord and Liberator.

A final weakness, often pointed out by critics who feel that one of the strengths of this model proves also to be a point of greatest vulnerability, has to do with its active attempt to relate Incarnation to Atonement. By the stress that Atonement is a thoroughly divine action, the human nature of Jesus seems to take on the appearance of a robot. Jesus' actions are so suffused with Deity that his humanity, the hard and vital choices that constitute his ministry, fade from view. While those choices are maintained in the second model at the price of distancing the reconciling God from the action, in this model the overwhelming Presence of the God who was in Christ blots out the human action, however formally insisted upon (while conquest is done *by* God, it must be done *in* and *through* a human). And thus the incarnational premise itself is rendered suspect, for God replaces the God-Man as the actor in the drama. And so we turn to a fourth model.

4. *Jesus as Presence*

The Incarnation makes a significant impact on the previous model. But there is a fourth type of Atonement thought in which the Incarnation is virtually identical with the Atonement. Such a view is related to the definition of the world's problem in terms of carnality itself. The *issue* in our fourth perspective is transiency and mortality. Decay and death are all around us. Who will bring life and light?

The *locus* of Atonement here is the moment of at-one-ment between time and eternity, the enfleshment of God at Bethlehem. The *focus* of the Work embodied in the very being of the Person is not the change of our hearts and minds, nor alteration of the divine attitude and behavior toward us, nor defeat of the powers ranged against the purposes of God, but the transformation of time and space. This happens in the union of Deity and humanity. For in the *action* of Incarnation the whole universe is taken up into a new reality. As a drop of dye colors a glass of water, so the presence of Deity at Bethlehem and beyond transfigures the cosmos. The *outcome* of this incarnate action is deification, the taking *in principle* of the world into the divine life, and *in fact* of those so joined to the Person by faith.

To see the Presence of God as the Work of Christ makes it utterly clear that Atonement is through and through a divine action. In so stressing God's enfleshment, this model underscores the fact that Incarnation is the presupposition of Atonement, that Bethlehem is the framework for Galilee, Calvary, and Easter. Furthermore, the ambiguities of life in this world, its passingness and mortality, are not ignored; we are destined for something more than decay and death.

Yet, as in the other models reductionism so scissors the fullness of the biblical witness that critical sections of the Christian Story are left out. The Galilean ministry and mandates do not receive the attention that is due to them; the preoccupation with one's own finitude, while helping us to come to terms with things that cannot be changed, does not make sufficient room for life and living and the imperatives to serve the neighbor in need, things that can be changed. Further, the exclusive focus on temporality obscures the anterior problem of human sin, our culpability and need for divine mercy. And the struggle against the historical powers and principalities in the battle for historical hope in the face of hopelessness get less than their due. Thus Jesus the Example and Teacher, Sufferer and Savior, Lord and Conqueror, have something to teach the exponents of this incarnational view.

The four models of the Work of Christ may be portrayed in this way:

Model	Issue	Locus	Focus	Action	Outcome
Example and Teacher	ignorance and apathy	Galilee	human attitudes and behavior	disclosure by word and deed of love of God and neighbor	illumination and inspiration
Substitute and Savior	sin and guilt	Calvary	relationship of God to humanity	vicarious suffering and death	judgment turned to mercy
Conqueror and Lord	evil and death	Easter	powers and principalities	resurrection victory	defeat of powers of evil and death
Presence	transiency and mortality	Bethlehem	temporality	incarnation	life and immortality

The Three-fold Work of Jesus Christ

Our typology of role models suggests that there is a process going on in the Church's exploration of the Work of Christ not unlike that to be found in the development of the doctrine of the Person of Christ. There is focus upon one or another important motif, elaboration of it, and a tendency to reduce the multifaceted richness of the meaning of Christ to that one theme. Whereas the reductionisms associated with the Person have to do either with the humanity or Deity of Christ, those that attend the Work gather around one or another of the stages on Christ's way: Bethlehem, Galilee, Calvary, Easter.

While there is no ecumenical consensus about the Work, juxtaposed to the reductionist models, as there is in the Person (holding together humanity, Deity, and unity), there is an ecumenical tradition that has sought to honor the pluriform Work of Christ. It has been called the *munus triplex,* the threefold office of Christ. The insights to be found in the models of Example and Teacher, Substitute and Savior, Conqueror and Lord are captured in the terminology of *Prophet, Priest,* and *King.* And when these roles are seen to be executed by the God-Man, and therefore the Presence enfleshed, then Bethlehem is viewed as the presupposition of Galilee, Calvary, and Easter. Some version of this imagery and conceptuality appears as far back as Eusebius, continues in Jerome, Augustine, Aquinas, and Schleiermacher, and appears in such recent thinkers as Bulgakov, Visser 't Hooft, and Barth. John Calvin has given it extended treatment in *The Institutes of the Christian Religion.* There is by no means universal agreement about this way of affirming and organizing the various Atonement themes, but it has proved to be of value in catechisms and statements of faith throughout the Church as well as in the theology of specific thinkers.

Interpreters of the idea have noted that as the three offices in the Old Testament were set apart by the act of anointing, so in the three-fold work of Christ, the "anointed One," we have the fulfillment of Covenant promise. While the continuity with the Old Testament is an important value in this formulation, both the specifics and semantics of anointing are not solidly grounded by historical research. The three-fold office must be rooted more fundamentally in the legitimacy of Prophet, Priest, and King as ways of expressing the themes in the Work of Christ and their interrelationships. We shall attempt to describe the fullness of Christ's Work in a way that incorporates the various motifs and resists the attendant reductionisms.

The Christian Story tells us that Jesus Christ is our liberator and reconciler. He works to defeat the powers of sin, evil, and death, and brings us together with nature, humanity, and God. He does this work as Prophet, Priest, and King. In language closer to our contemporary idiom, he is Seer, Sufferer, and Liberator. And the One who accomplishes this Work is the Person of Jesus Christ, truly human, truly God, fully one.

Prophet and Seer

The Old Testament prophet is a seer of the Vision of God. He is the forthteller who *makes it plain.* Jesus of Nazareth stands deeply in this tradition (Matt. 21:11; Luke 4:24; 7:16; 24:19). He caught sight of and pointed toward the coming Kingdom in which the will of God would be done on earth as well as it is in Heaven. He is the revealer of the future of God. In this New Time the mourners will be comforted; those who hunger, and those who hunger for righteousness, will be filled; the merciful will obtain mercy; the peacemakers and persecuted shall be vindicated; the poor, and the poor in spirit, shall be satisfied; and the meek shall inherit the earth (Matt. 5:3; Luke 6:17, 20–23). All human bondages shall be broken and the oppressed liberated (Luke 4:18–19). This deliverance is extended to all the alienations and disharmonies of nature as well, for Jesus preached and practiced the healing of the body and the restoration of a fallen creation (Matt. 4:24; Mark 4:39–41). The Kingdom of Shalom is more than horizontal, for it is marked by a freedom from the powers that separate humanity from God, as well as from neighbor and nature, and the overcoming of blindness to the Covenant partner: the arrival of Shalom means that "those whose hearts are pure . . . shall see God" (Matt. 5:8).

The coming of Shalom means judgment as well as fulfillment, justice executed against oppression and estrangement as part of the Vision of redemption. "Alas for you who are rich . . . alas for you who are well-fed now . . . alas for you who laugh . . . alas for you when all speak well of you; just so did their fathers treat the false prophets" (Luke 6:24–26).

The unmistakable sights of foreseeing and the notes of foretelling and forewarning that identify the prophet are to be found in Jesus' preaching and teaching about the Kingdom of God.

But this prophet penetrates more deeply into the Vision of God. In his description of the coming Kingdom is portrayed the *ground* as well as the *goal* of our pilgrimage. The characterizations of the future speak of the wellsprings of Shalom: *Agape.* Jesus points to the boundless unconditional Love which makes possible the final liberation and reconciliation of all things.

What is the nature of this Love that lies behind the ultimate freedom and peace? 1) It is *neighbor* love (Luke 10:25–37). Its focus is the one in need. The one in need is the victim on the Jericho road unseen by those who pass by. Agape is the sight to see and serve the invisible, those who do not come in range of the fallen world's vision. It includes all the helpless and hurt: the poor, the hungry, the sick, the oppressed, the stranger, the prisoner. It encompasses those of lesser estate and second-class citizenship: the widow, the orphan, women, children, the aged. In Jesus' teaching and in his conduct toward the debilitated and the dysfunctional, he healed the sick, treated women and children, the weak, the old, and the outcast with dignity and compassion, fed the hungry, and preached good news to the poor and those in bondage (Matt. 25:31–46; 15:22–28; 18:2–6; Mark 12:42–43). 2) Agape is a love that goes deeper than the care for the physically, mentally, and socially afflicted. It reaches out to the *lawless* as well as to the loveless. While Jesus did not scorn the law, he had compassion for those that breached it. In fact, he kept company with "sinners." The tax collectors against whom a case could be made for both conniving and collusion with tyranny, harlot and adulteress, those considered immoral and impious were the ones he sought out and with whom he related (Matt. 9:11; Luke 5:27; John 8:3–11). Why so? The unmerited love of the God to whom he bore witness and the Kingdom toward which the world moves also reach toward such people. "Your heavenly Father . . . makes his sun rise on good and bad alike, and sends the rain on the honest and the dishonest. If you love only those who love you, what reward can you expect? . . . There must be no limits to your goodness, as your Heavenly Father's goodness knows no bounds" (Matt. 5:45–46, 48). 3) The radical nature of Agape is demonstrated by its final reaches. It extends not only to the victim and to the unjust, but to the *enemy*. There is nothing that can turn aside the open arms of an unconditional Agape. It pushes past the resistance of those that hate it, and rushes toward those that despitefully use it (Luke 15:20). And when assaulted directly, it turns the other cheek and goes the second mile (Matt. 5:38–44). This capacity to accept the unacceptable and love the unloving is forgiveness. Forgiveness is fore-giving, readiness to give and go before without promise of reciprocity and in the face of rebuff. It is the always-open channel of communication, the in-spite-of care that persists no matter how deep the hurt or painful the wound. This is the quality that makes reconciliation possible. And we are enjoined to pursue it relentlessly (Matt. 18:21–22). 4) No radical love of the neighbor in need, the reprobate, and the enemy is possible if it is not ultimately rooted in selflessness. The self that is not prepared to abandon itself is not capable of dealing with this agenda. The cost-benefit analysis of Agape shows a pre-posterous balance sheet; its bottom line is written in the red of crucifixion. Agape is spendthrift, an uncalculating love that is the opposite of self-preservation, other-directed rather than self-directed. This is the unstinting servanthood that Jesus taught and was. "Whoever wants to be great among you must be your servant, and whoever wants to be first must be the willing slave of all. For even the Son of Man did not come to be served but to serve, and to give up his life as a ransom for many" (Mark 10:44–45).

Jesus was as good as his word. As a prophet sets forth the message in deed as well as in word, so Jesus enacted the Vision of Agape-Shalom which he preached. He did what he said, giving himself in abandonment to the needs of the unloved and unlovable. The issue of this Agape was the liberation of the enslaved and the reconciliation of the estranged. And as there is "no greater love than this, that a man should lay down his life for his friends" (John 15:13), he climaxed this Galilean ministry on Calvary.

Indeed Jesus did seal his prophetic office with his own blood. As it was the fate of the ancient prophet to be despised and rejected, so Christ evoked the wrath of those he called to account before the Vision. As he disclosed the contours of Shalom, an angry world thrust this embarrassing specter from its sight. In the destruction of Jesus on the cross the depths of the world's hate was manifest. Thus the work of the Prophet is both the disclosure of the ultimate reaches of the Vision, and also the *exposure* of the depths of resistance to it by the powers of sin and evil. That a larger meaning is to be found here we shall explore presently when we look at the work of Priest joined to the work of Prophet on Golgotha.

The Agape that suffuses Shalom is the love we are to have in the Kingdom that is coming and to which we are called right now. But it is this kind of love because it is the mirror of God's own love. The outcast, the oppressed, the malefactor, and the adversary are to be the object of our giving and forgiving because they are the object of God's giving and forgiving. The final ground of Shalom, therefore, is the *divine Agape,* the unmerited, spontaneous, uncalculating compassion of God's own heart. We are invited to participate in the liberation and reconciliation that God brings, and we are called to keep company with the wretched of the earth, to forgive the sinner 70 times 7 because the God to whom Jesus points is present with and ministers to the neighbor in need, the sinner, and the enemy.

This prophet not only points to this God, but understands himself to be in unique relationship to the divine Agape. Jesus addresses God in terms of special intimacy, "Abba" (Mark 14:36). In fact he calls people to relate to him as to the inbreaking Kingdom, and commands an authority that sets him apart from former models of teacher and preacher (Matt. 7:29). He pictures the Kingdom not just as near but also as here. It bursts into the present, and signs of its arrival are everywhere. The sight of the future is caught in the deeds that are done in the midst of the words that are said. The healing of the sick and the exorcism of demonic powers are the foretastes of Shalom that confirm the report that the Kingdom is coming. Misery and death are contested and ignorance is overcome, happenings in which the enemies of darkness begin to feel the light and heat of the new Day arriving. The most startling claim of the special bond with God is Jesus' assumption of the power to pardon sin (Matt. 9:2, 5; Luke 7:48). And it was this offer of forgiveness, the prerogative of God alone, that brought down upon him the wrath of the pious.

Jesus' self-understanding is confirmed to the Church in his resurrection, and proclaimed as a central article of its faith. The Prophet is not only the man of God but the God-Man; the Incarnation underlies all the Atonement offices. God was in the Christ of Galilee (II Cor. 5:19). Jesus not only sees the Vision but *is* the Vision. The light of God shines in the face of Jesus as well as toward the eye of this seer. He is not only the prophet of Shalom but he "*is* our Shalom" (Eph. 2:14).

Conceived by the Holy Spirit, the Power of the Vision makes this Light shine in and through him. The capacity to see the lengths and breadths of the Kingdom and finally to see into the depths of Agape and to enact as well as to portray the ground and goal of all things is by the Love and Hope of God made flesh in the Person of the carpenter of Nazareth. Jesus Christ: divine and human; Prophet and Seer of liberation and reconciliation.

Priest and Sufferer

As the prophets of Israel do not stand alone in the formation of a covenant that had the priestly tradition as partner, so the Work of Christ brings together priestly and prophetic offices. While the prophet casts up on the screen of the future the Vision of God and calls people toward it, the priest deals with the gap between the Vision and the reality of where the people are in their listless and rebellious journey toward the future. So the central act of the priest is to deal with the fact of sin—to make a sacrifice for the offense of the people against the purpose of God (Heb. 9:12). Jesus Christ takes this ancient office, presses it against the radical imperatives of his own prophetic work, and transforms it by the unique character of his sacrificial act. It is to Calvary that our attention is turned, for here the ultimate sacrifice is made.

Why the determined attack on Christ by both the power structure and the people to whom he came to show light and share vision? Paul tells us that love has a way of pouring hot coals upon its enemies (Rom. 12:20). It burns into us an awareness of what we are called to be. And we seek to put the hot brand away from our too tender skins. We are judged by Christ's life, and therefore we put him to death. We cannot stand the sight of our image as it was meant to be. Jesus Christ is the victim of the sinful humanity common to us and to our first-century counterparts. We were all there when they crucified our Lord.

That attack reveals who we really are, creatures prepared to go to any lengths to remove from our sight the embarrassing Presence of what we are called to be. Human nature demonstrates the depth to which it can descend, as Christ evokes the hatred of which we are capable. Jesus Christ's purity brings out the worst in us. We are ready with the nails and armed with the spear. This prophetic exposure of what we are is also the beginning of the priestly act of dealing with it. Effective engagement requires the full visibility of the enemy.

The exposure of the depths of the world's animosity is understood when Jesus of Nazareth is seen as an event in the history of

God as well as in our own history, the Presence incarnate. Here is the Shalom of God in our midst. What is done to Jesus of Nazareth on Calvary is done also *to God* (Col. 1:19–20). The nails that pierced his hands are driven into Deity itself. The blood of Jesus is the "blood of God." The sacrificial victim is the Lamb of God. One gasps at the horror of this happening. Our assaults reach into the Godhead itself. This is the measure of our sin.

When we try to describe the cross in the language we have been using to tell the Christian Story, we must speak of this profound wounding as an attack on the Vision of God itself (Col. 2:9). The crucifixion of Jesus, the incarnate God, is an enemy sally against the innermost sanctuary of the divine Hope. The death of Jesus is the passing away of Shalom, the demise of the Dream of God. This is not the death *of* God, but death *in* God (Jürgen Moltmann). There is "a cross in the heart of God" (Charles Dinsmore). Here on Calvary God died a little death. As the life of Christ discloses the Intention of God, the death of Christ exposes the depth of our sin.

But Jesus Christ not only suffers *from* but suffers *for* his assailants. Here is the Lamb of God who takes away the sins of the world. Atonement is expiation (Eph. 2:13–16).

Jesus Christ is the suffering Savior who redeems from sin and guilt. We have seen how our second model of the Work of Christ seeks to do justice to this crucial New Testament affirmation. Yet how easy it is to take the world's own understanding of expiation, the mollifying of God or the gods by altar sacrifice, as the key to Christ's work, and thus the rupturing of the unity of Jesus and God. Because God was *in* Christ on the cross reconciling the world, the priestly office is an act done *by Deity*, not the appeasement *of* Deity. The Incarnation is the presupposition of the Atonement. Just as it was God's own heart that was broken by our sin, so it is God's own heart that takes into itself the consequences of that sin. The consequences, the wages, of sin are death. In the righteousness of God there is no possible evasion of the scales of this justice. Death follows sin as night follows day. The aggression of the human race against the purposes of God is not indulged, overlooked, waived aside, or winked at. But the miracle of Calvary is that God the Judge goes into the dock for the sentencing. It is on Deity that the consequences fall. It is in Deity that the price is paid. Here the judgment that befits our crime was meted out, received, absorbed. Here in the heart of

God is where death descended and a cross formed.

In our metaphor-motif, the Vision of God was darkened on Calvary. Its Light was put out by human sin. Yet in this death a *suffering* Love bore our guilt. As the heart of God was broken, the profoundest depths in the divine life were reached. The suffering Love to be found there was drawn upon to deal with God's judgment. The pain experienced by God in those depths, the anguished receiving by God of God's own No to sin we can only dimly guess. In these inner regions of the divine life Shalom was borne up by Agape, the unconditional love that does not return in kind but accepts the unacceptable and loves the unlovable. Acceptance of the sinner is no cheap grace. It costs God to accept what righteousness must rebuke. The cost is the pain of judgment turned in upon God rather than out toward us. That is the suffering Agape that bears Shalom. Agape is the ground and Shalom is the goal of the history of God.

Jesus' story of the love of the parent for the prodigal son gives us a clue to the stirrings in the divine depths (Luke 15:11–32). It is a tale of the suffering Father whose son is what we also are. We can see in that figure of wasted gifts and violated hopes something of our own flight into a far country. And we can also see something of the anguished love in a parent that swallows his pride and hurt, who absorbs his own righteous anger and, more terribly, the sorrow of defeated expectations, receiving back the one who caused that hurt, yes running toward him! So the broken heart of God mends itself with suffering love. And the future comes to live again now on new terms. Here is offered a *new covenant* based on mercy, one that does not depend on our response, but one that goes before us as the father rushed to meet his son. The wrath and righteousness of the parent have been met and absorbed by the pathos of the parent. What we do toward the turned figure and outreached arms is a question of our own turning and running, a matter of which we must deal in the suceeding chapter when God's Story becomes our story.

The vulnerability of the Father that this narrative assumes and the Christian Story proclaims is a fundamental part of the priestly action, but one often slighted by the conventional wisdom of expiation. It is not only the tit-for-tat premises of ordinary experience that obscure this perception, but also secular notions of power trans-

The Christian Story

ferred into Christian context. Thus the Oriental potentate of ancient politics and the aloof philosopher who is truest when devoid of pathos were qualities attributed to God. With this conceptuality it was unthinkable that Deity would participate in the moil and toil of passion and crucifixion. At best it would be the human nature of Jesus to which suffering might be attributed, but never to God. This worldly wisdom about Deity has helped turn the crucial expiatory motif into the reductionist second model, polarizing Jesus with God. In fact, the Christian Story of Atonement as the action of an Incarnate Deity cannot be read aright without perceiving the passion of God in the crucifixion of Christ. Here is no anger of one bought off by the sacrifice of another, but the divine Wrath overcome by the divine Love, the "curse" absorbed by the "blessing" (Luther).

While the second model settles too quickly for the world's wisdom on sacrifice—done by humanity toward God—and does not grasp the vulnerable love of God in this event, it has held us firmly to history. Against any tendency to vaporize the event of Calvary, to project it so deeply into the transcendent realm that the human Jesus does not figure in the action, it has stressed the blood and tears of a real Savior. Calvary happened not only in the history of God but in our history as well. Without this tree and the man who hung upon it, without recognition of the choices of this figure there is no sound biblical interpretation of the cross. Jesus is not a robot acting out in our midst something that really only occurred in the heart of God. Suffering took place on earth by the hard choices made there by the historical Jesus (Mark 14:32–36 RSV). Without the real choices of the historical Jesus, in this case the decision to go to the cross, there would have been no enactment of the drama within the Godhead in the drama on Golgotha—and therefore no communication to us of the mercy of God for us. And more, Jesus represented the whole human race when he looked into the abyss and cried "My God, my God, why hast thou forsaken me?" (Matt. 27:46). He saw the death in God of the Vision of Shalom. He watched the Dream die. He experienced the sorrow of the broken heart of God, the withdrawal of the hand of God from the Hope of God. Jesus the Seer of the Galilean Vision also saw its suffering and passing on Calvary. In this sense too the judgment of God fell on the cross of Christ.

But why should the crucified humanity of Jesus be of such

consequence? The answer is obvious if the suffering of human innocence is necessary to mollify an angry God. But if the pain of judgment is taken up into the Godhead itself rather than executed on a third party, how can any meaning be given to the claim that *Jesus* died for our sins? And if the dubious notion of one guileless human being's death as providing an equivalent punishment of the race's guilt is also rejected (the strength of this assertion was always the Incarnational premise that only God had the power to deal with the debt incurred, the conviction implicit in our understanding here that equivalency of judgment means that only the pain of God can take away the sins of the world), how again can it be said that redemption from sin happened on the cross of Golgotha? If it is the suffering of God that accomplishes salvation from sin and guilt, what is the need and significance of the suffering of Jesus of Nazareth?

The answer to this question, given or implied, by many of those who have spoken about the passion of God is that the cross *shows* to us what goes on in the divine depths. If it were not for this window into ultimate Reality we would not know of the suffering love of God. This is, as far as it goes, an important meaning of the crucifixion. But it cannot be the last word on its significance. Standing alone, it represents a version, albeit a more profound version, of the exemplarist model of the Atonement. In it Jesus exists to disclose what God is like in order that we might be changed in heart and mind. But the work of priest not only reveals information and gives inspiration, but also participates in the very action that effects the new relationship between God and humanity. Without the deed of Jesus not only would we be ignorant of the forgiveness of sin, but there would be no forgiveness of sin. This is the astounding claim made over and over again in the New Testament, one that the Substitute and Savior model has sought to explain. Is there any other way to honor that claim without making the mistake of polarizing God and Jesus or bifurcating Father and Son as is done by this model?

A much scorned patristic tradition gives us a clue to such a way. Many of the Fathers spoke of redemption as the deceit of the devil, using the fishhook-bait metaphor to render it meaningful to ancient society. Jesus was portrayed as a tempting morsel presented to Satan in order to lure him from his hiding place in the undersea world. The bait that was dangled before him was too much to resist and he struck at the target. But in seizing Jesus, the Evil One was hooked. Thus the sinless Jesus served to conquer the enemy.

Embedded in this picturesque imagery is another way of conceiving the role of the human Jesus as Savior. For God to deal with the militancy of the world against the divine purpose, it was necessary to engage the enemy in its fullest manifestation. Incarnation means encounter with the total depth of bondage and alienation. Sin, evil, and death must show their truest and ugliest face. It is the presence of the purity of historical Shalom that enrages the powers and principalities evoking their true being. As in the patristic imagery, the innocence of Jesus draws from the depths the ultimate assaults of sin, evil, and death. Only by such a human being living on the plane of history where sin and evil make their home, and where death can do its most demonic work—the destruction of hope itself—can the enemy be induced from its lair and be what it is. Thus the very purpose of God turns on the obedience of Jesus, an obedience in life to the faithful pursuit of the Vision and obedience "unto death" in willingness to draw from the powers of darkness their mightiest effort. Jesus' steadfast loyalty to the Vision of God brought the monsters of the deep into engagement not only with human innocence, but in and with it the power of the enfleshed God whose very suffering Love proved to be the weapon able to deal with our enmity. Here on the cross is the Lamb of God that takes away the sins of the world.

Jesus Christ is suffering Priest. He offers himself as victim of the world's knife thrust through to the heart of Shalom. In the shed blood he is the God who suffers in our place, and the man who chooses that agony as the agent of our reconciliation with God and our liberation from sin and guilt.

King and Liberator

Sin and guilt meet their match in the priestly Work of Christ. But the powers of evil remain to be finally dealt with. So does the last enemy, death. It is in the kingly Work of Christ that these foes are met and overcome. This contest takes us out of the cavernous underground land of the spirit where sin dwells and onto the broad ranges of history and nature where evil and death roam. And it takes us also from the cross to the resurrection where this final engagement is decisively fought and won.

The work of Christ the Conqueror does not wait upon the Easter event but begins at Bethlehem. At Incarnation the battle is joined. Here the Vision of God enters the land to which the powers of evil and death lay claim and where they have had their way. It is into the flesh of humanity that sickness, sorrow, and mortality have driven their spears. It is on the plane of history that the thrones and authorities, the structures of power, have strutted and tyrannized. And it is among the birds of the air and the flowers of the field that the groans of nature can be heard. It is with this reality that the Vision of God comes to grips, and into this arena that it plunges. Here darkness meets the Light.

The battle with the powers of this world rages in Galilee. Christ reports the vision that empowers his struggle: "I watched how Satan fell, like lightning out of the sky" (Luke 10:18). Out of this perception of a foe already on the run, he meets the Tempter at the opening of his ministry, pursues him at every turn, and wrestles with him at the climax in Gethsemane. The work of evil in temptation is matched by its work in agonies of the body and mind. Again Christ confronts and ousts the power in healing and in exorcising the demonic powers (Matt. 10:1). The engagement with evil extends into the arena of political, social, and economic power structures which he meets at each turn of his ministry, from the Sanhedrin to imperial Rome (Matt. 26:59–68; 27:11–14).

But does this last encounter not tell another story? In the confrontation with the might of the power structures, all seems to be lost. For in the final assault by an alliance of political, military, economic, and ecclesiastical principalities, sin conspires with evil to bring death. In the crucifixion of Jesus Christ, it is not only a man that is destroyed, but also a Dream. Here is the last best Hope of the world, and it is gone.

If the narrative ended here, hope would be dead. In fact, the life and teachings and cross would themselves tell a different tale. It is only the next event in the unfolding drama that transforms the meaning of Galilee and Calvary. This sequel is the Work of Christ as Liberator from the powers of evil and death (Col. 2:15). On resurrection morning, Christ beats down Satan and all his hosts and destroys death. The very worst that the world hurls at the Vision cannot finally extinguish the Light of God (Col. 1:13). The resurrection of Jesus Christ means that evil in all its forms—the ills of the flesh, the disasters of nature, the holocausts of history—do not have the last word. The enemy does not control the future. The intention of God to bring the Kingdom cannot be turned aside; Shalom will be! And as doom is spelled for the powers of evil, and sin is overcome by the divine mercy, so too *death* meets its match. When Christ rose from the grave, he signaled the death of death and the coming of Life. Easter means that the Vision of God is victorious over its foes and the reconciliation of all things is the destiny of the Great Experiment of creation. "Courage! The victory is mine; I have conquered the world" (John 16:33).

What really happened in first-century Jerusalem to warrant these astounding claims? Something took place among a dispirited band of disciples that gave rise to this Easter faith and its dramatic consequences. These are the logical possibilities: 1) The physical body of Jesus was raised. 2) A "spiritual body" was raised. 3) The physical body of Jesus was raised and transfigured into a "spiritual body." (In the case of 1, 2, and 3, the event may have been perceived either through the eyes of faith or the eyes of sight.) 4) The Easter experiences were psychic events in the lives of the seers. 5) The Easter experiences were a resurgence of faith in the hearts of the early Christians.

It is possible to conjoin any of these five empirical interpretations of Easter to the fundamental *theological* affirmation of resurrection. Even the last two possibilities can be interpreted as veridical psychic or faith experiences. The fact that Jesus Christ "was raised up by God" (Acts 2:32) and defeated the powers of sin, evil, and death does not depend on that event's taking place in any one way. The heart of the matter is the *that* not the *how*. Yet it must be said that the nature of the apostolic testimony (Matt. 28; Mark 16; Luke 24; John 20–21; Acts 9:3–6; I Cor. 15:3–8) and the implication of this event for other chapters in the Christian Story point to option 3: the empty tomb and transfigured body seen by the eyes of faith. (The significance of history and the dignity of things physical in the Christian faith, and the clue in Christ's resurrection to our own eschatological hope underscore this interpretation.) For all that, the fundamental declaration of Easter faith is the victory of the Vision of God, Jesus Christ, seen by the apostles in the resurrection appearances. These are resurrection appearances in both meanings of the term: genuine experiences of real people, however interpreted, and an authentic arrival of the future of God, Jesus Christ, in and through these experiences. At the center of the resurrection events is a view of a triumphant Vision of God.

The light of Easter dawn is shed back upon the crucifixion disclosing it as the way of conquest over evil and death, and the weapon of victory over sin. The sword of the Liberator is the cross. Suffering Love is the way in which not only forgiveness of sin is made possible, but also the defeat of evil and death. God in Christ works to conquer all the enemy in a fashion commensurate with the divine nature: not by force but by "persuasion." The might of the Lord is suffering Love (Eph. 2:16). Agape is the road God takes toward Shalom.

As our understanding of how suffering Love conquers sin is helped by the parable of a grieving and forgiving father, so there are New Testament clues and human analogues that hint at the finally imponderable conquest of evil and death by the Agape of God. Thus the compassion of Jesus which conquers illness is portrayed in the anthropomorphisms of an exorcised demon (Mark 1:34), or the repentance of a symbol of the power structure, Nicodemus (John 7:50), or the raising of a Lazarus (John 12:17).

And from that elusive event in our own history when a soft answer turns away wrath, a power structure is humbled, and systemic change occurs by the life and witness of a Martin Luther King, healing happens, or the sting of death is removed through the agency of suffering love. But these are just clues, for until the final reckoning with evil and death in that eschatological goal toward which history now drives, suffering love continues as crucified love, and the Kingdom comes as portent and firstfruit and not fulfillment. Evil does not recognize its defeat, and our mortality is a sign of its refusal to acknowledge its Lord. Therefore, in the half-light of the Already–Not Yet of Christ's resurrection victory, it is not given to us to see *how* suffering Love achieves its end. We live by the eyes of faith not empirical sight.

Easter is the liberation from evil and death in portent and principle, thrusting toward the liberation in fulfillment and fact in the consummation of all things. Christ's conquest in the resurrection is a *finished* Work in that the rule of the powers of darkness is over at this Dawn. But it is a *continuing* Work, in that the acknowledgment and completion of this Lordship awaits the End. In the time between Easter and Eschaton we contest the forces that continue to militate against Christ the King. About the continuing and final Work of the Liberator in our age, and his call to keep step with him in the work of liberation today, we shall speak in our exploration of the present and future Work of Christ.

Christ the King achieves the Work of reconciliation in and through the Work of liberation. As the conquest of sin is the reconciliation of humanity with God, so the victory over evil and death is the reconciliation of nature and history with God, within themselves, and with each other. Won in portent and principle by Calvary and Easter, this coming together is looked for at the End when the wolf will lie down with the lamb, the child will put her hand over the viper's den, swords shall be beaten into plowshares, the creation will no longer groan, the New Jerusalem will descend, and the Kingdom come. It is looked for as well in the firstfruits of this Finale in the healings in, and hopes for, nature and history in this time between the Times. Thus the continuing Work of reconciliation in this world is one in which Christ saves from evil and death and brings wholeness to the fractures of this world.

Theodicy

The age-old problem of evil is an agony to be wrestled with in the Christian understanding of Christ the King, and so we deal with theodicy: the defense of God's goodness and omnipotence despite the presence of evil. While theodicy draws its most profound resources from eschatology, it is in the understanding of Atonement that the first word of faith is spoken about the engagement with the powers of evil.

An understanding of the Incarnation and Atonement as the encounter of Vision with reality affects the issue of theodicy by changing the terms in which the question is posed. This is true when the three ingredients in the problem of evil—the power of God, the goodness of God, and the presence of evil—are defined with reference to the Good Friday–Easter events rather than given content by cultural assumptions.

Traditional theodicies frequently accept uncritically a conception of power inherent in the original pre-Christian formulation of the problem, one that has been perpetuated since. Into it some premises of Greek philosophy and some perceptions of Oriental statecraft and patriarchal life intrude. When the question, "How can a good God, who is also all-powerful, countenance the presence of evil in the world?" is posed, what is assumed is the instant and omnipresent control of a being who has the characteristics of an Oriental potentate with the traits of a dominating masculinity and a timeless Greek form. To pass muster in the definition of Deity, he must have "in charge" credentials of that sort. To interpret theodicy from the atoning center of Christian faith, and thus to wrest it from these cultural assumptions, is to put these themes in the place of machismo and despot notions of power. 1) Power is to be understood as the power which in fact effects redemption, the Holy Spirit of suffering Shalom, not an invincible autocracy. 2) Power is power *enough* to fulfill the Vision of God, not totalitarian hegemony. 3) Power expresses itself, and therefore defines itself, along the time line of the Christian Story, not as instant fiat.

Taking the above as reference points, the Atonement illumines the problem of evil in this way: God overcomes evil in the crucifixion and resurrection by a vulnerable but victorious Shalom. The outcome will be that "He will wipe away every tear from their eyes; there shall be an end to death, and to mourning and crying and pain; for the old order has passed away" (Rev. 21:4). The sufferings of persons, history, and nature will be redeemed. Evil has been defeated, and therefore its work will be undone. The Deity who achieves this Purpose is no monarch who rules with an iron hand that gestures instant obeisance, but who rules in a fashion commensurate with the long-suffering nature of the divine Vision. God opens up maneuvering room for response to the divine beckoning, a vista of time from Easter to Eschaton. Here is a Dawn in which shadows persist, the ambiguity of an Already–Not Yet that continues until the high noon when God is all in all. The evil flailing about in this span of time is absolutely real, a darkness poised over against the Light. Yet it is "pro-visional," going before the Vision that is to be. It is the perversion of the freedom God grants a good creation, albeit a penultimate one, endemic to history but overcome in eternity. The Power of God secures the goodness of God in a world inhabited by evil that is moving toward redemption. The crucial distinctions introduced by a Christocentric definition of power make the difference between a triumphalist deity and a triumphant God.

The sensitive humanist or morally outraged atheist who deny

God because they feel the true horror of evil (though not sin) more than most, and the defensive theist who attempts to justify the ways of a Deity believed to be in some sense the cause of the world's misery, are at one in their misunderstanding. The atoning Power wages a victorious battle against the principalities of this world—on their terrain, but on God's terms. And the aesthetic and peda-gogical traditions in theodicy fail at another point, for they do not probe deeply enough the depths of evil in their attempt to protect the goodness and power of God. The defenders of a finite God fall into a dualism that grants the Devil more than his due and/or deny the omnipotence of God. When omnipotence is viewed from the perspective of Good Friday and Easter, "all-powerful" becomes the demonstrated potency to establish the divine End.

The Shared Work of Prophet, Priest, and King

As the humanity and Deity of Christ are in unity in the Person of Christ, and as the three Persons of the Godhead coinhere, so the offices in the Work of Christ mutually interpenetrate. It is the one Christ who accomplishes the Work of Atonement. Each represents a distinguishable role of Christ, but the exercise of each role merges with the others.

Christ as Prophet discloses by word and deed the Vision of Shalom. But this Work of revelation is also a Work of conquest, and thus a royal action. It is the blindness to the Light that afflicts a world turned in and away from its horizon that is conquered. In the Work of disclosure Christ liberates from the power of darkness, thus anticipating the resurrection victory. And the powers of evil and death have already begun to meet their master in those same Galilean events, as we have already noted. Here too is the anticipa-tion of the cross and the Work of Christ the Priest, for the ground of Shalom as well as its goal is revealed in the life and teachings of Jesus, the depths of suffering Love reached upon the cross. It is by the action of Agape that the Vision is uncovered in Galilee, one enacted in fullest measure on Calvary. Here too in the ministry of the Prophet is the forgiveness of sins proclaimed and shared, one whose final foundation is built on Golgotha. Thus the Galilean Prophet portends and embodies the Work of Priest and King.

Christ as Priest is of a piece with the Galilean ministry, for here is the crown and completion of the suffering Love manifest in the life, healings, and teachings of the Prophet. As such, Calvary in its darkest hour is also disclosure of the invisible Light of God. And the disclosure of the Prophet becomes exposure of the hostility of the world in the act of crucifixion. King as well as Prophet makes his presence known on the cross, for here the King is at work conquering sin in the sacrifice made. And evil and death are being confronted as well, for it is by the sword of the cross that they are finally felled. Thus Prophet and King enter into the Work of Priest.

Christ the King is in unity with Christ the Prophet, for the resurrection discloses the victory to which the Prophet points and authenticates the claims of Jesus the Example and Teacher of Shalom. Here also the way of the Prophet, Agape, is the way of conquest by the King, and that way embodied in the Galilean Christ is one and the same suffering Love wielded by the King on the cross. There too is the Liberator from sin, as well as the way of the Liberator from evil and death. The King is in, with, and under Prophet and Priest.

The Deed of Christ

What did Christ do? He brought us at-one-ment, liberation from sin, evil and death, and reconciliation with God, neighbor, and nature. How?

He saw and shared the Vision of God. He was the Prophet who perceived and pointed to the horizon Light of God's Shalom. A Prophet but more than a Prophet, for the Light that shone toward him also shone *in* him. The Vision became flesh and manifested itself in deeds of liberation and reconciliation.

He was a Seer, but also a Sufferer, a Priest, as well as a Prophet. He suffered for the Vision of God, exposing the hate of the world as it sought to extinguish the Light of God. And so too he suffered the sight of the eclipse of the sun of Shalom, obedient unto death. And he *was* the embodied Vision of God that suffered that death, and in that suffering took into the divine life our punishment, releasing the mercy that covers our sin.

He was the Seer and Sufferer, but also the Liberator and Lord. The sword of the cross pierced the armor of the powers and principalities. The risen Christ is the Conqueror who opens the future and assures the coming of the Kingdom. No more do we fear the thrones and authorities that rattle their swords in this world, for they have met their match, and we are empowered to resist them in the liberation and reconciliation struggles of our time, even as we meet the last enemy, death, in hope.

"Thanks be to God who has given us the victory through our Lord Jesus Christ!"

CHAPTER V

Church: Nature and Mission

NATURE

Divine grace is power as well as favor. The grace of God in Jesus Christ that offers the world liberation and reconciliation makes its presence felt in the liberating and reconciling power released into the world. And so we come to that chapter in the Christian Story that has to do with the pouring out of the Holy Spirit, the coming of the power of God on the day of Pentecost. Our exploration of the doctrine of the Church, ecclesiology, will begin with the original record of this event. The early chapters of Acts provide the biblical framework for understanding what the Church is and does, its nature and mission.

The Ascended Lord

The account of the Ascension in the first chapter of Acts builds a bridge from the Person and Work of Christ to the nature and mission of the Church. "As they watched, he was lifted up, and a cloud removed him from their sight" (Acts 1:9). In this striking visual imagery the risen Lord mounts to the "right hand of God." As with other chapters in the Christian Story, debate about the cosmology of the biblical narrator can deflect us from the Word to be heard and the Vision to be seen in and through the text. Attention to the *that* and *what* of the matter here, rather than the *how* and *when* of changing scientific world views, discloses a crucial act in the drama of redemption.

In traditional language the Ascension declares the glorification of Christ and, more specifically, the glorified humanity of Christ. The world in which we live is one in which Jesus Christ actively exercises his kingly rule. This same Jesus—truly human, truly God, truly one—now is the world's indisputable Lord; the world is "Christic." Indeed he reigns by the power of suffering Love, not by the instruments of the rulers of this world. The exaltation of Christ is the active regency of Shalom. "He's got the whole world in his hands."

The time of rulership is the occasion for "the continuing Work of Christ." Things happen on earth as well as in heaven. The *ascent* of the Son means the *descent* of the Spirit.

The Descended Spirit

The second chapter of the book of Acts reports the evidence of the sovereign power of the exalted Christ. The radiance of the Light that bathes the world comes as fire in the midst of it. "While the day of Pentecost was running its course, they were all together in one place, when suddenly there came from the sky a noise like that of a strong driving wind, which filled the whole house where they were sitting. And there appeared to them tongues like flames of fire, dispersed among them and resting on each one. And they were filled with the Holy Spirit and began to talk in other tongues, as the Spirit gave them power of utterance" (Acts 2:1-4). The power of the divine Light, the Holy Spirit, descends on a people enflaming them with the language of another land and sights of the Vision of God. The exalted humanity of Christ lets its glory shine in the world, taking form as the Body of Christ on earth. At Pentecost the Holy Spirit brings the Church to birth (cf. Eph. 4:7-16).

This happening occurs among the most ordinary of mortals. Those who see with the natural eyes ask "Why, they are all Galileans, are they not, the men who are speaking?" (Acts 2:7). In the same way the Church's later antagonists, seeing Peter and John "perceived that they were uneducated, common men. . ." (Acts 4:13 RSV). Thus in a different frame of reference the antinomies of Incarnation are repeated as the *Body* of Christ is paradoxically seen to be at one and the same time a *body* of ordinary people.

What are these fires of Pentecost? Those today with the "gift of tongues" trace their lineage to this event. Yet others distinguish the articulate languages described here from the glossolalia of the Corinthian congregation, finding in this Acts text the missionary call to reach the nations. Our guideline to the meaning of the text's "flames of fire" is their significance relative to the birthday of the Church. The language of Heaven and the sights of new Vision portray a new outpouring of the Spirit and its empowerment of a new People as the Body of the glorified Lord.

The illumination of the Pentecostal birthday comes from within the event itself. Peter declares, "This is what the prophet spoke of: God says, 'This will happen in the last days. I will pour out upon everyone a portion of my spirit; and your sons and daughters shall prophesy; your young men shall see visions, and your old men shall dream dreams. Yes, I will endue even my slaves, both men and women, with a portion of my spirit, and they shall prophesy' " (Acts 2:17–18). The work of the Spirit is the bringing to be of the Vision of God. At Pentecost the empowerment of Shalom takes place as the capacitating of persons to "see visions and dream dreams." It is the fulfillment of the Old Testament hope that there be a people who will see and serve the future of God. This new perception is an eschatological event: "In the last days. . . ." The birth of the Church is the beginning of the End. The Kingdom of God as the miracle of ocular newness when "the blind see" makes its impact on history in the creation of a *visionary community.* The scales fall from the eyes of these seers who discern the risen and ascended Lord and experience the power of his coming Kingdom. The sign that they have been invaded from the future is their report of "the mighty works of God" (Acts 2:11) in eschatological language. Whether those tongues that burst forth be interpreted as intelligible—"how is it that each of us hears in our own language?" (Acts 2:6)—or as a rush of unintelligible glossolalia—"Others mocking said, 'They are filled with new wine' " (Acts 2:13)—it is the language of the world to come, a universal Shalom that is not confined to the particularities of our finitude, nor does it settle into our neat and manageable coherencies. Therefore in this birth of the Church, the risen and ascended Lord takes to himself a Body on earth with eyes opened by the Spirit to see the future. These are the Dawn People, the children of Light empowered to see the Vision of God.

People who have had visions of the end for which we have been made, who have seen the future, are going to be restless with anything short of that destination. The Church's foretaste of the fruits of the Kingdom, its forevision of the Shalom to come, creates a dissatisfaction with present reality. Its eschatological perception makes the Christian community a stranger and pilgrim in this world. Herein lies its radical leverage. Because it knows how the world should be, it sets up signs in the Now pointing to the Not Yet. By the power of the Spirit that opened this new horizon, it seeks to orient reality to the Vision.

The effects of this Future shock are to be seen in the events that take place within the Christian community which we shall presently explore, ones that show its struggle to be a colony of the Future. And subsequently, as described in Acts 3 and 4 and beyond, this revolution within pushes its perimeters further and further into the world without.

The Acts report focuses upon the corporate nature of envisioning; it is about a new people. Yet the miracle of new sight is also an individual matter as the text soon enough suggests: "Whoever calls on the name of the Lord shall be saved" (Acts 2:21 ASV). We shall explore this individuating aspect of the Church's creation, personal salvation, in our next chapter. Here we are concerned to understand Pentecost as a deed of God that brings a singular community into existence.

A return to the original record in Acts of the Church's creation helps to root the doctrine of the Church in the inner ring of authority and also to draw upon its rich visual and visionary imagery. In the more conventional language of traditional theology, our exegesis has sought to express the dual nature of Church as a divine-human institution. It is an "earthen vessel" subject to the frailties of its membership and to the play of sociological forces. Yet it carries treasure. God is in the midst of this sinful and finite people. Jesus Christ is truly present by the Spirit that gives this Body life. The uniqueness of the Church consists in this special bond with its Lord. We have spoken of it as the empowerment of the people by the Spirit that abides in its midst to see the Vision of God. As such the Church is an eschatological community. The Future penetrates the present; the rays of its Light are seen by the opened eyes of faith. Indeed we do not see "face to face" the coming God. The Church can make no pretense of *being* the Kingdom. It is portent and firstfruit of what is yet to come, unfulfilled, broken, subject to error and ambiguity. But in our present period of ecclesiastical self-criticism, we cannot forget the Church's fundamental identity. A covenant bond has been forged by the Spirit with this people, in all their frailty. While there is no transparency of the future here, we do "see through a glass darkly." In this community we are offered communion with the coming God.

The Gifts of the Spirit and Marks of the Church

The Spirit sustains the Vision of God and strengthens the ties to the future with special gifts given to the people of God. The outpouring of the Spirit on the day of Pentecost manifests itself in the appearance of these "marks of the Church":

Kerygma

The presence of the Vision of God fires the people of God to say what it sees. The first act of the empowered people is *kerygma,* the report of the Good News, the proclamation of the Gospel. Thus Peter announces to the onlookers, "Men of Israel, listen to me: I speak of Jesus of Nazareth, a man singled out by God . . ." (Acts 2:22). So the Christian Story is told. And it is told against the background and in the idiom of the people of the Covenant out of whose history this new Word and Vision comes. Peter thrusts the narrative back into the Prologue, the "plan and foreknowledge of God" (Acts 2:23 RSV), and forward from that to crucifixion, resurrection, and ascension, and thence to the call to participate in the unfolding drama. The translation aside, that is how the message is addressed to the "house of Israel." The narration of the Tale of the deeds of God, the *telling* of the Story, is a sign of the presence of the Spirit, and a tool the Spirit uses to build the Church. The kerygma, therefore, is a constitutive factor of the Christian community. Where the Word is preached the Body of Christ takes form in the world.

Leitourgia

The stirrings of the Spirit continue. "Those who received his word were baptized, and there were added that day about three thousand souls. And they devoted themselves to the apostles' teaching and fellowship, to the breaking of bread and the prayers. . . . And day by day, attending the temple together and breaking bread in their homes, they partook of food with glad and generous hearts, praising God . . ." (Acts 2:41–42, 46–47 RSV). Prayer and praise, the waters of Baptism and the bread of the Supper, these gifts of the Spirit and worship acts of the people appear in the midst of the aborning congregation. *Leitourgia* joins kerygma as a mark of the Church. The Church *celebrates* as well as tells the Story. In the sacramental form of Baptism and Eucharist an "outward and visible sign" of the Spirit complements the verbal one of proclamation. Word and Sacrament keep company in sustaining the life of the Church. Yet the sacramental signs, which we shall examine more carefully later, do not exhaust the liturgical life of the Body. Corporate prayer and praise in its multifarious expressions, meditative and celebrative, are vehicles of the Spirit in maintaining and strengthening the Body of Christ. The prayers and songs of the Church keep the people of God in communion with the Vision of God. In worship we are put in touch by the Spirit with the future. On the one hand, our anchor is lodged in the Not Yet and our life is given direction and firmness. On the other, we are dislodged from the present, made restless with the givens, and thus strangers and pilgrims in the Now. In this manner the Spirit keeps the Body moving by the eye of faithful prayer and praise turned toward the Horizon.

The life of prayer is at the center of worship, communal or personal. Prayer, mental or verbal, is conscious communication with God. Here an I meets a Thou, the human person encounters the divine Self. In praying, we address the Envisioner of Hope. Prayer in Christian idiom is offered "through Jesus Christ our Lord." This means that Jesus Christ, the Vision of God, is the reference point for our supplication and adoration. As the Lord's prayer begins and ends with the Kingdom of Shalom, so the prayers of the believing Christian are made against this Horizon of liberation and reconciliation (Matt. 6:9–13). Our praise, petitions, intercession, confession, thanksgiving, and commitment are in and of the Spirit, the Spirit of the Vision, to the extent that they are empowered by, and can stand the exposure to, this radiance.

In the act of prayer we are catapulted forward to meet the coming Lord. As such, prayer frees us from bondage to the present moment, gives perspective on it and leverage in dealing with it. But it is not these pragmatic benefits of "spirituality" that justify prayer. In fact they can only be had when they are not sought. "Seek first his kingdom and his righteousness, and all these things shall be yours as well" (Matt. 6:33 RSV). Rather it is the love of God "for his own sake," the company kept with the One who comes, which is the ultimate warrant for what we do on our knees before our Maker and Redeemer.

Diakonia

"All those whose faith had drawn them together held everything in common; they would sell their property and possessions and make a general distribution as the need of each required" (Acts 2:44–45). As the Spirit opens the eye of faith to see the Light, so it empowers the visionary community as well to see *in* the Light the brother and sister in Christ. Illumination by the divine Light means in this instance a *diakonia,* a serving of the neighbor in need within the Christian community. According to the text this meant a very radical act of physical support in the primitive Church, a pooling of property and possessions and redistribution on the principle "to each according to his need." As this commitment worked itself out in the ensuing life of the community, it took the form of care for, and the honoring of the dignity of, the dysfunctional within ancient society, the "nobodies" of that culture: the widow, orphan, prisoner, slave, and poor. The Church demonstrated the meaning of Agape in its internal life, *doing* the Story, loving the unloved, and thus intuitively modeling the quality of life in the Kingdom to come. Servanthood comes naturally to be a gift of the Spirit of a Shalom in which the bondages of deprivation and indignity are challenged, and the broken *bodies* of human beings are made whole by bread and wine and water as well as broken *spirits* healed by participation in the sacramental life.

How diakonia is enacted changes with each new occasion. The form of servanthood may be the communitarian caring of the earliest Christians or the benevolent or justice ministries of later ones. And its neighbor may be the slave and orphan of the first century or the aged and poor of the twentieth century. But the fact of diakonia continues in each new setting to be a mark of an authentic Church. The care in body as well as spirit for the brothers and sisters in Christ is a constitutive factor of the Christian community, testifying to this people having been captured by the vision of Shalom, and to the presence in the midst of that people of the Spirit of liberation and reconciliation.

Koinonia

"They met constantly ... to share the common life.... With one mind they kept up their daily attendance at the temple, and, breaking bread in private houses, shared their meals with unaffected joy ..." (Acts 2:42, 46). Sharing the common life and meals was more than a ministry of material benevolence. In and through the diakonia was to be seen and felt the throb of *koinonia*. The Spirit gives the gift of *being* as well as doing: being together. Koinonia is the life together of sister and brother in Christ, *being* the Story. Luther, identifying it as a constitutive factor of the Church, calls it the "mutual conversation and consolation of the brethren." A sign of the Church, therefore, is its reality as a support system. Here joys are shared and burdens are borne. The tepid word *fellowship* does not convey the deep sharing that koinonia implies as it was lived out by the Acts community and is relived by people of God wherever the Spirit is at work. Koinonia happens when there is an authentic "common life," a sharing and caring life together in which the people of God dwell in the joyful unity of the Spirit.

What happened at Pentecost? The Body of Christ was born on earth, formed by and filled with the Holy Spirit and living under the known sovereignty of its exalted Lord. The sign of the birth of the Body and the presence of the Spirit is the seeing of visions and the dreaming of dreams by sons and daughters, young and old. The visionary people of God catch sight of the Vision of God. The rays of the future draw from them words and deeds through which the Spirit keeps the Vision alive and compelling. These are the organs in the Body of Christ by which the Spirit keeps it alive and alert.

The nature of the Church, therefore, is its existence as a divine-human organism, the Body of Christ manifest in a body of people, empowered by the Holy Spirit to see the Vision of God, to know who is Lord, and to tell, celebrate, do, and be the Story of the coming of Shalom. The gifts of the Spirit which keep the Body alive and alert, the marks of the Church, are kerygma, diakonia, koinonia, and leitourgia.

By making our way into this understanding of the Church through the first two chapters in Acts, however, we have seen only one dimension of it, made necessary by the chronological character of our narrative approach. Pentecost accents the Church's inner life. Its nature is embodied in its nurture. But the fullness of the Church's being includes outreach as well as inreach, *mission* as well as *nurture.* In the chronology of the primitive Church, this explosion outward comes in the wake of the Pentecostal implosion. Thus Acts 3 and 4 report the thrust of the Church beyond the boundaries of community that has just been created and described in Acts 2. We turn to the succeeding chapters of Acts to grasp the mission aspect of the Church.

MISSION

Reaching out is intrinsic to the saga of God. The Christian Story is about the *Missio Dei,* the mission of God in the pursuit of Shalom. The ancient Church interpreted the "economic Trinity" in terms of this going forth. The purpose of God was built up in the "missions" of the Trinity as the Father acted in creation, the Son in reconciliation, and the Spirit in redemption.

The mission of the Church grows out of the mission of God, by way of participation in the mission of the Spirit. The Spirit does not cease its ecclesial work by creating a community that tells and does the Story to itself, and celebrates and is the Story within itself. The Spirit nurtures this community with these gifts in order that it may be in *mission.* Light and fire are for warmth and power. Inreach is fulfilled in outreach. Indeed this is how the drama of the Church's beginnings unfolds. The ascent of Christ, descent of the Spirit, and birth of the Body of Christ described in Acts 1 and 2 are followed by the movement outward in mission narrated in Acts 3 and 4. The Vision that enters into this community and that is seen by this people at Pentecost leads them outside their own life to share the

Light and serve in it. The very gifts of kerygma, diakonia, koinonia, and leitourgia are honored, paradoxically, to the extent that they are given away to others. Let us follow the path of mission as it is charted in the texts.

Deed

"One day at three in the afternoon, the hour of prayer, Peter and John were on their way up to the temple. Now a man who had been a cripple from birth used to be carried there and laid every day by the gate of the temple, called, 'Beautiful Gate,' to beg from people as they went in. When he saw Peter and John on their way into the temple, he asked for charity. But Peter fixed his eyes on him, as John did also, and said, 'Look at us.' Expecting a gift from them, the man was all attention. And Peter said, 'I have no silver or gold; but what I have I will give you: in the name of Jesus Christ of Nazareth, walk'" (Acts 3:1–7). As in the Samaritan story (Luke 10:29–37), the eye of love was opened while the blind passed by on the other side, and the Spirit empowered the disciples to do a deed of Shalom. Mission is *diakonia*. It is the empowerment of the Church to see in the Light the victim "by the gate of the temple." The Spirit opens the eyes of the Christian community to see the invisible of the world, and seeing, to serve.

Servanthood is not doing the conventional, but the unconventional, the unthinkable, the miracle. How that miracle is performed depends on the resources the Spirit provides. Again, it is the *fact* not the *form* of grace that is integral to the Story. The heart of the miracle at the gate is not the supernatural powers in the narrative but the God of surprise who moves the Church to think the unthinkable and do the undoable in diaconal mission. The Spirit uses a variety of means to liberate from the bondage of the powers of pain and hurt when the rest of the world accepts these circumstances as unalterable.

Word

In the midst of this deed of Shalom comes a word of Shalom. The same Peter whose proclamation was an instrument of the Spirit's Pentecostal gathering of the Christian community again tells the Story. This time it is a kerygma thrusting out of the newborn people in mission toward the world. "Men of Israel, why be surprised at this? Why stare at us as if we had made this man walk by some power or godliness of our own? The God of Abraham, Isaac, and Jacob, the God of our fathers, has given the highest honor to his servant Jesus . . ." (Acts 3:12–13). A Vision is lifted before those who have not seen it. And it is told in translation, in the context of the language and history of its hearers. Mission, therefore, does not stop with the act of mercy and justice but brings the deed into companionship with the word. Evangelism, in its broadest sense, is the task of getting the Story out, flinging the Christian faith in the air. Evangelism in its apostolic sense as practiced by Peter and John, *Acts evangelism,* is the conjoining of word and deed. It is neither a deedless word nor a wordless deed but word *in* deed. The signature of the Spirit is seen where there are found evangelists empowered to give visibility to the Vision by a miracle of Shalom done to wounded bodies, and audibility to the Word by a courageous witness to broken spirits.

Call

Missionary kerygma is no academic exercise. The telling of the Story is a call to consider our own tale. So Peter's narrative concludes, "Repent then and turn to God, so that your sins may be wiped out" (Acts 3:19). Do you want to see the Light? If so, wrench loose from your mesmerism with the powers of darkness! Do an about face (*metanoia*). The teller of the Story comes with a call to decision and vision.

That invitation is corporate as well as individual. It beckons into the visionary community. Orientation to this Horizon is pilgrimage with the children of Light. Where the Spirit undergirds the deed and word yet another miracle takes place: "Many of those who had heard the message became believers. The number of men now reached about five thousand" (Acts 4:4). When the seed of the Story is planted in fertile soil it springs up. "Church growth" is an expectation of mission. The debate on the character of this growth is a vigorous one. But the rightness of this hope cannot be disputed. Mission includes the welcome of the five thousand into the Body of Christ, and the expectation that "God gives the growth" (I Cor. 3:7 KJV).

Confrontation

Sowing in mission goes on among the brambles and rocky soil as well as in fertile soil. In the Acts narrative resistance comes to both word and deed from those who have the most to lose from this outreach: the powers and principalities of the dying Age. The structures of power that took offense at the Good News, in this case, are made up of a military-political-ecclesiastical complex which felt its hegemony threatened by the visual and verbal signs of the New Age. "They were still addressing the people when the chief priests came upon them, together with the Controller of the Temple and the Sadducees, exasperated at their teaching the people and proclaiming the resurrection from the dead—the resurrection of Jesus. They were arrested and put in prison for the night. . ." (Acts 4:1–3). Later the occasion for the attack is described by Peter this way, "Rulers of the people and elders . . . the question put to us today is about help given to a sick man. . ." (Acts 4:8–9). Thus it was testimony to the Vision of the risen and ascended Lord whose sovereign power now rules the rulers, testimony given in both word and deed, that evoked the anger of the powers that be. Confrontation with authorities and principalities is a mark of mission. Because this aspect so easily gets lost from view in conventional understanding of mission, we give it added attention here.

Early in the career of the Church its mission found itself in controversy with the authorities and rulers. Whether we interpret these powers in ancient idiom as cosmic forces or personal beings or in modern perspective as institutions and systems, the common feature is the presence of social, economic, and political power organized into entities which are more than the sum of the individuals that comprise them. Peter and John confronted the same kind of power structure that Martin Luther faced at Worms, that Martin Luther King, Jr., met in the Birmingham jail, and that Christ encountered in Pilate. And as is regularly the case, the powers of this world are hostile to the forceful witness of word and deed.

Mission in and to the structures of power has included from the beginning at least two characteristics: 1) the readiness to confront the thrones and authorities, and 2) the calling to accountability of these structures of authority. To them must be said, "We must obey God rather than men" (Acts 5:29). They do not control the world but are subject to the Lordship of Christ.

How further the Church in mission relates to the powers and principalities is affected by its larger theological vision. Thus as the eschatological expectations of the early Church lengthened, and no imminent cosmic finale was any longer anticipated (one which would render superfluous any effort to change the structures of power, an effort also made improbable by the relative powerlessness of the Christian community itself), the sense of responsibility for the secular systems and processes increased. That expanded purview, at worst, has led to the captivity of the Church by the authorities and powers in its attempt to penetrate them, and at best to the prophetic challenge to and humanization of these structures in obedience to the Lordship of Christ. And the involvement of the Church in this mission has proceeded in a fashion not unlike that described in the Acts texts: the ministry to individual human needs is the entry point, one which leads ultimately to systemic confrontation, or in the current language, a movement from social service to social action.

To resist the powers is to court the enmity of this world. The counsel to love our enemies implies that we must be prepared to make some. Keeping company with the risen Lord who bears the marks of nail and spear is participation in the sufferings of God in the world (Bonhoeffer).

Life Together

The movement of mission whose outlines we perceive in these chapters takes place in living relationship to the continuing life of nurture. There is a rhythm of outreach and inreach, thrust beyond and return for nourishment. Peter and John come back for a renewing of the Vision in the life together of prayer and praise, fellowship and sacrament. "As soon as they were discharged they went back to their friends and told them everything that the chief priests and elders had said. When they heard it, they raised their voices as one man and called upon God. . . . All were filled with the Holy Spirit and spoke the word of God with boldness. The whole body of believers was united in heart and soul. Not a man of them claimed any of his possessions as his own, but everything was held in common" (Acts 4:23–24, 31–32). Mission returns to be rooted in the leitourgia, kerygma, diakonia, and koinonia of the visionary people. And thus the fullness of mission includes the central acts of nurture.

While the gifts of leitourgia and koinonia are not given explicit missionary direction in Acts 3 and 4, liturgical and fellowship outreach do emerge in the larger panorama of New Testament mission. Therefore the fullest picture of the exercise of these gifts both within and beyond the Body of Christ can be portrayed this way.

Nurture (Inreach)	*Gifts of the Spirit* *and* *Marks of the Church*	*Mission* (Outreach)
Preaching and teaching	Kerygma (Telling)	Evangelism
Servanthood within (Care for brothers and sisters)	Diakonia (Doing)	Servanthood without (Social service and social action)
Life together within	Koinonia (Being)	Life together without
Worship	Leitourgia (Celebrating)	Festival

The continuing Work of Jesus Christ as carried out by his Body on earth is the witness to the Vision of God in the acts of kerygma, leitourgia, diakonia, and koinonia. When nurture and mission involve these marks of the Church, we see a living Body animated by the Spirit and moving toward its destination.

Sect and Church

To interpret the meaning of the Church in an eschatological framework tends to move it in the direction of the "sect-type" view (Troeltsch) of ecclesiology. If the Church is to be what it is called to be, it must emphasize radical obedience to God's will. The pressure of final Vision makes for an understanding of the Church as the company of those truly committed to the Vision and therefore separated from fallen humanity. Somewhere the demands of this *sect principle* must be honored in ecclesiology, or else the Church is tempted to settle comfortably into its environment, taking its cues from the surrounding culture and losing its ultimate Vision. Such visionless accommodation is the hazard of the "church-type" ecclesiology with its loose membership requirements and culture-Christianity.

While the sect principle must make its contribution, the *church principle* has an important witness as well. In contrast to the exclusivist view of the former which limits the Christian community to the "committed" or "pure" or "saints," the latter is inclusive, letting the "wheat and tares grow up together" (Matt. 13:30) and making room for both the saints and the sinners. More exactly, it views the holiness of the Church as an objective status conferred by the Spirit on a company of sinners, not as a state of moral and spiritual attainment subjectively demonstrable by a company of saints.

To honor the validity of both principles means that we conceive the Church as an eschatological community but one living under the conditions of this present age. It is the *ecclesia,* those called out of the present and toward the future, but not yet living in that future. As it is Dawn and not High Noon, the shadows permeate this colony as well as its worldly environment. In its common life Shalom is present as *foretaste* and not as fulfillment. What constitutes the impingement of that future is not the moral and spiritual rectitude of its members but the presence of the Vision. It is the reality of God in the midst of the sinful people that establishes the Church's singular being and constitutes its holiness. This is the validity of the church principle with its insistence on a catholicity and inclusiveness of the last and the least, and its stress upon the divine objectivity and initiative. And it is through the gifts of kerygma and leitourgia that the real Presence of Christ in and through Word and Sacrament that the Vision comes to the people.

But where there is Light there is also Fire, and where there is Fire something happens as it did on the day of Pentecost. The Power of God accompanies the Vision of God. The Spirit bringing Christ to this community stirs up this Shalom. This is the validity of the sect principle that witnesses to the evidence of empowerment wherever the Spirit is at work. Thus there are true signs of the Spirit's movement in spiritual and moral vitality that make the authentic Church. Where the Spirit is, there is life and light struggling against death and darkness. The Church always lives under both the imperative and expectation of radical obedience, even as it lives out of its existence as an inclusive company of forgiven sinners.

The partnership of exclusion and inclusion, commitment and catholicity, can be embodied institutionally in terms of the ancient notion of "ecclesiola in ecclesia," the little church within the Church. That is, within the broad institutional life of the Christian community there is a place for a sub-community of special visionaries. Just as the body part of glossolalia serves the function of keeping the Corinthian church off balance, so the Church in every period needs those who talk the strange language of the Not Yet, those who peer further into the future, strain toward that goal in their attitude and behavior, and hold the community to attention before the Vision. It is not that these visionaries are necessarily more advanced in their spiritual and moral life, for the sin of pride and self-righteousness visits them more habitually and intensely than most, precisely because of their intensity of purpose, thus keeping them in the company of sinners. It is their role as critics-in-residence that gives singular meaning to their fervent witness and calls the Church away from its easy-going accommodation to the world. The orders within the ancient Church and the renewal movements of the present Christian community (including the charismatic movement itself when it has learned to relativize its role and is open to other gifts given to the Body, I Cor. 12–14) serve this purpose. This visionary role is always exercised as a part of the Body and is not to be mistaken for the whole, as in the case of the sect type whose reductionism excludes those with other gifts and ministries. Rather, the visionary is part of an inclusive community of those who see and serve the light that shines upon them. "The eye cannot say to the hand, 'I do not need you. . .' " (I Cor. 12:21).

Church, World, and God

Related to this question of the purity of commitment within the Christian community is a current debate on the interrelationship of God, Church and world, a theme to which we shall return in our chapter on salvation. Thus there is a conception of the connections that can be portrayed in this fashion: God→ Church→ World. In its most stringent form, it is expressed as "no salvation outside the

Church." In general it can be taken to mean that God is to be encountered redemptively by passage out of the world and into the Church, for God offers truth and life only through this particular channel. Against this "ecclesiocentric" view of grace and salvation it is argued by others that the proper relationship is as follows: God→ World→ Church. God works first and foremost through worldly action. To be authentic, the Church must gravitate to these places and processes of healing and hope and participate in them. In this role the Church is a "postscript" to the world, relinquishing the claims made by the church-centered view, and existing only by a secular grace to which it appends itself.

As a corrective to the ecclesiocentricism of the first position the second perception must be affirmed. We shall address ourselves further to this in the section on soteriology. However, this view cannot stand alone as a doctrine of the Church for it ignores the promise of Christ to be with his people in all their frailty. As with the sect view, this secular view assumes that the reality of the Church can be materialized by our good works. The validity of the Church does not rise or fall on our good works but exists by the promise and presence of Christ. Further, there is a gift to be given through this undeserved union of Christ with the Church; here the Vision and Word is offered. This fuller understanding of the relation of God, World, and Church might be so portrayed:

God's saving grace meets us through both the Church and the world. In the Christian community the Vision is seen; Christ opens our eyes to see who he is. In the world, Christ comes to us incognito wherever there are movements of freedom and peace (Matt. 25). We shall explore the Emmaus road passages subsequently for another perception of this question. Here we note that the Church is *fully* the Church not only when it sees the Vision and hears the Word, but also when it goes into the world in pursuit of Shalom. On the other hand, the life with God in the world finds its fulfillment when it leads into the Christian community where the Vision is to be seen.

THE MINISTRIES OF THE CHURCH

There is great confusion in the Church today about the meaning of ministry. At one time, either in the dogmatic formulations of "high church" traditions, or in the common practice of many avowedly "low church" ones, it was an unquestioned premise that ministry belongs to the ordained clergy. Whether this was defined in sacerdotal fashion as bestowal of the mark of priesthood by the laying on of apostolic hands, or functionally as the setting apart of some to the office of Word and Sacrament, or operationally as those who "run the church," the clergy were conceived as the Ministers, and the rest of the Christian community as the Laity. In practice this meant that some were subjects and others objects in the life of the Church.

In the past few decades this view of ministry has come under sharp attack in both theory and practice. Both the ascendency-submission pattern and the sharp distinctions of the earlier view have been challenged by a conception of "the ministry of the laity."

Sometimes the ministry of the laity is interpreted to mean that there is no privileged caste, either ontologically or institutionally, and that all services by both clergy and non-clergy are of equal importance before God and in the life of the Church. At other times, the ministry of the laity is conceived as the complete mobility of functions within the Church, each person being empowered to perform any function. In other settings it is understood to mean that the real ministry of the Church is in the world, and thus the laity constitute the fundamental ministry of the Church, with the clergy serving as resources to, and enablers of, the laity in their secular mission. And at yet other times, the ministry of the laity is seen to be the only ministry, with baptism as the act of ordination, and the need for clergy in any sense of the word is put radically in question. In this last sense it is the laity who assume the functions normally associated with the clergy in the inner life of the Church, as well as in the ministry to the world.

A new vision of the ministry of the laity has had a salutary effect in many areas of the Church's life. But it has also contributed to the loss of a sense of identity among clergy who have attempted to honor this enlarged perception of ministry. And the reaction against the oversimplifications of some of the more recent theories of the ministry of the laity has prompted a too quick return in some places to authoritarian clergy models. In the midst of these tendencies and counter-tendencies is a rising generation of women seeking ordination and equal participation in the Church as pastors. This crucial struggle carries with it the assumption that there is a unique and important meaning to the ministry of altar and pulpit.

The context for our discussion of the meaning of ministry is the nature and marks of the Church. As the ministry is viewed in the light of the Acts charter, both the wholeness and the particularities of ministry come into clearer perspective. And with it come compelling mandates to bring our practice in line with the biblical vision.

The General Ministry and Special Ministries

The Body of Christ lives by the breath of God, the Holy Spirit. The signs of its life are the gifts given to it by the Spirit: kerygma, diakonia, koinonia, leitourgia (see above, pp. 151–155). Baptism, in one of its meanings, as entrance into the Church, is the seal of membership in this Body. Membership is to be understood in its most elemental sense as being one of the members, one of the organs of this Body. Baptism, therefore, is ordination to the general ministry of the Church. It is a seal of a gift of the Spirit, the claim of God on a person to be a living member of the Body and thus to exercise some gift given for the life and work of this Body. In baptism all are called to be living parts of the Body of Christ (I Cor. 12:4–31; Eph. 4:7–16).

The growth of a member of the Body is the coming to consciousness of the gift that has been given and the faithful exercise of that gift. The gifts of the Spirit for the preservation and vigorous life of the Body are of two kinds. There are gifts which assure the *identity* of the Body, and there are those that guarantee its *vitality*. One kind of gift is the vehicle of the *memories* and the other is the organ of the *hopes* of the Church.

The gifts of kerygma and leitourgia, the telling and celebrating of the Christian Story, facilitate the identity and memory of the Body of Christ. Without these gifts the Church falls into amnesia; it does not know who it is or where it has come from. Without these gifts the Church cannot see its Vision or know where it is headed. There must be some within the Church who are the custodians of the gifts of kerygma and leitourgia (I Cor. 3:5; Acts 6:1–6; II Tim. 1:11). They do not monopolize them but they do guard and facilitate them. They preserve the memories of identity, they remind the Church of where it came from, and they perceive the future and point to the Vision. These are the ears and mouth and eyes of the Body of Christ. Thus the Church requires stewards of the mysteries, of the visions, of God (I Cor. 4:1). This stewardship is exercised by the proclamation and celebration of the visions, by the custodianship of kerygmatic and liturgical gifts, by the preaching of the Word and the administration of the sacraments. This is a special ministry within the general ministry of the laity, "to stir into flame the gift of God" (II Tim. 1:6). And it is set apart from the general ministry for that unique purpose. It is a particular ministry with its distinctive functions signaled by a special act of ordination. Its gift and function are essential to the health and wholeness of the Church. Without it the Body runs the risk of being deaf and dumb and blind.

But a body can see and hear and speak and still be lifeless and inert. A body is made to walk and work, run and dance, embrace and reach out. So too the Body of Christ. Its purpose is fulfilled not by the longest memory, its most intense stare, or its mellowest voice, but by its life and movement. The Spirit's gifts of this vitality are diakonia and koinonia. The beating heart, reaching hands, and moving feet of the Body are those signs of life. To ninety-nine percent of the membership of the Church are given these organs of vitality. The laity, those called to the upbuilding and outreaching in love of the Body of Christ, are the stewards of enablement of the Vision (Rom. 12:4–8; I Cor. 12:27–31; Eph. 4:11–12).

Inasmuch as the Body of Christ exists to walk and work in the world, it is the ministry of the laity that is in the foreground of the mission of the Church. The laity is the presence of the Church in the rhythms and structures of society. In the places of work and leisure, governance, education, science, social change, marriage and the family, laity turn occupation into vocation as they live out their own priesthood. *How* this ministry is to be rightly exercised is still a moot point: as individuals in these systems and patterns? Or corporately in churchly or extra-churchly forms of Christian life and witness? *That* the laity are the leading edge of mission is not to be questioned. And *what* is to be done there is first and foremost the employment of the gift given by Christ, the serving ministries of rehumanizing love.

While baptism into general ministry does in some sense claim and accredit the laity for mission in the world, there is something manifestly missing in the practice of the Church at this point. If clergy are called by special ordination to their special ministry of kerygma and leitourgia, why are not the laity called and confirmed in a special way to the exercise of their particular gift? There is some precedent for this kind of commissioning, and therefore some tacit recognition of the void, in the consecration of laity to churchly functions such as church school teaching, choir participation, and other forms of intra-church leadership. And in some traditions there is the ordination of laity to the offices of deacon and elder, and commissioning for mission in and through church agencies. And in some cases there is even the consecrating of laity for ministry in their own secular work. But we have a long way to travel yet to become what we are in the Body of Christ. The recognition of full membership in that Body is the setting apart through special ordination by the Church of its gift-ministries of diakonia and koinonia, as well as kerygma and leitourgia. The present practice of ordaining deacons is the first timid step in this direction, for here the diaconal gift is honored. But its current interpretation is far short of the logic of the biblical pattern, for it is either understood as a step toward the priesthood and thus clericalized, or it is confined to the inreach aspect of the Church, and not infrequently trivialized in even that limited arena. The ordination into the diaconate should be a high and holy commissioning of those whom Christ calls to servanthood both within and without the congregation, and with special thrust without in mission. It acknowledges the gift and publicly commissions those who see in the Light the wretched of the earth and those who minister to elemental human need, and therefore minister with Christ in the world. The equivalent consecration for the ministry of koinonia is yet to be acknowledged and enacted.

Our emphasis on different responsibilities for ministry should not be hardened into a rigid division of ministry. A living organism is an inter-related whole. Even more so is the Body of Christ, as is suggested by Paul's moving discourse on love in I Corinthians 13, directed to the different gift ministries mentioned in I Corinthians

12. There is no faithful stewardship of kerygina and leitourgia that does not issue in diakonia and leitourgia. Nor is there faithful stewardship of diakonia and koinonia that is not grounded in and illumined by kerygma and leitourgia. Further, an open Church is one in which each steward of the Vision needs the other stewards and learns from them what that mutuality means. And where there is weakness or lack of opportunity in one section of the Body, then those with other gifts may feel the claim to move beyond their formal call to support and strengthen the Body at its point of need or opportunity. It is interesting that in recent decades of Church history clergy have acknowledged the open-ended character of their own gift ministry by moving beyond kerygmatic and liturgical responsibilities, out of loyalty to the Vision they saw, to diaconal and koinonial ministry. Thus in the 1960's we experienced the vigorous clerical involvement in the common life in diaconal movements of human rights, poverty, peace; and in the 1970's we see the ministrations of koinonia in the counseling and small group interests of many clergy. At the present time we see many laity performing a similar ministry as they attempt to orient the Body to kerygmatic and liturgical needs. Thus the call by laity for Bible study and theological depth, the growing interest in evangelism, and the search for a more meaningful spirituality.

Inasmuch as this movement beyond the particularity of gift does really achieve its purpose of inter-relating the gifts—the involvement of clergy in humanization movements encouraging the laity to exercise their ministry, and the laity initiatives in biblical and liturgical concerns pressing the clergy for growth in their own stewardship of Word and Sacrament—this mobility of ministry is vital to the life of the Body. But when either clergy or laity usurp the other's role and thus neglect their own special call, this dynamic movement within the Body becomes a cancer growth that consumes the other parts and makes for death, not life.

Yet another distinction between differing responsibilities and rigid divisions is assumed in our attempt to honor the variety of gifts within the Church. To be *responsible* for the kerygmatic and liturgical gifts does not mean the exclusive monopoly of kerygma and liturgy. The clergy are the guarantors of these organs functioning within the Body; they do not thereby carry out all the activity of these organs. For example, the stewardship of kerygma in mission and evangelism means that the minister of kerygma sees to it that the Good News goes forth from the Church. But it may be that the most effective sharing of the Christian Story is done by laity, either organized and trained by the Church, or equipped to witness in a more individual way. By the same token a lay diaconate is called to keep the human needs of the world and the congregation before the eyes of the Church and facilitate the Church's reach of neighbor love. In that ministry there will surely come a time when clergy can play a vital role in the execution of that corporate or personal Samaritan act. Ministry is stewardship, not overlordship, of a gift of the Spirit. It is consecrated by the whole Church in order to enable its happening, whatever form that execution may take and by using all the available resources of the Church for its exercise.

A final observation: all the gifts are given by the Spirit to the whole Body. It is the Body in its unity and totality, therefore, that tests and then sets apart the special ministries of kerygma, leitourgia, diakonia, and koinonia. While the personal call to be eye or mouth, hand or foot of the Body comes in the intimacy of one's communion with the Spirit, the public confirmation of that call and consecration in it comes through the Christian community. It is not a part of the Body that does this testing of the Spirit and setting apart to special ministry of its own gift or all the rest, but the whole company by the action of the people or its representatives. And this dispersion of the power of the Spirit among all the people includes universality in the opportunity of the people of God to enter into any ministry for which personal call and publicly validated equipment have prepared them. The debate about the ordination of women to the ministry of kerygma and leitourgia has sharpened this question of universality of option. An unambiguous answer is given in the Petrine framework for ecclesiology. In the charter language of the Church he declares, "God says, 'This will happen in the last days: I will pour out on everyone a portion of my spirit; and your sons and daughters shall prophesy. . . . Yes, I will endue even my slaves, both men and women, with a portion of my spirit, and they shall prophesy' " (Acts 2:17,18). Reflecting the eschatological goal in which there is "neither male nor female," the capacity of seer of the Vision of God is given to all. Thus no aspect of the stewardship of the visions, the ministry of the Church, is denied to any part of the people of God, least of all that unique ministry in which mysteries of God are seen and celebrated.

Identity and Vitality

There is a variety of other issues that relate to the question of ministry: origin and order, organization and oversight, call, style, and duties. The origin of ministry from Christ through the apostles to the Church and into its several expressions is the route here implicit. The threefold order of presently ordained ministry—bishop, presbyter, and deacon—enjoys increasing ecumenical consensus, especially in union negotiations, and is assimilable to the foregoing discussion if the diaconate can be enriched by our discussion of lay ministry. On matters of organization and oversight, the plenitude of gifts in the Church and the encompassing work of the Spirit argue for a fully participatory form of governance. And the way of Christ's own ministry as that of one who came "to serve, and to give up his life as a ransom for many" (Matt. 2:28) is surely the style appropriate to all our ministries. But we have not dwelt on these questions that have to do with *how* and have concentrated instead on the *that* and *what* of the matter: that there is a general ministry to which we are called in baptism, that there are special ministries of identity and vitality all of which are authorized by Christ and empowered by the Spirit, and what these are in their facilitation of the Vision by kerygma, leitourgia, diakonia, and koinonia.

To set the foregoing exploration in the larger context of the continuing Work of Christ, we may summarize this understanding of the ministry in the following way.

The continuing Work of Jesus Christ in the Church is the same done in his ministry of life, death, and resurrection. The same Christ is present in the Body as Prophet, Priest, and King. Our ministry, therefore, as it shares in the continuing Work of his ministry, participates in that threefold office. The whole ministry of the people of God continues his ministry of Seer, Sufferer, and Liberator. It does so in the modalities fitting to the ministries of identity and vitality.

The ordained ministry of identity is an agent of the Work of Prophet as it proclaims the Word and clarifies the Vision in its custodianship of the kerygma. And it serves the Work of Priest in its stewardship of the sacramental mysteries and in liturgical leadership. It is an agent of the Kingship of Christ in its role of enabler of the life of koinonia through both support and governance. And in each aspect of ministry is carried out the meaning of the word itself, diakonia, suffering servanthood.

The ministry of vitality given to the laity is the empowerment of the Body by the Spirit that enables it to walk and work in the world, embodies the office of Seer as it bears witness to Shalom by deed and word in the secular structures, and enriches the work of the stewards of kerygma by bringing a secular context to the biblical text. The Work of Sufferer lives on in the participation of the laity in the suffering servanthood of God in the world as they seek to live out the life of the Body in all the ambiguities and agonies of secular existence, and as they bring this experience to the liturgy whose very center is the broken Body and shed Blood. The Work of Liberator makes its presence felt to the extent that the laity are agents of liberation and reconciliation in the world and take responsibility for freedom and peace in the governance and life of the Church. Thus, the ministry of the whole people of God, shared according to their several gifts, is continuous with the threefold ministry of Christ in word and worship, work, and redemptive suffering (Consultation on Church Union).

THE SACRAMENTS

The identity of the Church is sharpened by the central events of leitourgia cited in the second chapter of Acts, baptizing and breaking bread. They have been with us ever since as the rites of birth and nurture in the Christian community, baptism and the Lord's supper. These events of initiation and nourishment, the "mysteries" (I Cor. 4:1), are the *sacraments* of the Church, "the outward and visible signs of an inward and spiritual grace." They are the sign language of faith, the visible Word which portrays and declares the Good News of liberation and reconciliation. They are the happenings that give visibility to the Vision of God. But they are gestures of the Church which *do* what they *say;* the sacraments are "effectual signs" that convey grace as well as display it. Sometimes this twofold quality is expressed in the idea that they are "signs and seals" of the Promise.

The ingredients of valid sacramental action are usually considered to be the matter or external element, the form or Word said in conjunction with it, the one who administers the sacrament, and the honest intention that this event be what it is biblically asserted to be. *Validity* of action becomes *efficacy,* the sacrament becomes salvific, when faith is present to receive the grace offered.

Through these signs the Holy Spirit seals her people within the community of faith. Indeed there are other visible acts through which the Spirit works to strengthen our ties to the Vision and to one another in the envisioning community: confirmation at coming of age in faith, marriage at conjugal union, ordination at vocation, confession and counsel—public and private—in the pilgrimage of faith, and burial at the end of our journey. These *ordinances* are radii from the sacramental hub. We focus here on the central acts, rising out of the ministry of Christ manifest in the originating events of the Church's birth, and integral to any participation in the Body of Christ. Here the Vision becomes physical in the water, wine, and bread, creating and sustaining the visionary community.

Baptism

While there have been a few significant recent studies on baptism and some interest in its implications for ecumenism and mission, this rite still dwells in the shadows of contemporary Christianity. Moreover its traditional importance and meaning have come under heavy attack, especially regarding the practice of baptizing the newborn. The demise in many places of a triumphalist mentality, the pluralist society in which the Church lives, the stress upon the diaconal and koinonial credentials for the Christian community, a neo-universalist and eschatological framework for theology which is reluctant to make soteriological claims for the Church, all work to put in question this entry point.

For all the modern uneasiness about baptism, any contemporary faith that takes the Storybook seriously will have to come to terms with its strange assertions about this rite. It is described in the New Testament as the cleansing laver of regeneration (John 3:5; I Cor. 6:11; Eph. 5:26; Titus 3:5), the remission of sins (Acts 2:38; 22:16), being buried and rising again (Rom. 6:3–4; Col. 2:12), putting on or entry into Christ (Rom. 6:3; Gal. 3:27), engrafting into the Body of Christ (I Cor. 12:13), the pouring out of the Holy Spirit (Acts 2:38; 19:1–6; I Cor. 12–13; Titus 3:5–6), and in general is associated with God's saving action (Mark 16:16; Eph. 4:5; I Pet. 3:21). And if we join the Church's testimony to that of the Bible, there is to be found among its classic interpreters similar claims: forgiveness of sin and divine illumination (Justin), "the seal of eternal life and our rebirth in God" (Irenaeus), the bestowing of the Spirit (Tertullian), freedom from the power of the devil (Origen), participation in the mystical Body (Augustine), unity with the Godhead (Athanasius), deification (Gregory of Nyssa), putting on Christ (Calvin), and bathing in Christ's blood (Luther). The collision between ancient wisdom and contemporary perception presses for a restatement. The vision motif that serves as our organizing principle throughout provides us with a fresh angle to view the meaning of baptism.

Baptism is the enactment of the Church's vision of parental embrace in the Prodigal Son story, "the open arms of the Father" (Aulén). It is the affirmation that the eye of God rests upon this child of God. It is the ray of the divine Light that reaches toward this "single one." But in this individuating reach there is a gathering as well as a calling. Baptism is the welcome of Christ into the community of the Vision. It is the doorway into the household of faith.

Where the water is joined to the baptismal Word in the community of faith these things happen. 1) The baptized is placed in the *environment* of the Vision. The baptized is taken from the shadows and brought into the pilgrim band moving toward the horizon Light. The direction in which this company moves is that in which the risen Christ can be seen by the eye of faith. In other metaphors, baptism is engrafting into the Body of Christ, the entrance into the new Covenant, translation into the Kingdom of grace. 2) The baptized is brought into a new *relationship.* The "I" of Christ makes a "Thou" of the baptized, signalled by the giving of a Christian name. The wide-open arms of God close in their reach toward this individual. Here is the self-presentation of covenanting Love. The offer of mercy effected on Calvary is particularized to this one human being. The face of God is turned toward this person. A perception of Easter's risen One is granted to this potential seer. In other metaphors, baptism is regeneration and new birth, unity with the Godhead. All these ancient terms point to a new bond forged between this self and the divine Self. 3) In baptism a personal *claim* is made and a *call* is issued. This person now is invited to make response to the invitation of grace, to open the eye of faith to the Light and engage in the works of love responsive to the divine Love. In the latter case, baptism is ordination to the general ministry, the call to servanthood. And it carries with it the impulse to special ministry as well, insofar as a unique gift is given by the Spirit to be exercised within and beyond the Body. In ancient idiom this aspect of baptism is being buried and rising again with Christ, or putting on Christ. Jesus Christ calls this human being to be an actor in the drama of redemption. Baptism as call and claim is an indelible mark, the insignia that identifies the soldier and convicts the deserter (Augustine).

The environmental, relational, and imperative aspects of baptism are the work of the Holy Spirit. As membership in the mystical Body, and as individual relationship to its Head, it is the Spirit that signifies and seals the action. It is grace, not our works, that make baptism "illumination," the shedding of divine Light on one for whom Christ died and rose again.

Grace and Faith in Baptism

Grace in baptism is the Self-offer of Christ and all his benefits. Faith is the reception of that Presence, the open arms of the daughters and sons responding to the divine reach. "Be it unto you according to your faith" is a sacramental word as real to baptism as to the supper. The presence or absence of personal faith does not materialize or destroy the reality of baptismal grace. Baptism is valid with or without our response. But it is not baptism "unto salvation" without personal faith. It is grace appropriated in faith by which we are justified. The meaning of this great Reformation theme we shall explore in the subsequent chapter. Here we anticipate it by making a crucial distinction between the *offer* and its *acceptance.* The baptismal waters are the lens through which the divine Light is brought to focus on a single self, and on that called-out community of visionaries. Whether that self or society opens its eyes to see the Light and walk in the Light depends on the act of faith, itself the fruit of grace.

"Faith comes from what is heard" (Rom. 10:17 RSV). This is why the proclamation of the Word is companion to the celebration of the sacraments. The Vision lifted in the telling of the Story is seen by the eye of faith. Faith is born in the conscious confrontation with the mighty acts of God in Jesus Christ. The believer comes to the baptismal event to accept the welcome of Christ there portrayed and enacted. Thus the Holy Spirit works faith in the preaching of the Word and seals it in this sacrament, binding the faithful to one another and to Christ. The grace of baptism, therefore, *saves* when it is received in *faith*. When the "Yes" of God in baptism is answered by the "Yes" of faith, it is "unto salvation." As the love of God can turn to hot coals before its enemies (Rom. 12:20), so the divine Love that comes to us in baptism can be burning fire rather than healing Light, damnation and not salvation. And so the awesome reminder by Karl Barth that the casually taken ritual stands as a sign of judgment on the faithlessness of western Christendom. But those who receive it in a faith busy in love receive it unto life and Light and not unto death and darkness.

Household Baptism

If faith alone can receive the grace of baptism, then can the sacrament be administered to the newborn? While it is possible to speculate about the seed of faith in an infant, the high view of baptismal grace we have taken here demands serious attention to the preparation for this gift, and at the very least a profession of faith, one that is responsible only at the age of discretion. Is baptism then to be limited to the mature believer? Do the open arms of Christ reach out only to individuals who are "old enough to decide for themselves"?

"God setteth the solitary in families" (Psalm 68:6 KJV). Our individualistic culture finds this to be a hard saying. The ambiguous state of the family in contemporary society makes it further suspect. The corporate framework of biblical faith is not the conventional wisdom of modernity. But the theme that "no one is an island" is part and parcel of the Christian Story, expressing itself in a variety of ways, from the corporate personality of the people of Israel, through the koinonia of the Christian community, to the belief that the intercessory prayers of one can help another and that the faith of one can count for another (Matt. 17:14–21; Mark 2:3–12). The vicarious act on the cross itself attests to this truth. It comes to expression in the practice of infant baptism or, better, *household baptism,* the biblical word which puts the emphasis where it belongs, on the communal meaning, rather than acceding to the individualist connotations of the former phrase. While a clear but not convincing case can be made for household baptism in four New Testament passages (Acts 16:15, 16:31, 18:8, and I Cor. 1:16), and while there is no mention of the adult baptism of the children of believers (and such other arguments as parallels with Jewish proselyte baptism, the evidence for a fairly universal practice in the early centuries, etc.), it is on theological grounds that the question must finally be resolved. If baptism is the sign and seal of the reach of God, and if the self is more than solitary, then a household reception of the divine Love is one way of responding to the beckoning of God.

The family that receives the divine invitation is an inclusive one. Those who represent the newborn child, making the act of faith for that child until he or she can make it personally at the age of discretion, and preparing the child for that option, are first and foremost the parents to whose conjugal union the Spirit adds the child as a blessing. But the nuclear family does not exhaust the circle of support, extending as it does to "sponsors" or "godparents" and to the congregation itself which takes the vows.

The corruptibility of the practice of household baptism is well known and much to the foreground of contemporary discussion, especially in lands where there is some form of State Church, but also anywhere that the Church has settled comfortably into its surroundings. The integrity of Church membership becomes a passionate concern where accommodation and bourgeois mediocrity are the order of the day. To this end the deepening of the meaning of a faith commitment within the congregation preparatory to the baptism of a child, and the strengthening of the ordinance of *confirmation* deserve eminent attention. In the latter case, the confirmand is prepared to take upon herself or himself the profession of faith which receives the offers of baptism and through which the Spirit renders them "unto salvation."

To summarize the thrust of household baptism we return to both the Acts charter and to the imagery of vision. In the call issued by Peter against the background of an End thought to be imminent, we hear "Repent and be baptized, every one of you, in the name of Jesus the Messiah for the forgiveness of your sins: and you will receive the gift of the Holy Spirit. For the promise is to you, and to your children . . ." (Acts 2:38–39). The inclusion of the children of our household in this promise means that the pilgrim band moving toward the Easter horizon, seeing and walking in the graceful Light, gathers to itself in baptism also its children. The sleeping child is carried in the arms of this company travelling by the sense of direction given to it by the Spirit through its eyes of faith. But there comes a moment in that pilgrimage when the child must descend from the arms that have supported it, open its own eyes to the Light, and choose for itself whether it will continue in that line of march. It must itself confirm the faith of its father and mother, and its sisters and brothers in Christ. This is the journey of household baptism, begun in the gift and claim of the Light of God, received by the eye of supportive faith, confirmed by personal vision and decision. The apparent divergence of practice in the Church today is actually not as theologically polarized as it would appear to be, for the rite of "dedication" of children widely observed in adult baptism denominations signifies the welcome into the arms of Christ represented by the baptismal waters. And the growing stress upon the decisiveness of confirmation where household baptism is practiced is recognition of the importance of the personal act of faith at the age of discretion. As the Christian Vision is perceived in greater ecumenical reality, a catholicity of teaching about baptism will follow.

Supper

The Pentecostal flames burn again in "the altar fire" (Olive Wyon). As the Light of God invites us in baptism, it comes to strengthen us in the holy supper. The Vision comes toward us and we to it in the initiatory sacrament, and we are rekindled by it and in it through the grace of communion. Illumination happens because at the Lord's table we are guests proleptically at the heavenly banquet itself. Here is the presence of the Future. The eschatological Vision is imparted in the eucharist and we participate in things yet to come.

The Vision of God is given visibility in the last supper. Christ is Host, his disciples gather in communion with him and each other, the wheat and wine of the earth are consecrated. In this event is to be seen the liberation and reconciliation to come; sin, evil, and death are passed away and the broken relationships with God, neighbor, and nature are healed. In the upper room Christ gave his disciples a taste of the heavenly banquet with its union with him and unity with humanity and the earth. And the price paid for that final victory, the sacrifice of Jesus and the suffering of God, is the modality in which the Future comes to us through the medium of bread and wine, a broken body and shed blood.

Our re-enactment of that meal in the sacrament gives like visibility to the Vision. In the Lord's supper we remember that event and the sacrifice to and through which it pointed toward Shalom. As such, it is a memorial of what has been and a whetted expectation for what is yet to come. Together with the first guests at the table who were present with the Host, who partook mystically of his sacrifice through the bread he broke and wine he poured, and who shared in the feast to come (Luke 22:14–19), it is for *us* also a participation in the Vision, as well as its recollection and anticipation (John 6:41, 48–51). In our celebration of the supper we keep company with the same Host and taste of the same feast of final liberation and reconciliation. We do it under the mode of a sobered hope by the same symbols of sacrifice. And the claim upon the partakers and the praise that they offered for these gifts are ours as well. Let us examine these aspects of the holy meal.

Memory and Hope

The sacrament of an historical religion will be rooted in earthy happenings. Our supper points back through the upper room to the crucifixion. It is a " *memorial* of the blessed sacrifice of his Son." The participant remembers the formative event of the community's history and of personal pilgrimage. The meal fixes on the reality of suffering and death, its cost on Calvary and in Deity. But *this* historical religion by looking backward is thrust forward. The Lord's supper then and now is portent of the eschatological banquet with its celebration of the final coming together of all things. This is the sacrament of mourning and joy, memory and hope (I Cor. 11:24–26).

Communion with Christ

This is the *Lord's* supper. He is the Host at this table. The Church which is his Body on earth takes its most decisive embodiment in this event of breaking bread and pouring wine. Here is not only memory and hope but also the real presence and thus *communion* with the risen and ascended Lord (I Cor. 10:16). Here is where the Vision is seen with the eyes of faith. "He broke the bread and offered it to them. Then their eyes were opened, and they recognized him" (Luke 24:30–31). We come face to face at this table with the One who is to come, participating mystically in his glorified humanity. This is why the sacrament of the Lord's supper has always been considered by the Christian community "the innermost sanctuary of the whole Christian worship." The bond of the believer with the Lord is strengthened with greatest power, and the Vision is kept clearest by regular communion of guest with Host (I Cor. 11:23–30).

Communion of Saints

The coming Kingdom is not an ethereal communion of "the alone with the Alone." It is a *life together* with the brothers and sisters in Christ (I Cor. 10:17). As foretaste of that reconciliation among neighbors, the sacrament is communion now with all the visionary people, all those who see the Light and live in it. The children of Light are the saints of God, for saintliness is not spiritual virtuosity but living in relationship, turning to and walking in the Light that has shined toward us. The saints of God are the whole company of believers, present and distant, living and dead. At this table the communicant is joined to a world-wide fellowship and a time-long "cloud of witnesses" who have gone before us. Thus the communion of saints joins communion with Christ in a prolepsis of the eschatological life together. And as testimony to life together, the supper is claim as well as gift, calling us to challenge all the bondages and alienations inimical to the final vision of Shalom.

Unity with the Earth

The Vision includes the knitting together of all the ruptured relationships with nature as well as with self and society. Our neighbor the earth is represented in the sacrament by the wheat and the wine. The sanctification of the earth, the healing of the wounds it has sustained in this fallen world, is symbolized by the setting apart of these symbols in anticipation of that fulfillment. And our eating and drinking is an anticipatory union with that new heaven and new earth (Rev. 21:1–4).

179

The Christian Story

Sacrifice

The New Jerusalem is yet to come, swords are yet to be beaten into plowshares, we do not yet live face to face with the Vision, the new heaven and new earth are still to transfigure this groaning creation. Whatever sacramental participation we have Now in this Not Yet is in cruciform presence. Christ and all his benefits come to us through broken body and shed blood. It is as *sacrifice* that the future comes into our midst in the sacrament. The One who offers himself to us here is the crucified Lord. And all the healed relationships share in this ambiguity, a communion with brother and sister and union with the earth that is still under the sign of the cross, living toward the crown (Mark 14:24).

In this sacramental union we are joined to the One whose single perfect sacrifice is here re-presented to the vision of faith (Heb. 10:19–25). And we see the sacrifice for what it is, the bleeding body of Christ and the broken heart of God taking the consequences of our sin and communicating to us the forgiveness of sin in the bread and wine.

Thanksgiving

The sacrifice we make is of our praise and thanksgiving. We offer on the altar our gratitude for Christ and all his benefits, remembering the past deeds of God, anticipating those to come, and rejoicing in the Presence. This meal is the supper in which we join Christ in giving thanks (Luke 22:19). That the Vision given to us in this liturgy was, and is, and is to be, makes this event, climactically the *eucharist.*

Grace and Faith in the Supper

Grace in the sacramental meal is the Self-offering of the Host and all his benefits. He is there by his promise not our performance. That promise and presence is received by faith, and therein grace becomes "efficacious," and the promised renewing of relationship and refreshing of visions is fulfilled. As with baptism so with supper, this faith is itself a gift of grace. In prospect we act as if it were up to us; in retrospect we know it is of the Spirit. In this prospective context we speak of it as the fit preparation for the receiving of the sacrament. The gracious personal relationships of the supper require of the guests a readiness. Whether it is there or

180

not will determine, not the Presence, but how that Presence will make itself felt, "unto salvation" or "unto damnation" (I Cor. 11:29).

Preparation means penitence, the antechamber of faith. The cleansing of the heart is given form in the confession of sin before the rite. Preparation means belief in the promise of Presence and trust in the suffering Love there exposed, an inner act given outer expression in the confession of faith in the liturgy. Where there is authentic penitence and faith, the meal is one in which the Host's welcome is honored by the guest and the Host's blessing is upon its partaker. A faithful response also is one that is claimed by the Shalom there shared; the authentic Vision issues in mission. In the encounter with the Vision of liberation and reconciliation there comes a commission to witness to the One who there discloses who he is, and to embody in acts of servanthood in the world the communion with neighbor and nature experienced at the table. A sign of the joining of grace to faith at the supper is the empowerment of the guest to keep company with the Christ of the table as he makes his way from Room to Road to be present there, incognito, as the crucified Lord in the sufferings of the world.

CHAPTER VI

Salvation

The Spirit descends from the ascended Lord to form the Church and empower mission. In and through this continuing Work of Christ goes on the work of *salvation.* "And I shall draw all men to myself, when I am lifted up from the earth" (John 12:32). The Christian doctrine of salvation is the focus of intense debate in the Church today. Contributing to the confusion is unclarity about the word "save." It is taken from a common usage that often means the accumulation or preservation of things, from money in the bank to time on a clock. The meaning of the term in the Scriptures and tradition of the Church is otherwise. In these contexts it is used in two other ways. On the one hand, to be saved means to be rescued or delivered from a foe. On the other hand, it signifies healing or making whole. Thus we are saved *from* something and saved *for* something. From what and for what?

In our discussion of the Atonement, we have already met the enemies and the friends to be found in this encounter. The Work of Christ is the beginning of the doctrine of salvation. Sometimes the Atonement is treated as the *objective* aspect of "soteriology" (the doctrine of salvation) which is complemented by the *subjective* side that deals with how salvation reaches us in grace and is personally appropriated by us in faith. Here we organize the chapters in the Christian Story in a slightly different way in order to honor the integrity of the Atonement and also to see those aspects of "Salvation Now" (the theme of a recent World Council of Churches inquiry) sometimes hidden from view in the notion of "subjective soteriology."

The distinction in salvation between God's action and its consequences is better expressed by the use of categories appropriate to the narrative character of Christian faith: the time segments of past, present, and future. As H. Richard Niebuhr is said to have replied to a zealous street evangelist who asked him if he was saved: "I *was* saved by what Christ did; I *am being* saved right now; I *shall be* saved when the Kingdom comes." Salvation is a process launched in the saving events that take place in Jesus Christ. It continues into the present as the Spirit moves to deliver and make whole. It reaches a climax when the enemies of God ultimately surrender and the friends of God are finally brought together. We shall focus on the present in this timeline. The historical roots of salvation have been examined in our discussion of the Work of Christ. And we reserve the exploration of the end point of the processes of salvation for the last chapter of the Christian Story, "Consummation." (It is possible also to interpret the chapters from Christ through Church and Salvation to Consummation as all parts of eschatology, the doctrine of the End, in so far as the future breaks into history in Christ and we live now in the tension between Already–Not Yet.) It is the meaning of salvation in the "time between the Times" to which we address ourselves.

The enemies of God are sin, evil, and death. The Work of Jesus Christ, the finished work accomplished once and for all in the life, teachings, death, and resurrection of Jesus Christ, is deliverance from these foes. Herein is the meaning of *salvation from.* They can no more imperil the purpose of God; deliverance has *already* taken place. We are saved from their assaults—liberated!

The salvation accomplished for us in Jesus Christ is *reconciliation* as well as *liberation.* It brings together God, humanity, and nature. No more barriers exist to their friendship. Both God's favor and power have been turned toward us, and the breach has been healed. Herein is the meaning of *salvation for.* The Light of God has shined upon the world, and that world shall be drawn into its intended unity.

SALVATION NOW

The tendency toward reductionism we have met in previous chapters reappears here also. Because of the immediacy of this belief and its personal import, the intensity of partisanship increases. How passionate is the proselyting and how ready are the partisans to consign their opponents to damnation! Those who believe that the essence of salvation is freedom from the judgment of God on our sin and guilt, bought by the blood of Christ and received by joy in faith, will hear of no other point of view. Those for whom salvation means deliverance from political and economic oppression will call all else flight from reality and the opiate of the people. But the Storyline carries with it a richer understanding of salvation now, and we strive to catch sight of that more encompassing vision.

Salvation now, however conceived, comes to us by *grace* (Acts 20:24; Rom. 4:16; I Cor. 15:10). Grace is the ancient Christian term for the initiative taken by God, the going-before-us of Deity, the divine "prevenience." Grace is a gift of God, given not earned; we are *saved by grace* (Eph. 2:5). God reaches toward us first. Grace in the larger setting of salvation *already, now,* and *not yet,* is the flow of the healing waters from their source in the saving work of Christ toward the parched lands of the present and future. Grace extends to us through the deeds of God. Grace is the reach of Jesus Christ toward the present and the future. And because this reach is to the present and future, it is the work of the Holy Spirit. Grace is another word for the activity of the Spirit. Salvation now is the gracious work by the Holy Spirit of bringing Christ and all his benefits to us in this time and place.

SALVATION FROM SIN

On Calvary God took the punishment for our sin. The divine Love absorbed the divine Wrath on the cross. Out of this suffering is born the mercy that covers our guilt. So Jesus Christ saved the world, liberating us from the bondage of sin.

But this freedom in Christ now available to us must be received by us. It is by God's personal grace that we are reached by the action that took place on Golgotha. Grace is the divine favor that accepts the unacceptable and loves the unlovely. The offer of forgiveness for *our* sin is communicated through the proclamation of the Good News of divine mercy. This Word of liberation from sin and reconciliation with God comes to us in the Bible and it is set forth by the Church faithful to this Gospel. The image of speaking and hearing has been part and parcel of our understanding of this aspect of salvation, as grace is understood as a gracious personal Word.

Grace is also understandable in visual terms. Grace is the cross of the dying Savior, the open arms of suffering, Love receiving the sinner. Grace is the overflowing compassion of the parent welcoming the prodigal. Just as grace as Word is communicated to us in preaching, grace as Action is displayed to us in an "outward and visible sign," the sacrament of baptism. Envisioning takes form in visibilities, the open arms of the Church, our mother, drawing us into life with God. The sacramental entry of the newborn into the Christian community is dramatization of the nature of grace as a divine favor which is in no way contingent upon our demonstrated merits but is poured out unconditionally. So also the gifts of the Body of Christ, diakonia and koinonia as well as leitourgia, are gracious gestures of the beckoning God.

The open arms and the word of welcome invite response. Salvation now happens in our life when the embrace of God is received in trust. We enter those arms in the act of *faith*. Faith is our response to God's initiative. It is made possible by the same grace which reaches toward us, now empowering us in turn to reach out to God. *We are saved by grace through faith* (Eph. 2:8).

To be saved from sin, right now, is to receive in faith, by the power of the Holy Spirit, the offer made by God on Calvary. It is to be made "right with God" after having been "in the wrong." Another way of speaking about this new relationship to God is *justification*. To be justified is to receive the pardon offered by God on Golgotha. The declaration of pardon to humanity now becomes the declaration of pardon to this believer.

While our language forces us to speak about faith as a *response* to grace, and our practice suggests that we appeal in Word and Vision for a human decision of faith, Christian spirituality grasps the grace-faith equation in other terms. "In my labors I have outdone them all—not I, indeed, but the grace of God working with me" (I Cor. 15:10). This "I . . . not I" paradox (Donald Baillie) expresses the sense that faith (and its issue, labors of love) is a choice to which we are called, one that is ours to make. Yet, we make it not on our own power, but only by grace. Put another way, in *prospect* we feel it is all up to us, but in *retrospect* we know that it was all of God. It is not "partly us, and partly God," not even "some us and mostly God" as the variety of synergisms in Christian history have suggested. Jonathan Edwards said it this way: "In efficacious grace we are not merely passive, nor yet does God do some and we do the rest. But God does all, and we do all. God produces all, and we act all. For that is what he produces, *viz.* our own acts. God is the only proper author and founder; we are the proper actors."[5] Psychologically, prospectively, linguistically we enter the faith movement as the actor in this drama; theologically, retrospectively and spiritually, we know who its Author is. We are, therefore, justified by *grace* which expresses itself in us as *faith*.

The Pilgrimage of Grace and Faith

A great gift that Martin Luther brings to the Christian community is his exploration of the depths of the soul's struggle with the meaning of justification. We are indebted as well to that tradition of piety which testifies to the experience of personal salvation by grace through faith for mapping this terrain of Christian spirituality. The perennial encounter with the Christ of faith may come to us in our way and time through the wrestle with social visions as well as individual commandments, but the issues of sin and grace remain the same. We call upon the classic guides to help us understand the meaning of justification today.

Luther felt the claims of the Law and sought to pursue its perfections, a quest that led him into the rigorous self-abnegations of monasticism. The Christ who beckoned from on high seemed to be reachable only by the ascent of the ladder of moral and spiritual achievement. Yet the grasp of each rung brought with it the self-congratulatory whisper, "Good work, Brother Martin!" The act of righteousness became the occasion for self-righteousness. Sin in its ugliest form, pride, kept company with the climb toward virtue. The harder he tried, the more intense the temptation, and the more despairing the pilgrim. Luther's sensitive conscience saw the face of Christ astride the rainbow above as full of wrath and prepared for punishment. In this impossible struggle to attain the righteousness demanded of us how can we find a gracious God?

In the search of the Scriptures carried on in the midst of this pilgrimage he found his answer. Righteousness—being right with

God—is not a prize won by the moral and spiritual athlete. He learned from Paul: "I am not ashamed of the Gospel . . . because here is revealed God's way of righting wrong, a way that starts from faith and ends in faith; as Scripture says, 'he shall gain life who is justified through faith'" (Rom. 1:16–17). Righteousness cannot be earned by good works. It is freely granted by God in Christ, and receivable by us in trust. We are "justified by Christ's sacrificial death" (Rom. 5:9) and we appropriate this gracious act through faith. Hence, the fighting words of the Reformation, *justification by faith.*

In this pilgrimage, the Law plays an ambiguous role. On the one hand it is "in itself holy, the commandment is holy and just and good" (Rom. 7:12). After all, it is the statement of the divine intention for the race, obedience in its relationships to fellow-humanity and to God. And Luther read the decalogue in the light of Christ's counsels of perfection with monastic rigor. But the Law becomes something more than a sharp and clear imperative when it strikes home to us in a fallen creature: "When the commandment came, sin sprang to life . . . sin found an opportunity in the commandment, seduced me, and through the commandment killed me" (Rom. 7:9–11). The perversity in the human heart uses the mandates of good for its own ends. Not only does it prompt us to want to do what we are told not to do, but our obedience to it stirs up the vainglorious pretension which exudes "Thank God I am not as others!" Yet, in this struggle, the Spirit turns our abuse of the Law into a sound "schoolmaster" use, the apprehension of our plight, the realization that we have to do with a lethal factor in the self which is far more profound than our first efforts in virtue conceived: "What I do is not what I want to do, but what I detest. . . . For I know that nothing good lodges in me—in my unspiritual nature I mean—for though the will to do good is there, the deed is not. The good which I want to do, I fail to do; but what I do is the wrong which is against my will. . . . Miserable creature that I am, who is there to rescue me?" (Rom. 7:16, 17–19, 24). Our sojourn with the Law brings us to despair about ourselves. But by grace this despair grows into repentance, a wrenching loose by the power of the Spirit from the bondage to the self, and finding a new freedom in faith. Repentance is turning (metanoia) from the powers of darkness toward the Light.

The response of faith to God's gracious pardon is both *assen-*

sus and *fiducia,* both *assent* and *trust.* It is assent, a conviction about who God is and what Christ does. As such it entails an affirmation about the way things are, a belief, a Yes! to the telling of the Christian Story about the suffering Love on Calvary that takes away the sins of the world. It is a commitment of the mind to the Tale that is told about the journey of God into the world to obliterate our guilt by an act of sacrificial mercy.

But this belief is not only intellectual. It is a profound inner event, an act of "soul," in which the self hurls itself on the mercy of God. Thus faith is *trust* as well as belief, one that engages the deepest level of emotion and the total being of the believer. Yet trust does not exclude assent, whatever the current pressures upon it might be from the visceral, metaphorical, or existential currents of our time. The love of God which is the act of faith is one of the whole self done with "all your heart, with all your soul, with all your mind" (Matt. 22:37).

Grace and Faith in a Time of Vision and Reality

The pilgrimage of faith continues. The struggle with the Law, the reach of grace, and the truth of justification are enacted on ever-changing terrain. The dreams of perfection that drew Luther into the monastery come to our time in visions of liberation and reconciliation, personal, social, and cosmic. An era of hope believes it can bring the Kingdom of God into its history, and its visionaries pursue this righteousness in a variety of ways. By political thrust, social transformation, economic engagement, and more recently personal self-renewal, freedom and peace can be won. Scenarios of corporate redemption and individual transfiguration are everywhere to be found. Once again it is the quest for righteousness that exercises its attraction in these efforts in secular salvation, coming more as the vision of the prophet than as the law of the patriarch. But this envisioning is pursued as Law in its promise of a changed world or self by a good will and good works.

For the serious pilgrim who heeds the imperatives of liberation and reconciliation, who gives his or her all to them with the dedication of a Luther, there comes the moment of truth when vision confronts reality. That reality has to do with the collision of aspiration with a recalcitrant world. And at its deepest level it is the awareness of the pretension and self-righteous fury that destroys the noblest of motives. This moment of perception of the ambiguities of self and society can lead to despair and retreat. It is the occupational hazard of visionaries whether they pursue their dreams in a monastery or in a movement. But they may shield themselves from the truth by a hard-driven fanaticism fed by self-righteousness. Thus visionaries can succumb to apathy on the one hand or arrogance on the other. This torpor which counsels retreat from the vision, or vanity which hides its own vulnerability is on a continuum with the sins of concupiscence and pride spoken of in the classic tradition. But the slide into lethargy or the imperial claims of self-sufficiency are themselves rooted in the deeper fact of our fallen nature, the idolatry of the self, the substitution of one's own visions for the divine Vision.

Freedom from bondage to this foundational idolatry comes when the depth of the Vision of God is set before the pilgrim visionary. Here is exposed the broken heart of God, the suffering Love that is the ground of existence as Shalom is its goal, one that takes into itself the aggressions of the world and absorbs its most death-dealing blows. Here are to be seen the "open arms." Here is shown the other side of the cross, the accepting Agape that lies behind the demanding Law of Shalom. It is by faith in this undeserved mercy that the grace of God is received. The visionary does not have to create the vision, and the dreamer can face his or her own subversion of it. In this encounter the imperilled visions are themselves renewed, regrounded in both a realism about self and society and a hope in the God who empowers Shalom and shall bring the Dream to be. The Word and Vision of pardon and peace belong to us today as they did to Luther and to Paul.

Pardon and Power

Personal salvation is *power over* as well as *pardon of* sin, *Christus in nobis* as well as *Christus pro nobis*. The Reformation's emphasis on the depth and stubbornness of our sin makes it rightly suspicious of any claims of virtue, leading as they do to self-congratulation and "works-righteousness." This sobriety in its extreme form, however, may fall prey to an abstract and excessively juridical understanding of grace. But grace is *sanctification* as well as *justification,* the making of persons whole (holy) as well as declaring them forgiven. Grace is power as well as pardon. Salvation is liberation from the act of sinning as well as from the guilt of the sinner. Where the Spirit has brought the believer into a new relationship with God, the same Spirit confirms this bond with grace upon grace. "The harvest of the Spirit is love, joy, peace, patience, kindness, goodness, fidelity, gentleness, and self-control" (Gal. 5:22). The greatest fruit of the Spirit is love. The sanctification intertwined with justification is growth in the life of love and its issue, good works.

Faith is a seed planted and nourished by the Spirit that springs up in the fruit of love. By these fruits the reality of faith is demonstrated. Or in our visual language salvation is not only seeing the Light but seeing *by* the Light. It is seeing in that Light the wretched of the earth. It is the vision of the neighbor in need as well as the vision of God. The works of love are directed toward our wounded neighbor who cries out for help and also our neighbor the earth, scarred and ravaged. And the works of love that flow from faith have at their core the love of God as well as the love of neighbor. This is the life of spirituality directed toward Deity, in and through the life of service toward the neighbor in need.

We would have learned poorly from the great insight of the Reformation if we did not add to this hope for progress in good works the realism that sin always clings to the healthiest of spiritual and moral growth, stunting it and pulling it back upon itself. The grace that must finally save us is the mercy that reaches from the other side of a gap left unbridged by the longest stretch of our good works.

By *faith* we receive the saving grace of God that delivers us from guilt and sin. In *love* we participate in the victorious struggle of God against the principalities and powers of evil. To this aspect of the saving work of Christ we next turn.

SALVATION FROM EVIL

Christ prays, "Deliver us from evil." That prayer is answered. Through him God has delivered us: as sin meets its match in Christ, so do the principalities and powers. The suffering Love that covered guilt also cowered the armies of darkness. Wielding the sword of the cross, Christ invaded the realm of the demonic authorities. These powers, which we have characterized en masse as evil, run from the intimate enemies which afflict body, mind, and spirit, through the historical forces of political, economic, and social tyranny, to vast natural perils of disease and pollution and the mysteries of earthquake, fire, freezing, and flood. The liberation won in the life, death, and resurrection of Christ ended our bondage to these powers. But liberation is a process begun then, continuing now, and completed only in God's final future. It is the "freedom now" which we here speak of, salvation as it is at work in the liberation struggles of this present time between the Times.

The Liberator now at work is Jesus Christ. Wherever the world is freed from foes that separate human from humans, nature from itself, humanity from nature, and all or any from God, there Christ is present and active. Wherever the barriers of evil are removed and the life together of Shalom breaks through, there is the hidden Christ present by the power of the Holy Spirit bringing the mighty from their seats and exalting those of low degree. There is the Son of God, the Vision of God, exalted to the right hand of the Father, ruling over all the authorities and powers that seek to challenge the divine regency.

Where Christ is liberating now is where Christ was liberating in the days of his flesh. And his work is done with the same weapon of suffering love with which he vanquished the enemies that beset his world.

In his Galilean ministry Christ exorcised the demonic powers that enslaved persons, and healed the sick. Wherever and however bodies and minds are mended today, by the methodical sciences or imaginative arts of healing, often by the best of modern medicine but sometimes mysteriously, there is the same Christ touching the infirm. Here is the light of Shalom penetrating the darkness, burning away by the hot fires of its love the enemy powers.

As liberation is freedom from the ills of the flesh, it is also freedom from the cares and oppressions of the world. The New Testament word to us is that Christ our contemporary is to be found, incognito, wherever the hungry are being fed, the prisoner attended, and the naked clothed (Matt. 25:34–46). This ministry is no genteel benevolence but is fraught with the same kind of conflict

and struggle that Christ faced. This is made clear in Christ's declaration of war against the powers and principalities at the inception
of his ministry. "The spirit of the Lord is upon me because he has
anointed me; he has sent me to announce good news to the poor, to
proclaim release for prisoners and recovery of sight for the blind; to
let the broken victims go free, to proclaim the year of the Lord's
favour" (Luke 4:18–19). In this battle he engaged structures of
power, a political-economic-military-ecclesiastical complex that
saw his claims of Lordship as a threat to its own tyrannies and that
finally brought him to court and to death. Yet not without important
skirmishes that give us a clue to his present work: the driving of the
money-changers out of the Temple, forewarning us of the corrup-
tions of economic power, and, through the confrontation with Cae-
sar, putting us on notice to the onslaught of political power. How
the contemporary Christ is present in our midst, liberating from
economic injustice and political tyranny, is illumined by the words
and deeds of the prophetic tradition in which the Liberator chose to
stand by the just-cited declaration of Isaiah quoted in Luke. Even
though he transfigured this tradition by a more searching perception of the depth and range of enslavement and the height and
breadth of its promise, he maintained its vision of the wretched of
the earth and the God who breaks the yoke of slavery and makes
the wounded whole. Salvation now is the presence of the Liberator,
wherever the shackles of human bondage are being torn off and the
oppressed set free. In our time we discern his footprint in the
struggles of the developing nation to be liberated from colonial
domination, the ravages of hunger, and its own internal political
tyrannies. And we see it everywhere there is to be found the struggle
of the ethnic, racial, and religious minority, the unfree majority, the
unrepresented young, the ignored aging and elderly, the exploited
women, the trampled class and caste. Christ is alive and at work
wherever "the least of these" raises a cry of anguish and hope.

"Liberation theology" has heightened the awareness of the
Church in our time to the presence of systemic evil and has given
Samaritan sight to see the invisible poor and plundered. And in its
de-ideologizing campaign it has also reminded us that our incapacity to perceive injustice in the shadowy valleys is inseparable from
our taking up ecclesiastical residence atop the peaks of political,
economic, and social power. To see the unseen victim we must leave

the pinnacles and learn to live in the narrow defiles where Christ is to be found in the press for visibility and dignity. "Where the Spirit of the Lord is, there is liberty!" (II Cor. 3:17). Liberation in the Christian vision is, perforce, all-encompassing. It can settle for no partial perceptions of the disenfranchised, enlarging our horizon to see the present work of Christ in the empowerment of the old as well as the young, the oppressed sex and race as well as class, the middling citizen as well as the minority group, the disabled as well as the dispossessed.

The Liberator is at work wherever evil is contested and bread and freedom won. But Christ is present not only in victories but also defeats, in times of agony as well as hope. He is Sufferer as well as Liberator, victim as well as victor, experiencing the anguish of the oppressed, the cold, the hungry, and the homeless. He is the God-Man of sorrows acquainted with our grief (Isa. 53:3). And as one who knew the abandonment of the Father on the cross, the Son participates in the sense of God-forsakenness that attends so much human misery. The cost of liberation is the pain of co-suffering with those in chains.

Bondage comes in many guises. The crutch of dependency as well as the club of tyranny makes for unfreedom. When benevolent patriarchies do for us what we must do for ourselves, offer assuagement for our troubles when we might better deal with them in courage and imagination, invite lassitude and acceptance of the way things are, then the pursuit of the Vision is challenged by a more benign but no less dangerous foe. Here religious ideas and institutions in the form of a "Deus ex machina" may be the instrument of evil as they cripple the world's coming of age (Bonhoeffer). And here Christ the Liberator is at work setting us free wherever humans are empowered to take responsibility for their future. He works in, with, and under the creativity of scientist and artist, the secular movement and ministration that expands our insight and increases our ability to humanize society. While the exuberant secularization theories of the recent past have been properly sobered by a growing understanding of both the limitations and corruptibility of human ingenuity (a sobriety appropriate as well to many current liberation theories), the truth that God wills and works the adulthood of the race cannot be lost. "If then the Son sets you free, you will indeed be free" (John 8:36).

Our consciousness of the range of evil has been raised in this time of ecological sensibility. Liberation is freedom from the poisons and imbalances of earth, air, and water caused by the arrogance and shortsightedness of humanity, and also the hostilities to Shalom that are endemic to a nature red as it is in tooth and claw, sundered as it is by earthquake, fire, disease, and decay. The eyes of faith also see in this realm of nature evidence of a cosmic Lord. The New Testament bears witness to One who stills the storm and marks the sparrow's fall. The story of Christ walking on water is the testimony of a faith that nature too comes under the Lordship of Jesus Christ. That there shall be a new heaven and a new earth as the issue of the liberation wrought by God in Jesus Christ means that even now this Vision is at work in creation, freeing it from forces inimical to the divine will and empowering mutuality in its rhythm and patterns. A relentless Love is at work making the desert bloom, sternly judging and setting boundaries to the destructive chemistries of nature, and inviting the human partner to cooperate in the healing of nature, just as that Spirit does in the healing of nations and persons.

The redeeming work of the Vision of God in history and nature is no more confined to the agency of human envisioning than the power of the Word of God in the world is limited to verbalizing. Our use of the metaphor of vision must not be understood in terms of a philosophical or political idealism which discounts the role of material factors. The Vision and Word of God, our suffering Liberator, works in and through the social-economic-political-natural processes as well as by the lure of the dream and the power of the idea. While the former are not the sole determinants of social change, they are critical factors in any advance made by the incognito Christ against the demonic principalities and authorities.

As grace brings Atonement to bear as mercy to the sinner now, so the same grace of God carries deliverance from evil to the world now. We are saved by grace from sin and saved by grace from evil. It is the initiative of the Vision of God, Jesus Christ, that makes for healing of self, society, and nature. And as we are called to participate now in the salvation from sin offered to us, so we are also beckoned to enter into these healing streams. The entrance to one is by faith, to the other by love.

The Works of Love

Presence with the Christ who is suffering with and struggling for the hungry and the hurt exists by way of compassion, according to the tale of the sheep and the goats. We are companions of the hidden Christ to the extent we keep step with him in his quest to liberate his companions from the tribulations of this world. Alongsidedness with him happens in the love of the neighbor in need. Where the Samaritan reaches to bind up wounds there is fellowship with Jesus Christ.

The relation of faith to love and the revealed and hidden Christ is suggested by the Emmaus Road story (Luke 24:13–35). In that episode the disciples experience two different relationships with the risen Christ. First on the road they travel with a stranger who "caused their hearts to feel on fire" (Luke 24:32). Then in the upper room at the end of the journey, the stranger identifies himself at the table: "He broke the bread and offered it to them. Then their eyes were opened and they recognized him" (Luke 24:30–31). Christ is present with us, so to speak, on the road and in the room. We keep company with him in profile, as our comrade in acts of mercy and struggles against the powers of evil. It is neighbor love that puts us on the road alongside the incognito Christ present wherever the hungry are fed, justice is done, and peace is made. But we also meet him face to face in the intimate encounters, cognitive meetings, disclosures of identity, of personal piety and Christian life together. At the holy table in sacrament, word, worship, and prayer, faith opens our eyes to recognize him and opens our ears to hear the Word in which he says who he is. In the life of the Church, Christ encounters us by grace through faith as an I meets a Thou. In the life of the world, Christ meets us by grace through love as an I travels with the He.

Those who are agents of worldly liberation and reconciliation, engaged in ministry to the hungry and oppressed but who do not know him or confess his name, nevertheless do meet and suffer with him according to the testimony of Matthew. Therefore they participate in *that aspect* of Christ's saving work, deliverance from the powers of bondage and estrangement. And those who do know him and confess his name yet fail to follow him from the room to the road in ministry to and with Christ among the neighbors in need are judged with the eschatological rigor set forth in the same account.

What is not often said by those who cite this passage as evidence of the liberating and reconciling grace at work in secular action and people is the complementary truth that those who do not personally know Christ as the Liberator from sin and guilt, the One who discloses himself in Word and Sacrament, have yet to participate in the fullness of his atoning Work. Herein lies the Church's evangelism mandate.

Authentic faith is one that keeps company with the Christ of the road as well as the Christ of the room, a faith busy in neighbor love. A fulfilled love is one that has learned to love God as well as neighbor, one that has traveled with Christ to the upper room and there discovered in faith the name of this worldly companion.

To be with Christ in the world is no serene stroll in the garden. Jesus Christ is present in the agony of hunger, nakedness, prison. To be with him there in neighbor love is to "participate in the sufferings of God in the world" (Bonhoeffer). And to be alongside the suffering Christ is to take part in the battles for liberating the prisoner, the hungry, and the homeless. This is a painful journey that goes through dark valleys and along dangerous trails.

As faith is impossible except by the gracious initiative of God, so love cannot be manufactured by human effort. A love that participates in the suffering and liberating activity of the worldly Christ is a gift of grace. Wherever salvation happens, it is not earned but granted. We are saved by grace.

The love that God uses to put us in touch with the hidden Christ expresses itself in different ways. The works of love vary according to the needs of the hour. Here is a way of identifying the kinds of behavior in which love can embody itself: *the works of heaven, earth, and hell.*

Heaven

The works of heaven are those in which our conduct takes the form of the perfect self-abnegation of Christ. This is the kind of cheek-turning, coat-sharing, second mile love that *will be* in heaven, that *was* in Christ, and that *is* in the heart of God. It is eschatological love, the perfection for which we are ultimately intended, an agape of selfless behavior that matches the agape of selfless disposition issuing in a perfect Shalom.

In the perfection of the Kingdom in which God is all in all and there is no sin or evil, the reach of this love is reciprocated in kind: Love evokes love. But on earth in this time before the Kingdom's arrival, sin and evil take their toll. In such an unfulfilled world the powers of darkness trample selfless behavior; perfect love ends on a cross. Samaritan cheek-turning to the bandits on the Jericho road during an assault eventuates in two victims instead of one, and no subsequent resources of servanthood. The failure to recognize this, rooted as it is in a too sanguine view of human nature and history, results in an ethical *perfectionism* unable to set bounds to these rampages of sin and evil. The perfect ethics of heaven cannot be exported in packaged fashion to earth.

But radical selflessness in behavior does have relevance to day-to-day decision-making. As the perfect Law of love, embodied in and taught by Jesus Christ, it is the lure and judge of all lesser conduct. It is a Vision that attracts us toward the conformation of our life to the divine Agape. It keeps us off balance, goading us to higher approximations of selfless conduct in both personal and social relationships. And as judge of lower forms of conduct that are too ready to settle for less, as well as condemnation of manifestly self-serving agendas, it is the Law that exposes us as sinners and marks our world as fallen.

The fact that there are evidences on earth of selfless conduct sharpens our vision of the heavenly goal of all decision-making. Jesus Christ is our chief model of self-forgetting love. However, in the intimate relations of the conjugal bond, the family, friendship, and Christian life together, some measure of agape can be reached, although always conjoined with *eros* or *philia* in which there is some return assumed in the relationship, rather than being completely spontaneous and unmerited. A perfectionist understanding of love is also sustained in small visionary communities. These communities can serve as potent witnesses to the final Vision and as a conscience to the larger society. And in special historical moments when some evil of that larger society comes to high consciousness, the purity of the Vision translated into non-violent strategies for social change, as in the movements of Gandhi and King, may have intense historical significance. But these times pass, and even their moment of ripeness is not unfree of practice that sits uneasily with the theory (as when one marches in non-violent protest protected by the guns of the National Guard). In the matter of day-to-day decision-making in which all available choices lead to some harm to someone, we take heaven as our reference point, as guide and judge, but must make our way along the rutted and poorly marked trails of the earth.

Earth

The work of love on earth is to translate moral vision into the reality of claim and counterclaim, of intractable and self-regarding tendencies. Love in this land means setting bounds to the destructive possibilities and expansionist inclinations of human nature. It means honoring and protecting the dignity of each. And it means aspiring toward whatever measure of mutuality can be achieved in this world of competing claims. These forms have shaped earthly love: moral law, code, and covenant. *Moral law:* Human societies have tended to share common perceptions of fundamental right and wrong; survival and growth have depended upon the pursuit of values that set limits to the lethal tendencies of the race and facilitate its development. Among these universal imperatives are justice, freedom, order, and mutuality. Moral law in the hands of Christian love reads justice as equality of option to fill every need, freedom as liberation from all tyranny, order as the civilizing boundaries that make social existence tolerable, and mutuality as the community necessary for a human life together. *Code:* Human experience in general is particularized in the code of the biblical community. Here the abstractions of a universal moral law reach one step closer to concretion in the form of the decalogue. Like moral law, these imperatives also are mandates of the earth that presuppose the fractious material of which we are made. Hence, their construction as "Thou shalt nots." In its three thousand year laboratory the people of two covenants have learned that such acts as murder, stealing, adultery, and lying rend the fabric of human community. *Covenant:* The human community and the biblical communities have also learned that there are social structures integral to survival and humanization, as, for example, the state and the family. Commitment to the state by Christian love is an acknowledgement, on the one hand, of the need to set limits to the self-interest of humans living together, and on the other, to make possible human growth. Its vision of Shalom will predispose it to that kind of state in which freedom and justice for all, and a community supportive of the needs of each is the rule. Commitment to the family by Christian love will mean a conjugal union, with children as the way sexuality finds expression and the next generation is born and nurtured.

Out of the general laws, codes, and covenants of earthly love come a wealth of derivative guidelines for conduct with greater specificity. Thus from the universal axioms of moral law grow "middle axioms" that take on special relevance in a particular time or place. Justice becomes, for example, in an era of raised consciousness or manifest injustice, justice for black citizens in housing, education, and voting; freedom for the undeveloped country under colonial domination; order for an urban community paralyzed by crime. And beyond these is the hammering out of perspectives on new moral issues prompted by technological innovation or other developments for which there is no obvious lore either in the human community or in the biblical communities: medical issues such as abortion and euthanasia and biomedical issues such as the creation, control, and extension of human life.

What is common to all the wisdom that grows out of the experience of earthly love is its communal matrix. Whether it is learning from the experience of the race as it emerges in the ethical refrains from a variety of societies as found in moral law, or whether it is the points of assent of fresh formulation within the biblical peoples past and present, it is the community that is at work in honing the guidelines for conduct on the earth. This itself is part of both the communal vision of Shalom that is the reference point for all the works of love, and also the realism which knows that in a fallen world the sin in the self has to be subjected to public tests and corporate scrutiny.

The simple and uncritical adhesion to the rules of the community because they are there is an invitation to reductionism, not unlike the perfectionism discussed earlier which insists upon utopian behavior as the only norm of love. With regard to earthly love this temptation comes in the form of *legalism*. The legalist gives unthinking obedience to the laws of earth. As such they remain unchallenged by the higher possibilities of heavenly love, on the one hand, and on the other, they do not allow for the "exception to the rule" made necessary by the life of love in hell. To this perilous terrain we shall next turn.

Hell

Hell is that circumstance in which both the horns and all the cloven feet of the devil appear (Reinhold Niebuhr). Hell is confrontation with the full malignancy of the powers of sin, evil, and death. Satan and his hordes do not play by the rules of the game. Therefore, in hell one cannot look up in a book of the codes, laws, and covenants what must be done. Here is the exception to the rule.

Yet the Light penetrates even the shadows of hell. The stars of Agape and Shalom shine in this night. Our attitude and behavior take their bearings from these orientation points. Decision-making in hell is the union of faith with lethal fact, love with ambiguous circumstance. Agape-Shalom, therefore, lives contextually in the land of the demons. It makes judgments case by case as it is given Light by the Spirit of love. Let us examine some cases.

In heaven selflessness evokes selflessness and its fruit is mutuality. In hell selflessness is exploited as weakness and the innocent are slaughtered. In the fact of this radical attack on the Vision of freedom and peace, and the violation of the earth's laws of humanity and justice—let us say in a case of political tyranny—Agape must be translated into behavior that "resists the powers of evil." The right of revolution, in 1776 in the American colonies or in 1976 in African colonies, becomes an option in Christian ethics. Just revolution has its counterpart in macrocosm in "just war" and in microcosm in "just abortion," however severely restricted the former in our awesome nuclear context, or carefully interpreted the latter amid the rampant oversimplifications. In other no less oppressive circumstances, when the political covenant of law and order (Rom. 13) descends to hell (Rev. 13), the ethical imperative may be the non-violent civil disobedience of the first-century martyr or the twentieth-century resister. And in yet another example of the limits of earthly covenants, when the powers of evil have so destroyed partners and offspring in the bonds of marriage and family, it is a work of love to sever the ties.

It has been the contribution of situation ethics to bring to our attention the ambiguities of context and the limitations of codes.

This is the hell in which Love is our only Light, and law is set aside in the shadowy arena in which Love does its work. Yet as with each insight in ethics, the temptation to absoluteness is overpowering, ironically even in a perspective that disavows it. Christian ethics cannot be reduced to *situationism* any more than it can be to legalism or perfectionism. Contextual ethics must itself be taken contextually, and that context is hell. It is not a norm for day-to-day decision-making, for in the continuities of earth the corporate lore of the biblical peoples and the human community serves as a critical resource.

One other gift of heaven, in addition to the dispositional Light of Agape, that makes its presence felt in hell is the communal theme of Shalom. The self-serving agendas that are always operating, and especially so when we bracket the codes and covenants of earth and choose to live by Love alone, come under public scrutiny when the brothers and sisters are partners in painful exceptional choices. Thus the choices of violence or non-violence in challenging the oppression of the state should be done in mutual conversation and consolation with the brothers and sisters in faith. That presence of the other is, of course, at work as well in the counselor or pastor at hand as third party in the hell of marital breach. Decision-making in extremity calls in the community.

The three motifs in Christian ethics we have discussed can be visualized in this way.

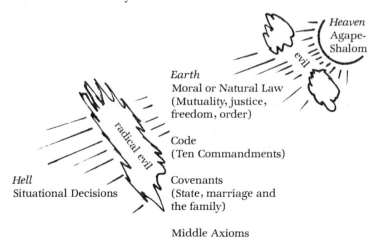

Heaven
Agape-
Shalom

evil

Earth
Moral or Natural Law
(Mutuality, justice,
freedom, order)

Code
(Ten Commandments)

radical evil

Hell
Situational Decisions

Covenants
(State, marriage and
the family)

Middle Axioms

SALVATION FROM DEATH

And what of the "last enemy," death, and salvation *now* from death? On the face of it, our enemy death is mortality. The present preoccupation with death and dying surely understands it that way.

In the broad Christian tradition death is no less than the fact that our days come to an end as a tale that is told. But it is also more than that. The death that is the "wages of sin" is, in its deepest sense, *separation from God*. And in its broadest purview it is estrangement of all the intended partners to Shalom: God, humanity, and nature. Death is alienation. It is the enmity of the world toward God and itself. And in turn, it is God's sorrowful judgment upon this rebel creation.

As the fracturing of all the intended relationships of Shalom, death is the crushing of God's Vision, the destruction of the divine Dream. It is the darkness that threatens when the Light is assaulted. When sin and evil swagger, and especially when they make their all-out attack on the Light that comes into the world, the shadows of death lurk about us. At the darkest point in human history, when the Light of God was extinguished on Golgotha, there was a death *in* God. The fading of the Vision of God portends the demise of the world, the abandoning of the Great Experiment in Shalom. The wages of sin and evil are death and damnation.

The flickering inner light, the image of God in us, is not so dim that it cannot at least disclose something of the shadows to be seen. Hence the fear humans have of mortality, their suspicion that this Dream may be unreal. And indeed mortality is a sign of the peril to the Vision of God, for it brings to naught the finest hopes and achievements. Now in an era of lengthened time perception the anxiety about the finitude of persons is extended to the finitude of history and ultimately the cosmos. Thus the futurist warns of ecological disaster or nuclear holocaust, and the scientist speculates about the heat death of the universe. Fear of death, and times preoccupied with mortality in any of its expressions, is loss of confidence in the future of God, expectation of the slaughter of Hope.

In the Christian Story the Good News of salvation from death is bodied forth in the resurrection of Jesus Christ. Here is announced to us that the Vision of God has triumphed over the power of death!

The Dream did not finally die on Calvary but was reborn in a suffering Love that overcame sin and evil.

The resurrection of Christ is more than an announcement. It is an event of triumph itself. If sin and evil were whipped on Calvary, then the "last enemy, death" met its match on Easter morning. As death is nothing less than mortality, so the empty tomb declares that finitude is not the last word. The death of this body, and also of this history and this cosmos, is not the end toward which the world moves. Our history in time, as self or society or universe, does not conclude as a tale futilely told. The finish is not the finale. What shall be is given to us in the earnest of the risen Christ. Here is the Life that overcomes death, the light of Dawn that defeats the night powers. About this we have spoken in our christological exploration. Here we re-affirm Easter as the grounds for liberation from physical death in any form.

As our earlier discussion indicated, the freedom conferred upon us at Easter is far more than breaking the shackles of mortality. In its profoundest meaning it is liberation from the *consequences* of sin and evil: the alienation from God and the partners of God. Liberation from death *is* reconciliation. In the resurrection, the world is granted in an anticipatory way, proleptically, the unity with God, humanity, and nature that will be its final destiny. The risen Christ is the down-payment on that time of ingathering, a preview of the "coming attraction." As the death of Christ was the death of the Vision of God, so the resurrection of Christ is the restoration in a transformed way of the Vision of God. Now the future of God, Shalom, is assured. And the way to that future is the suffering Love that triumphed over sin and evil, and now the last enemy, death.

What then of the process of liberation as it reaches us now, salvation *now* from death? What is achieved for us in the resurrection of Christ is communicated to us by grace, by the Holy Spirit that empowers the risen Christ to beat down death in our own time and place. The risen Christ is the enabler of new life in the world. He brings God, humanity, and nature together. Wherever the power of death and darkness is in retreat, there is life and Light, the risen Christ. Wherever reconciliation happens, there death is in flight. After resurrection all the manifestations of unity in the world are the work of a triumphant Providence. The reconciling action of the risen Christ means that death does not control the future of persons, history, or nature. Here in this phase of its pilgrimage toward fulfillment, time is open to fresh possibilities. As God's Dream has been reborn, so it is right that we too should dream. The empowered vision of God is given a new lease on Life by the resurrection; our hopes for this world have a foundation in the renewed nature of things.

It is *hope* that is legitimated by the resurrection then, and the life and work of the risen Christ now. As we are saved from sin by grace through faith and participate in the salvation from evil through love, so we share in the liberation from death by hope. It is through the eyes of hope that we see the powers of darkness being thrust back at the Easter dawn and on our own historical horizon. Hope makes a report of an open future, and eschatological hope of an open final Future. Hope knows that mortality is not the last fact. But more, hope is our perception that alienation is not our destiny. Hope is seeing the coming together of all things signalled by the resurrection of Jesus Christ, the firming of the future of Shalom. To hope is to catch sight of the fulfilled Vision and to track the rays of its Light from the future back into the present. By hope we participate not only in the suffering but also in the victories of God in the world.

While the eyes of hope perceive the Light to be, that same Vision sees what human sight also knows: the persistence of sin and evil, and the stubborn fact of physical death. Arrogance and apathy still work their ways on the self; history and nature are under constant attack from demonic power structures and drives; mortality still is our portion, and estrangement is everywhere to be seen. The pall of death, in every sense, hangs over this fallen world. Hope is no illusion of instant sweetness and light. Hope is not utopian, knowing we do not live at the Noontide when all the shadows pass, but in the half-light of the Already–Not Yet. Hope's symbol is a Dawnburst, not Sunburst, one that knows that there are dark shadows still on the land. Hope is *sober* hope, not giddy fantasy. And it knows that its rising sun metaphor is at best ambiguous, for there is no gradual dispersal of the clouds as Sol rises to meridian. Each liberation thrust in history, each ascent, is harassed by the continuing gloom, the resistance of the powers of darkness that continue to the End of time. "If it is for this life only that Christ has given us hope, we of all men are most to be pitied" (I Cor. 15:19). Hopes for *this time* between the Times are modest, the expectation of rays that pierce the darkness, signs and portents of that which is yet to come. The final conquest of death awaits the full Day.

But the "sting of death" is taken away by hope. We know that mortality can do us no final harm. The estrangements of this world cannot erase the Unity that awaits us. And the removal of the sting of death also means the freedom to quest for anticipatory victories that an open future promises in *this world.* To face our own approaching death and the world's demise without the anxiety of defeat is already in a profound sense to conquer death. And to be able to look for and rejoice in the victories of Shalom in our history is a like triumph.

Hope has a way, itself, of making a contribution to these victories. While despair *paralyzes,* hope *mobilizes.* The perception that the future is open right now empowers the hoper to stride into it. The tactic of entrenched power, the intimidation of the change agent by the swagger of those who pretend to control tomorrow, is undercut by the sight given to the eyes of hope, the sight of power structures that are only dust and ashes. The risen Christ is the Lord of the future, and this confidence enables the hoper to "resist the powers of evil," those forces that appear to the eyes of ordinary sight to be impenetrable.

The end-point of liberation from death and therefore the reconciliation of all things is the final chapter toward which the Christian Story moves. We shall examine the cluster of Christian visions that make up that eschatological reality in the next chapter, "Consummation." Their capstone is the Kingdom of God and the everlasting Life in which the shadows of death finally disappear. The fulfillment of the promise of God to bring Shalom can mean nothing less than that all the enemies are brought under the feet of Christ. No darkness lingers in the ineffable Light to be.

The Good News of salvation Now is a *word of faith* about the mercy offered to us on Calvary that covers our sin and guilt, a *work of love* that keeps company with the Presence in the world, and a *vision of hope* of a future opened by the risen Christ.

CHAPTER VII

Consummation

The Christian Story moves to its climax, the account of the *eschaton,* the "last things." The last chapter is about eschatology. For many people the turning of the final page of life has to do with our own approaching death. What is the meaning of death? What happens to me when I die? Where now is that loved one who was so much part of my life and is now no longer in our midst? Can we communicate with the dead? The issues of "death and dying" have come dramatically to public consciousness in recent years. This preoccupation with death has been further accented by the biomedical issues surrounding our personal end, questions running from organ replacement and the establishment of the moment of expiration to the humane treatment of the terminally ill and comatose.

It is not unusual to hear the subject of eschatology treated in the foregoing context and therefore understood to mean the belief in "life after death." And the Easter Sunday sermon will confirm it with intimations of immortality. Eschatology becomes here, or in the funeral homily, the declaration of postmortem existence. Its descriptions may range from theories about the immortality of the soul to counter-cultural speculation about reincarnation.

Still others in the Christian community, more attuned to the claims and burdens of history, seek to relate eschatology to the present world, the time before, not after, death. New eschatologies arise that speak of "the future." Some versions of a "theology of hope" (by no means all), connecting with the nineteenth-century emphasis on "building the kingdom of God on earth," interpret eschatology to mean the hopes we can have for our historical future, particularly aspirations of justice and peace.

Still another point of view of eschatology is to be found in which the notes of finality and decision are considered to be definitive of the last things. It transplants the stark confrontation with Christ spoken of in the Bible into the present moment. Right now, as one is encountered by an ultimate choice, the end is present with us, one before which we stand accused and called to decision. Under the influence of the existentialist thought of Rudolf Bultmann and others seeking to demythologize the cosmologies and chronologies of the biblical eschaton, the presentizing of eschatology is offered as compatible with the modern mind.

There are things to be learned from all of these efforts to do justice to the aspects of New Testament eschatology, aspects that include personal death, historical hope, existential choice. Yet they all fall short of what is, after all, the main thrust of this final chapter of the Christian Story, the affirmation of the end of the saga. This end is one characterized by both meanings of the word *end* — *telos* and *finis*. The story has a *purpose* and it has a *conclusion*. And there is a point of convergence of these two: a finale toward which history moves and at which its purposes will be fulfilled, a meeting point of Vision and Reality. The Christian Story is one that records the movement from invitation through alienation and connection to intersection and convergence. There is no responsible reading of this narrative's last things without taking seriously the Omega point beyond the finis of our personal existence and the telos manifest within history or existential choice. The penultimate matters of our personal death, the futures within human history, and the choices we are called to make point beyond themselves and are in turn illumined by the fulfillment of the purpose of God. That is the central matter addressed in the eschatological chapter of the Story. In our exploration of it we shall seek to show how the Light from the ultimate Future illumines our penultimate future in life and death. The last things thus merge into the "next-to-last things," the absolute future into our personal, historical, and cosmic futures.

MYSTERY AND MODESTY

What does the Christian Story have to say about the end? It is important to realize first what it does *not* say, especially in times when there are too many zealous offers of a detailed Cook's tour of the World to Come. "Travelogue eschatologies" (Hans Schwarz) with their lush apocalyptic imagery and confident descriptions of "the temperature of hell and the furniture of heaven" sometimes claim to know more than the Son of God about the how and when of his coming. His own counsel sets the tone for all our discourse here about the end. "About that day and hour no one knows" (Matt. 24:36). Christian Storytellers at their best observe this proper modesty as they seek to honor the final mystery. Thus "We see through a glass darkly" (I Cor. 13:12 KJV) when peering through the biblical window of the future. The glass is not transparent giving us a full and clear view, but translucent. We have enough light by which to see and to discern some of the shape of things to come.

While the Christian Story does not yield up encyclopedic knowledge about the *how* and *when* of the Consummation, it does give us bold affirmations about the *that* and *what* of the matter. In this respect the doctrine of the End is much like the doctrine of the Beginning. The factuality and form of Creation and Consummation are the things of interest to the Storyteller. *That* God shall fulfill the divine Intention, *that* history moves toward its Omega is fundamental to the meaning of the Christian saga. *What* the dimensions of that fulfillment are is equally important. The latter is summarized in the classic creeds of the Church. The Storytelling community has sifted through the Storybook in its own struggle age after age with human questioning and has fixed upon certain biblical refrains: *the resurrection of the dead, the return of Christ, the last judgment, everlasting life.* These comprise the kernel of Christian teaching about the End. These are the last things.

The kernel is surrounded by a husk. The color and sheen of this covering have a way of attracting the seeker, sometimes causing him or her to settle too quickly for the surface instead of probing to the center. There is a range of rich metaphors and images—the Anti-Christ, a thousand-year reign of peace, golden streets and pearly gates, numerology, the conversion of Israel—in which the great affirmations are housed. Three things should be noted about them: 1) They are not dominant or ubiquitous New Testament motifs, but random assertions. 2) They rise out of particular historical circumstances (Nero, Rome, etc.) and are often calculated to shore up the faith of the early Christians faced with oppression and martyrdom. 3) Most of them fall short of being eschatological affirmations since they do not deal with the transfiguration *of* the world, but with events *in* the world. Christian eschatology is not secular forecasting but the futurology of the World to Come. While these exuberant scenarios provide material for the armchair speculations and sometimes frenzied imaginations so popular in periods of travail in human history, Christian thought about the End has in the main chosen to be agnostic about the how and when, focusing rather on the that and what centralities of resurrection, return, judgment, and eternal life.

SCIENCE AND FAITH

One other introductory concern must also be taken into account before probing those centralities. It has to do with the relation of Christian eschatology to the projections of the scientific community. Does not the Christian faith intrude upon the terrain of science by making statements about this time-space continuum? Should not the faith community confine itself to inner space or trans-temporal realms so that faith and reason do not collide with one another? This policy of accommodation has been a favorite one since Immanuel Kant laid the groundwork for the distinction between fact and value, with reason taking responsibility for the former and our spiritual and moral intuitions for the latter.

Science and faith do have different foci and fields of inquiry. Yet theories emerging out of both the science community and the faith community may come into conflict. A case in point is the debate about Creation. There is a legitimate division of labor here between science which deals with the particulars of the origin of the world and faith which is concerned with its meanings. Yet what cannot be given up in this debate is the *source* of this Creation and also the *fact* of its beginning as noted in the first chapter. If it is a real saga with which we have to do, then the latter is as important as the former, something not always recognized in Christian apologetics. The reason it was not given its due is because the regnant theories of the origin and growth of the universe have posited a beginning. Evolution is out of a point in time, so both evolutionary theory and the Christian Story point toward an inception.

The bearing of this nineteenth-century debate on eschatology comes in the affirmation of an end point as well as a beginning point. This is a necessary faith statement. What is not of the essence of faith is how the world reaches its termination. Indeed if the scientific accounts and those of the Storybook do not agree, we must choose the best light we can get from scientific sources, as we have done with the question of the origins of the world. And that can include projections of a thermonuclear holocaust or environmental exhaustion as it pertains to this planet, or a theory of entropy about the running down of the universe itself. Eschatological faith speaks fundamentally about the nature and meaning of the end and is not tied to one or another scenario of natural or historical evolution or devolution. And it can live with the prognostications of the human community about the how and when of the end as well as of the beginning.

THEMES BASHFUL AND BOLD

In the primitive Christian community the last things tended to arrange themselves in a certain sequence with an obvious logic: first the resurrection of the dead, then the return of Christ, then the combination of the two—a judgment by Christ of the resurrected dead—then everlasting life. Several things have happened to this primitive scheme as each subsequent generation sought to use it to shed light on its own future. A tendency developed to accent one or another of these motifs: *judgment* of evil by Christ in times when oppressive forces loom large; *resurrection* of the body in times of heady spiritualization of the faith that ignored things material and fleshly; *everlasting life* in times which call for words of hope. Also different aspects of one or another of these motifs were brought to the fore according to the needs of the hour or the inclinations of the interpreter. Thus everlasting life came to be interpreted as a vision of God granted to the redeemed, an image powerful where the quest for truth or mystical experience was to the foreground; again, a full-blooded restoration of the poor to their rights in times of social struggle and in the throes of the oppression; plentiful crops, singing mountains, a joyful creation replaced a world of disease and drought and a groaning creation; eternal rest in times of weariness of body and spirit.

While each of these exercised a certain power with those to whom it was addressed or among those for whom these metaphors had special meaning, the same images for other folk and other times proved to be meaningless, or even stumbling blocks to faith. Thus an affluent and activist culture finds it impossible to believe that the goal of history is "eternal rest," an image that becomes a favorite target for skeptics who take pleasure in pointing out how boring such a heaven is. To realize that the appeal of this imagery is to oppressed people who are not so fortunate to have their elemental problems hidden by middle-class creature comforts, nor have the attendant energy or leisure, is to be less disdainful of these hopes of the hopeless. It is also true that there are other biblical images of the end that suggest anything but bovine serenity, such as a lively city, a festive banquet, the growth of seeds and kingdoms. In any case, we need to honor all the motifs, and to locate the images that speak to us, without reducing eschatological faith to just those which reflect our limited experience.

In our own translation of the Christian Story it is the image of liberation and reconciliation that has been to the fore and the motif of vision that has provided our refrain. Associated with this theme is an accent upon everlasting life. For here is the affirmation that the hope of God cannot be defeated. Yet such a dominant note for this last chapter must also do justice to the basic accents in each of the companion themes. And it must provide as well a holistic conception of everlasting life, the liberation and reconciliation of all things.

THE RESURRECTION OF THE DEAD

The Christian Story cannot be what it is unless all that ever has been participates in the culmination. There can be no thread of history that is not gathered up and woven into this final tapestry. The memory of God is total. Therefore when the time of fulfillment comes, it reaches into every nook and cranny of the past. An awesome thought!

But this is not simply an act of remembering analogous to our capacity to recall what has been. It is a memory that acts to bring to be what is remembered to have been. The phrase *resurrection of the dead* underscores the bringing into existence again of the least and the last of the history that has transpired. What has died is not lost but is recovered and placed as an actor in the final scene. All things are in the last things (I Cor. 15; Acts 24:15; John 5:28–29).

This includes our bodies, a foreground theme in those times and places in which more elusive spiritualized versions of the faith or popular religion have tended to denigrate the body both here and hereafter. The appearance of the phrase *resurrection of the body* in the Apostles' Creed was connected with the repudiation of a world-denying and body-rejecting Gnosticism and Docetism. It recurs in periods which ignore the issues of justice for trampled victims whose bodies are racked by hunger and pain. The resurrection of the body serves to comfort the afflicted as well as afflict the comfortable. We are reminded that our bodies are part of the final design of God. In the Christian Story there are no glittering generalities or elusive talk about the immortality of the soul as in an over-Hellenized Christianity or "religion-in-general."

The resurrection of the dead has already begun. Jesus Christ is the first of this new race. The Christian hope is that what he was at Easter we too shall be. The resurrection appearances of Jesus are in both continuity and discontinuity with his pre-Easter being. While the New Testament accounts portray a Jesus visually the same as his Galilean self, the flesh so perceived is not of equivalent temporality and mortality. Hence Paul's elusive description of our own resurrection bodies: "What is sown in the earth as a perishable thing is raised imperishable. Sown in humiliation it is raised in glory; sown in weakness, it is raised in power; sown as an animal body it is raised as a spiritual body . . . flesh and blood can never possess the kingdom of God. . ." (I Cor. 15:42–44,50). The prolepsis of the universal resurrection in Jesus Christ points toward the imperishable but embodied selfhood that shall be ours as well.

The resurrection of the dead in this tale refers to unbeliever as well as believer, the damned as well as the saved (Rom. 14:10). Nothing and no one escapes the last things. The resurrection of the dead is both final resolution and final reckoning, good news and bad news. It not only consoles but also warns that there is no place to hide in either the convenient theories of disappearance into nonexistence, or the pleasant illusions that twittering birds and laughing nymphs are all that await us as we go to an eternal Forest Lawn.

THE RETURN OF CHRIST AND THE FINAL JUDGMENT

The Apostles' Creed asserts, "He will come again to judge the quick and the dead." The Christ who last lived in this fallen realm was a suffering and crucified figure. As the world reemerges now in a new frame of reference, it must deal with the one who has preceded it to a new plane of history (I Thess. 4:16). The Christ who makes himself present at the culmination point is not the suffering victim but the triumphant victor. Here is not defeat and disaster but a liberator and reconciler! The King who reigns in heaven in the time between the Times now comes at the end of this age into a trans- figured history and into his complete glory. This is the Day that ends the night. Here the shadows disappear, and even the dawn passes away as the sun ascends to its place at the meridian. Shalom is victorious.

When the Son of God shines in the new world, everything comes to light. All that ever was is exposed for what it is in the Light of Shalom. Dark alleys are no longer hiding places. The world shall know who its friends have been all along—God, neighbor, and nature. They shall see them in the Light. And, on the other hand, we shall see ourselves for what we really have been: "He will bring to light what darkness hides" (I Cor. 4:5).

It is no accident that the coming of Christ is linked with judgment, for the flight of the world from its true goal must be reckoned with if the hope of God is to be fulfilled. Judgment is exposure to a searching light. Such radiance burns as well as shines. It is little wonder that images of fire recur within the history of eschatological preaching and teaching.

If Jesus Christ is our tribunal, we are to be judged in the light of Shalom. And all of us must stand that scrutiny, both believer and unbeliever. "For we must all have our lives laid open before the tribunal of Christ, where each must receive what is due to him for his conduct in the body, good or bad" (II Cor. 5:10). What can this stern declaration mean, one that is a refrain in the New Testament? Our imagery of light gives us a small clue. To be judged in the light

213

is to see with total clarity what we have been. The first fact apparent is our slavery to the powers of sin, evil, and death and our alienation from neighbor, nature, and God. To see the ugly fact of our self-centeredness and its effects with blinding clarity is the excruciating pain of judgment. More so indeed for those who have made professions of loyalty to Shalom and have given lip service to liberation and reconciliation. What deepens the agony of this self-disclosure is the other fact that comes clear in this moment of judgment—that the light of judgment is the light of Love. The harshest judge of a conscience that knows what it must do or what it should have done is to know the hurt it has caused. To know that we have broken faith with the One who has brought us to be, and to know the suffering we have caused God, culminating in the act of crucifying the Vision, that is horror indeed. It is why Paul spoke of love pouring hot coals upon us. The hot coals of last judgment are the knowledge of the injury we have done to God. On the other hand, the New Testament witnesses that there will be joy in heaven for the deeds of Shalom that are disclosed in deeds of sin, evil, and death (Rev. 20:12). In those acts of life Christ will be seeing his grace returned.

The wrath of God on judgment day falls heaviest on the agents of bondage and alienation. It is they for whom the Jesus of the parable of the sheep and the goats reserves his direst warnings. Those who have not fed the hungry, clothed the naked, cared for the sick, the prisoner, the stranger will have to answer to the Christ they spurned in the least of these brothers and sisters (Matt. 25:41–46). Thus the vindication of justice, the final accountability of the people and powers that trod upon the poor, despoiled the needy, and dehumanized all those of low degree is an eschatological promise.

But if the central chapter of the Story has any meaning at all, it signifies that the final judgment will not be made in terms of the deeds done (John 3:16). Paul speaks of adjudication by deed on the day of the Lord, but makes terribly clear that it is not by works but by faith that we shall be "saved from the wrath that is to come." Is this not a sheer contradiction? We give Paul and the other writers of the New Testament little credit to think that this seemingly irreconcilable testimony has no deeper unity. There is such a coming together of faith and works in the final judgment just as there is in the penultimate judgment in this life. The Christ who comes to judge the quick and the dead is the Shalom which suffers for our sake, taking away the sins of the world. The divine Love is more ultimate than the divine Wrath. That is the ground for his unceasing quest for us and finally taking upon himself the judgment we deserve on Calvary. Jesus Christ is by that reach of suffering Love the one who stands between us and the Wrath we so genuinely deserved. On that day Christ is not only our Judge by his suffering love, but more ultimately our Savior.

How then do we stand before the judgment seat of Christ our advocate? We stand only as we are behind him, yes *in* him. He is the advocate of the Father's Love before the Father's Wrath. We are saved from the wrath by that participation. The act of this affiliation is faith. It is by faith that this protection comes. How many different figures are used to capture this connection in the New Testament! It is clear from all of them that only as we have him as our shield can we stand in the latter day.

Faith, of course, is no faith unless it expresses itself in works. Faith is not just belief—even "the devils have faith like that" (James 2:19)—but belief busy in love. Without the love which expresses itself in works there is no faith. That is why in Matthew 25:31ff. the tests of authentic faith are the works of love. What counts on the last day is a faith demonstrating its reality and love—feeding the hungry, visiting the prisoner, seeking justice, making peace (I John 3:15–18).

A faith working in love confronts Christ who is our Advocate on the day of judgment. He is both judge and advocate! By his suffering love he takes the punishment of righteousness into himself and overcomes the wrath by the blessing. This faith is the fruit of the grace that comes through the testimony of the Body of Christ on earth. Yet it cannot be confined to that. Paul speaks of the faith of Abraham, citing him as the architect of faith. There is little evidence in the New Testament about this kind of faith possible outside the Church. Understandably so, for in this period the Church was fighting to establish its own identity and validity. Yet there is the implication of an implicit faith in the God who is not bound. "There are other sheep of mine, not belonging to this fold" (John 10:16). A redeeming Love can plant the seeds of inarticulate faith where it chooses. Our task is not to speculate about that but to seize and share what is offered to us. Where one "has been given much, much will be expected" (Luke 12:48).

HELL AND DAMNATION

What is the fate of the faithless? What is the destiny of those who have turned a deaf ear to the Word, a shut eye to the Vision? As in other Christian teachings, so here, too, Storytellers have been drawn in two directions each claiming biblical warrants. Each has a simple and clearcut scenario of the End.

Scenario 1: Light and Darkness

Clearly a majority opinion in traditional Christianity, this view of the End forecasts a double destination for the human race: the faithful go to heaven and everlasting bliss, the faithless go to hell and everlasting damnation. The saved receive their reward in the Kingdom and the sinners receive what is their due, the fires of eternal judgment. By a strict reading of the arithmetic of both the New Testament ("straight is the gate and narrow the way and few there be that find it") and the empirical calculation that only a small portion of world's population have even the opportunity for the choice of explicit faith, this option must be prepared to consign the better part of the human race to the curse of everlasting punishment.

This perspective has been expressed in a variety of ways, from hard to soft line interpretations. In its harsher form double destination can mean double predestination, in which God foreordains some to eternal life and others to eternal death. In its milder form the distinction is made between the eternal salvation of the faithful and a cessation of existence, the nothingness of death, for the unworthy.

Scenario 1 is able to assemble a set of New Testament texts that speak of hell and damnation for the sinner and heaven for the saved, the future division of the sheep and the goats, the fires of eternal hell for those who in this life have gone astray (Matt. 25:31–46; 10:28; Luke 16:19–31; John 3:36; 5:25–29; II Thess. 1:9; Heb. 6:8; 9:27; Rev. 14:10–11). Built on these texts, and shaped by a theory of punishment and reward which gives tit for tat, Scenario 1 assigns to some a destiny of Light and casts others into the outer Darkness.

Scenario 2: Light and No Darkness

Clearly a minority opinion in historic Christianity but a popular option on the margins of the Church, this view is rooted less in biblical texts and more in an appeal to the logic of love and also in a more sanguine assessment of human nature. It holds that there is no hell and damnation but only a future of love and light. There are no damned for all shall be saved.

This belief in universal salvation and no damnation—"universalism"—is usually associated with a confidence in the essential virtue of human beings. If human nature is basically good, there is no reason for dire forecasts of hell and damnation. We deserve a better fate. Moreover, a God of love would not treat us in such fashion, not even those of us who break the moral laws. "God forgives. That's his business."

This view also appears in a variety of forms. It is to be found in the simple Deism that links immortality with God and virtue as the essence of religion, and assumes that a heavenly immortality is our immediate and common destination. Or it may appear in more sophisticated forms of "neo-universalism" which have a much more critical view of human nature and a more sober understanding of the judgment of God than conventional universalism, but believe that after Calvary and Easter all the world has been saved.

Scenario 3: Light Overcoming Darkness

At many points along the way in our narration of the Christian Story we have found a polarization between reductionist views and the search of an excluded middle that holds in creative tension themes that would prefer to be autonomous and finally imperialistic. We meet this duality again on the present question and strive to hold the elements of each together in productive unity.

As often is the case, the excluded alternative is more elusive and difficult to state than the trim and simple, and therefore oversimple, polarities. Especially so is this true with regard to the third eschatological option. Because it has to do with what is yet to be, talk about it must carry the same modesty and mystery appropriate to the subject of eschatology as a whole. The modesty is increased and the mystery deepened in this aspect of eschatology by two additional considerations: 1) The biblical material to which we go for final perspective moves in two different directions. Depending on the texts, a case can be made for certain themes in both scenarios. Apparently it is not given to the biblical seers to penetrate this ultimate veil. 2) In dealing with the future, and eminently so with the ultimate Future, the sovereign freedom of God is intrinsic to the Christian Story. God will be who God will be. For us to prescribe in advance how that freedom will be exercised is a violation of that prerogative. All our projections here, as they are built from the New Testament and from the thrust of the Christian Story itself, stand under what we might call this eschatological proviso: God will be who God will be. For these two reasons, therefore, Scenario 3 is not a disclosure of what shall be, but a hoping for what *might* be. All our ruminations here about the destiny of the faithless and loveless must be put in this context of *Christian hoping*.

Scenario 1 is right in its serious assessment of the reality of sin and its demand for accountability. The righteousness of God is no simpering indulgence that overlooks the horror of human sin and its assaults on the divine intention. We are responsible for our turning away from the Light and our own plunge into darkness. There is judgment on our pride, punishment for our faithlessness and idolatry.

But Scenario 1 fails to hold this necessary emphasis on judgment in dialectical relationship with the thrust of the Christian Story. The forward momentum of the saga is toward the fulfillment of the divine purpose. To believe in that end when "God is all in all" is to affirm that there is no last resisting rampart, no unconquered territory. The biblical end is one in which all enemies are put under Christ's feet (I Cor. 15:26) and "all" points toward, in the words of the hymn, "death of death and hell's destruction." How is it possible to declare this kind of final victory of the Lord of Lords and King of Kings and still maintain the fact of accountability and punishment? We shall presently explore this difficult but crucial excluded middle. (See also Matt. 19:28; John 12:32; Acts 3:21; I Cor. 3:13–15; 15:22–28; Eph. 1:9–10; Phil. 2:10–11; I Tim. 2:4; II Pet. 3:9, 13.)

Scenario 2 is right in its instinctive resistance to the horrendous assumption of Scenario 1, that God creates a human race only to consign it in large measure to everlasting perdition. But this loving scenario contesting a loveless one is finally too naive about both the virtue of humanity and the indulgence of its Maker. It does not measure the depths of sin in the human heart and the accountability to God for this lethal resistance. It does not know how profoundly the heart of God has been broken by this breach of faith. The righteousness of God holds humanity responsible for its abuse of freedom, and that means the coming of the darkness of punishment for those who have turned aside. Yet how can the love of God that projects the Vision of Shalom and the power of God to keep the promise of fulfilling it be reconciled with the manifest conclusion that sin shall not go unpunished by the righteousness of God? We face again the quest for a way of affirming the kernel truths in each scenario.

One basic clue to finding that way is a self-awareness of how the *setting* of the Church's thinking about its beliefs has influenced the way the Christian Story is perceived and told. Enlightenment views of human nature and destiny have obviously contributed to the universalism of Scenario 2. What is not often acknowledged, however, is that cultural assumptions have also had their effect on the understanding of punishment to be found in Scenario 1. The milieu of traditional theories of hell and damnation has been judicial and penal practice of a punitive and retributive nature. Punishment was conceived as a way of paying back in equivalency for the harm the criminal had done to society. Little or no thought was given as to how that punishment could be shaped toward the rehabilitation of the offender for return to responsible participation in society. And so the New Testament themes of punishment were read in the light of the culture's practice of retributive justice.

That there are other ways of accountability and other methods of executing punishment than the punitive practices of another day is a common assumption in contemporary penology. Indeed current ideas of rehabilitation and restoration may well have had their rise out of fermenting work of the Christian vision of redemption challenging secular notions of retribution. Be that as it may, the eschatological affirmation of the Christian faith cannot be controlled by cultural categories, past or present. But the change in these categories serves to make us more critical of the too easy assumptions that the Last Judgment must look just like the judgment rendered in a sixteenth-century British court or prison or on a scaffold.

Yet another clue to avoiding the oversimplification of Scenarios 1 and 2 is to be found in the time line of the Christian Story. As in the parallel question of theodicy discussed earlier, so too here we have to do with an open Love which leaves the partner the maneuvering room of freedom, but a stubborn Love which persists in the unswerving pursuit of the Vision, and an empowered Love which will not relent until the Hound has ended the chase. Thus evolves a Story of the moves and counter-moves of God in the reach toward fulfillment of the Goal. And this divine persistence reaches beyond the limits of this world, as an ancient tradition recognizes when the declaration in the Apostles' Creed that Christ "descended into hell" was understood to mean that there Christ preached to those who had not yet heard the Word so they too might be given the chance to participate in the fulfillment of all things.

The disengagement of punishment from its retributive context and the affirmation of the Christian faith as a Story that takes time seriously and moves to the real fulfillment of the promise of redemption are elements in our third scenario. In this view judgment is utterly real and punishment of sin on the Day of judgment ineluctable. Indeed, the light of that day brings with it the fire of the divine Love, as is suggested by the visual and verbal art forms in Christian tradition. But fire can cleanse. The fires of the divine love can purge the dross and fashion new forms. While there are no biblical warrants for the teaching of purgatory as it is held in traditional Roman Catholicism, the passage to which it points (I Cor. 3:13–15) does speak of the last Day's fire that "will test the worth of each man's work." In an even more important reflection set in the middle of his long discourse on eschatological hope in the fifteenth chapter of I Corinthians, Paul speaks of the acts in the final drama of redemption which thrust toward a single destination, yet not without the pains and progression of chastening conflict: "As in Adam all men die, so in Christ all will be brought to life; but each in his own proper place: Christ the firstfruits, and afterwards, at his coming, those who belong to Christ. Then comes the end, when he delivers up the kingdom to God the Father, after abolishing every kind of domination, authority, and power. For he is destined to reign until God has put all enemies under his feet; and the last

enemy to be abolished is death . . . and thus God will be all in all"
(I Cor. 15:22–27, 28).

The New Testament passages that portray in vivid colors the
judgment on sin make unmistakably clear our accountability to the
righteous will of God. Written in the midst of persecution from
without and the risk of defections from within, they serve as warn-
ing and prophylactics, heightened in rhetoric by the life and death
circumstances and the perils to the survival of the faith community
itself. The stridency of these admonitions which not infrequently
call to decision with the promise of everlasting curse and everlasting
blessing should not prevent us from searching for the truth within
the hyperbole. And to see that truth as the prospect of the lasting
but not everlasting fires of divine Love does not take away from the
same evangelical Word that is part of the Church's mission today.
On its positive side, the offer of salvation by grace through faith is
the invitation to participate *now* in the eternal life that shall be then.
And its refusal is a reckoning *now* with the judgment that is and
shall be until all things are put under the feet of Jesus Christ.

The judgment on that Day in which the sun of Shalom rises
over all is one in which the fires of liberation and reconciliation
refine and its light so burns away the shadows that the last darkness
is overcome. The God whose "will it is that all men should find
salvation and come to know the truth" (I Tim. 2:4) has the power of
the Holy Spirit to keep that promise and accomplish that Dream.
The agony of this final contest of light and darkness cannot be
understated, as the proponents of Scenario 1 have been at pains to
point out. There *is* hell and judgment. But the last word in the
Christian Story is not that of a half-accomplished purpose, but of a
promise kept and a Vision that becomes Reality. Eternal hell is the
burning love of the eternal God, not everlasting death. The God of
power defeats even this last enemy, the death of the Dream, and
brings Light and *everlasting Life.* This is a Christian hope, *tempered
by the eschatological proviso*, yet shaped by the promise and power
of the God who will be all in all.

EVERLASTING LIFE

As we began the Christian Story with the Vision of God, so we
conclude there. In the end, the Vision becomes Reality. The promise

of Shalom is kept. The world that God brought to be out of the divine Hope reaches its fulfillment, the Kingdom comes, and God's will *is* done on earth as it is in heaven.

If the wages of sin and evil are death, then liberation from these foes is life. And their destruction is *everlasting life*. How can humanity still trapped in the valley of the shadow of sin, evil, and death understand what this Light and Life mean? For our dimmed vision there are the translucent metaphors of Revelation. Here in the final accounting of the final event we receive some illumination, albeit in the stained glass colors and shapes of this terrain. The rich imagery of the Apocalypse, to be taken for what it is, symbols from this world that let in the light of the world to come (not seeing "face to face"), gives us our clues. They express the reconciliation of all things which issues from the liberation of all things.

1) Reconciliation of Humanity with God. "How blest are those whose hearts are pure; they shall see God" (Matt. 5:8). When the purifying work of liberation is completed, its gift to us is the vision of God. John portrays this beatific vision in the richest images at hand: "There in heaven stood a throne, and on the throne sat one whose appearance was like the gleam of jasper and cornelian; and round the throne was a rainbow, bright as an emerald" (Rev. 4:3). Now the long-blind eyes are opened and we behold this ineffable Light. We face the One from whom we had turned, so that we may live and love in communion with God.

To see the Envisioner is to see also the Vision, to know its suffering and its victory. "I saw standing in the very middle of the throne . . . a Lamb with the marks of slaughter upon him" (Rev. 4:6). And to see by the Spirit the Father and Son is to exult "Thou art worthy, O Lord our God, to receive glory and honor and power. . . . Worthy is the Lamb, the Lamb that was slain, to receive all power and wealth, wisdom and might, honor and glory and praise!" (Rev. 4:11; 5:12). To see the Light is to celebrate. The joy of thanksgiving, portended in our eucharistic worship, is the service of worship and praise that issues from seeing.

2) Reconciliation of Humanity. Seeing the Light is seeing *by* the Light as well; the biblical portraiture of fulfillment has a horizontal as well as a vertical dimension. We see in the Light of the glory of God the brothers and sisters in Christ. The estranged shall

dwell in unity: "By its light shall the nations walk, and the kings of earth shall bring into it all their splendor" (Rev. 21:24). The Vision given to us is described in Revelation not only in interpersonal metaphors of life together in joy and love but in social and political images. The powers as well as persons of this world will come together, give obedience and praise to their Maker and Redeemer, and become agents of reconciliation instead of alienation. "He showed me the holy city of Jerusalem coming down out of heaven from God. It shone with the glory of God; it had the radiance of some priceless jewel, like a jasper, clear as crystal" (Rev. 21:10–11). The description of pearly gates and golden streets, disdained by both the spiritual and secular, are in fact important symbols of the earthy and corporate hopes of the Christian faith. Nothing is too worldly for the Vision of God, for ultimate redemption includes the bringing of all things under the feet of Christ, including the principalities of this world which have used their power and glory for their own ends. Now the kingdoms of this world shall give way to the Kingdom of God, and the new city will displace the tyranny and injustice of the old metropolis. We have noted earlier the ethical imperatives that this vision of a new city generates as we are called to set up signs in this world to the just and peaceable Kingdom to come. Thus the book of Revelation maintains the communal, corporate, and structural hopes of the prophetic tradition of the Old Testament. The new city and Kingdom which are to come are the world of Shalom in which swords are beaten into plowshares and spears into pruning hooks and there shall no more be the trampling of the poor or the waging of war.

While the portrayal of everlasting life juxtaposes the wrongs and hates of the world to the justice and love to come, there are continuities as well as discontinuities in Christian hope. There are signs of life as well as the pallor of death in this world, earnests of the Kingdom which are not destroyed but ennobled and fulfilled at the Consummation. One such firstfruit of the Kingdom is the conjugal union spoken of eschatologically in the marriage service: "So live together in this world that in the world to come you may have life everlasting." While on the one hand we know that "at the resurrection men and women do not marry" (Matt. 22:30), on the other the use of conjugal and familial metaphors to express the ultimate suggest that the richest unities in this life will participate in the final reconciliation. Such union is a candle lit in a dark world. When the Day comes it will not be extinguished but drawn into a larger radiance. "Love never ends."

3) The Reconciliation of Nature. The Apocalypse places "living creatures" around the throne of God in its vision of things to come. And John declares, "I saw a new heaven and a new earth" (Rev. 21:1), a revivified nature that includes crystal waters, abundant crops, and flourishing forests whose "leaves . . . serve for the healing of the nations" (Rev. 22:2). Thus the New Testament continues and completes the prophetic vision of Shalom in nature in which the wolf and the lamb lie down together, the child is a friend of the snake, and the desert blooms. The creation no longer groans but rejoices, for "I heard every created thing in heaven and on earth and under the earth and in the sea, all that is in them, crying, 'Praise and honor, glory and might, to him who sits on the throne and the Lamb for ever and ever!'" (Rev. 5:13).

God's is a cosmic Vision. Its fulfillment is the restoration of all things. The ecological imperative of the Christian faith is grounded in this Hope of God for the created order. As with the healing of the nations, so with the ministry of compassion to a wounded earth, we are beckoned to set up Franciscan signs here and now to the new creation.

The vision of an everlasting life that brings an end to the death we see about us is portrayed in that panorama of liberation and reconciliation lifted before the eyes of faith at Christian burial: "I saw a new heaven and a new earth, for the first heaven and the first earth had vanished, and there was no longer any sea. I saw the holy city, new Jerusalem, coming down out of heaven from God, made ready like a bride adorned for her husband. I heard a loud voice proclaiming from the throne: 'Now at last God has his dwelling among men! He will dwell among them and they shall be his people, and God himself will be with them. He will wipe every tear from their eyes; there shall be an end to death, and to mourning and crying and pain; for the old order has passed away!" (Rev. 21:1–4).

AFTER DEATH?

What happens to us after death? As confident chronologies and cosmologies about the end of time proliferate in an era uncertain about its future, so too do self-assured descriptions of our destiny after the last heartbeat. Postmortem existence is the favorite playing field of the cult and the occult. Its territory is carefully mapped by mystical cognoscenti, many of whom claim to have precognition or periodic reports from those who have arrived before us. Compared to the charts and graphs of these seers, the small candle lit in this darkness by the Christian faith seems unimpressive indeed. But as with the last things, so also here with the next-to-last things, we do see through a glass darkly, and mystery and modesty is our best light.

The pattern we have discerned in other Christian teachings, being pulled from two sides—spiritual and physical—is also manifest here in the penultimate arena of eschatology. Two very different scenarios have emerged around these poles, ones that have claimed Christian credentials as vigorously as have their christological counterparts, Docetism and Ebionism. Scenario 1: The first and more dominant point of view declares that upon death that indestructible segment of the self detaches itself from the body and returns to God. This is the doctrine of the immortality of the soul. It comes in a variety of formulations. The merging of the soul with Deity can be conceived in more impersonal terms on the analogy of the drop of water being absorbed into the ocean of Spirit. Or it can be interpreted in more personal terms as the communion of the soul with God. Very often, but not always, this destiny of the self is considered the final one, with little or no connection to the eschatological themes of resurrection, return, and judgment, as is pointed out in Oscar Cullmann's famous study of the question "The resurrection of the body or the immortality of the soul?" Cullmann and many other biblical scholars have underscored the fact that the idea of the immortality of the soul can be traced to Greek philosophical assumptions which are negative about the world of time and space, matter and the body, and therefore rejoice in the release of the soul from this "prisonhouse of the flesh."

Though the attempts are constant to force this teaching of the immortality of the soul into the Christian system, so much so that many pulpits in an acculturated Christianity offer it as the yearly Easter diet, it must finally be declared indigestible. Christian faith has too profound and critical an understanding of human spirit to consider it the "divine" segment of the self worthy of immortality, and too high a view of the body to disdain and separate it from our final destiny. Both something less and something more must be said about our penultimate and ultimate futures.

Scenario 2: In recent theological exploration of the subject of eschatology, a forceful criticism of the immortality of the soul has been made and what seems to be the clear alternative offered in its place, one that has also appeared before in Christian teaching. Thus it is boldly asserted on the basis of the psychosomatic unity of body and soul that characterizes Hebrew thought, and the belief that the eschatological resurrection of the body at the end of history is the definitive Christian teaching, that "when you're dead, you're dead." Upon death our body and soul, being inseparable, disintegrate and die to wait upon the end when we shall be reconstituted and resurrected in the flesh. Sundry interpretations of "secular Christianity" are glad to have some traditional allies at this point, for they too affirm that death is the end, the difference from the neoorthodox eschatology being that there is no talk of a final resurrection. There are as many variations on this theme as there are in the first scenario, with traditional interpretations stressing that the time between death and the end is as a "twinkling of the eye," and they often use the analogy of sleep, as in several New Testament texts (Luke 8:52; I Cor. 15:20; II Pet. 3:4). Some have spoken of the continuance of the dead "in the mind of God," or more recently in the language of computer technology in the "memory bank" of God available for "printout" on the last day.

The criticisms by Scenario 2 of Scenario 1 are to the point. And its affirmation of the resurrection of the dead as the end is surely a faithful reading of the Christian Story. But there is a theme in Scenario 1 which echoes some notes in that saga which are drastically muted in Scenario 2. It has to do with the bond forged by grace through faith with the believer. By faith we live and see the Light. Such a union with God is described in the Gospel of John as "eternal life" (John 3:36; 5:24; 6:40). What is eternal is indestructible. This bond cannot be broken. Death does not sever the tie that binds us to eternity.

There is a "putting on of immortality" by faith active in love upon which the life on the earth does not intrude nor can death interrupt. Slogans like "when you're dead, you're dead" do not do justice to this grace from which "neither life nor death" can separate us.

How can we give expression to truths embedded in both of these partial perspectives: the unsunderable bond of eternal life that persists after death, yet the fulfillment that awaits the last day? The "asleep" passages of the New Testament point to a proper modesty about the time between our death and the end. Yet the "awake" passages (Luke 16:19–31; 23:43; Rev. 6:9) bear witness to a richer reality than the reductionism of Scenario 2. And as John Mbiti and other Third World theologians remind us, the classic Christian teaching about "the communion of saints" is too easily forgotten by a secular Western theology and must be recovered in our dialogue with cultures that have a sense of relationship to the dead. The "cloud of witnesses" who have gone before us in some mysterious sense still surround us as they make their own pilgrimage toward Shalom.

Our metaphor of light is a clue to how we might perceive the Already–Not Yet paradox which is so difficult to conceive. The light of the divine Vision shines from the end of history toward us. But this is no cold and distant radiance. Its rays penetrate our terrain. It comes as revivifying warmth. Light shining *on us* is also power working *in us.* Just as personal salvation is not only pardon but also power, justification productive of sanctification, so the eschatological favor of the ultimate future pours into our penultimate future as power *now* over death—eternal life on earth and after death. Those empowered to see the Light and walk in the Light traverse the shadowy valley in hope. As a summary that both honors the mystery yet affirms the majesty of the eternal life which death cannot destroy, it is impossible to improve on Paul's own ecstatic utterance. For this reason it is the climax of the service of Christian burial: "Who shall separate us from the love of Christ? Shall tribulation, or distress, or persecution, or famine, or nakedness, or peril, or sword? . . . No, in all these things we are more than conquerors through him who loved us. For I am sure that neither death, nor life, nor angels, nor principalities, nor things present, nor things to come, nor powers, nor height, nor depth, nor anything else in all creation, will be able to separate us from the love of God in Christ Jesus our Lord" (Rom. 8:35, 37–39 RSV).

HISTORICAL HOPE

If Light streams from the future toward us *after* death, so it does *before* death. Jesus insistently struck this note in his own teaching about the Kingdom of God. Here in *this world* there are signs of the coming of Shalom, as the sick are healed, the blind see, the captives are released. Easter confirms and transfigures these intimations of the coming Kingdom. The resurrection is the foundation of Christian hope for portents and earnests of the Not Yet.

When speaking of historical hope, the doctrines of salvation and consummation merge. Eschatology at this point lies on the boundary of soteriology. The chapter of the Christian Story on salvation speaks of the thermal current of grace flowing in the lives of persons and in the structures of history and rhythms of nature. The eschatological chapter points forward to the possibilities of that grace in all the little tomorrows that stretch toward the final Tomorrow. Christian hope seizes this prospective work of the Holy Spirit. It is its charter for dreaming dreams and seeing visions.

That hope includes the possibilities of personal growth in grace, the pilgrimage of Christian turning to and walking in the Light that we have earlier explored. But it reaches far beyond to look for and hope for what the Spirit can and will do in the environment of nature and the theater of history. Thus both the givens and the perils of nature do not confine or define the future. That future is open to possibilities of historical Shalom in which the blind do see, the deaf hear, the lame walk, and the dead are raised, as dreamed and envisioned in the still blue sky forecasts of medical and biomedical futurist. And that same tomorrow is not closed to the social and political hoper who is able to say with Martin Luther King, Jr., "I have a dream!" Visions of liberation and reconciliation in the world are part of what penultimate hope is all about. It has taken the "theology of hope" to remind us of this kind of Light and Power which penetrated our human future.

Eschatological dreaming for our personal, social, and natural futures is lured by the Great Vision but it is also grounded in reality.

We live in the half light of the Already–Not Yet, at Dawn not High Noon. The last chapter does not tell of the building of the Kingdom of God by us in this world. The Commonwealth awaits the coming of and culminating Work of its Lord. As the Spirit gives us strength to erect signposts to the New Jerusalem, we struggle with the powers of sin, evil, and death that continue their harassments. Christian hope, therefore, is *sober* hope aware of the impossibilities as well as the possibilities of the historical future. Its visionary realism knows that the best and brightest of human advancements are plagued with ambiguity, afflicted by the temptations to arrogant power, corruptible and mortal. It tempers the giddy expectations of both the technological futurist and the political visionary with sobriety about sin, evil, and death. And it warns the moral and spiritual perfectionist about self-righteous fury and fanaticism. But visionary realism is not cynicism. While perceiving the shadows ahead in the corridor of the future, it knows that Jesus Christ has torn down the "No Exit" sign at its end and shouldered upon its dark door. While not thrust wide open to instant sunshine everywhere, there is a crack of light in the historical future. The powers of darkness do not control tomorrow or Tomorrow. Despair about the future paralyzes. Hope mobilizes. The eyes of Christian faith enable the seer to dare to hope and to act.

EPILOGUE

God

"Immortal, invisible God only wise
in light inaccessible hid from our eyes."

"I am the Alpha and the Omega, says the Lord God, who is and who was and who is to come" (Rev. 1:8). Our telling of the Christian Story began with the Prologue's portrayal of the eternal origins of the drama of salvation in the Godhead. As the Story has unfolded, what was implicit in its beginning has become explicit. The character of the God who envisions and empowers takes form in the deeds that fulfill the Vision. It is, therefore, appropriate to go beyond the sketch of the nature of God given in the Prologue and paint a portrait of the chief Actor who emerges from the drama. While traditional theology positions the doctrine of God early in its development, anticipating themes from subsequently expounded beliefs (for example, the Person and Work of Christ), here in conformity with our narrative structure we have chosen to use Prologue and Epilogue as the appropriate places to introduce and conclude reflection about the nature of Deity. In the Prologue the sparse trinitarian framework gives us resources to launch the epic. The Epilogue draws upon the rich material of the history of God so recounted to fill out that picture.

The inner-trinitarian Life in which the Christian drama originates—Envisioner, Vision, and Power—expresses itself in missions commensurate with the modes of its being. Envisioning takes form as the parental work of creating and preserving, as we have seen in the chapters on Creation, Fall, and Covenant. The Vision is enacted in the liberating and reconciling mission of the Son at Bethlehem, in Galilee, on Calvary, and on Easter morning. And the redeeming work of the Holy Spirit, the Power of God, is to be seen in the birth of the Church, in the rush of the winds of salvation, and in the consummation of the purposes of God.

The first mission of the Trinity includes both the bringing to be of the divine partner, the world, and its preservation. The divine creativity brings to be the things that were not. Its grace is revelatory as well as formative, for the Light of God's purposes shines on nature and in humanity. The paternal and maternal labors of the Envisioner also keep company with the world in its rebellion against the divine intention. Thus Providence supports the Vision in the maelstrom of history and nature and sets limits to the destruction that the powers of sin, evil, and death would wreak upon the world.

The mission of the Son, the eternal Light, comes to a burning point in the Incarnation and Atonement. The Vision becomes flesh and discloses the intention of God in the life and ministry of Jesus, is assailed by the full hatred of the world on Golgotha, makes the wrath of humanity serve the purposes of God by turning the cross into the moment when suffering Love defeats sin and evil, and finally brings life to the death of Hope on resurrection morning. Liberation from the enemies and reconciliation of the friends take place in the Person and Work of the Son of God.

The Holy Spirit brings the liberation and reconciliation accomplished for the world in Jesus Christ *to* the world and works them *in* the world from Pentecost to Consummation. The doctrine of the Spirit, pneumatology, has been implicit in our charting of the work of the Power of God in the sending of the beams of Light and Life from the Easter horizon across the world. The Spirit makes the Vision known and its influence felt in the birth, life, and witness of the Church, the flow of its saving grace in persons, history, and nature, and in the final coming of Shalom. Its work is the effective redemption from sin, evil, and death in the time between the Times and at the End of time.

While the operations of the triune God manifest themselves in these three great divisions of the Christian Story by the foreground activity of one or another Person, the mission of each interpenetrates the others. ("The works of the Trinity are one."—Anselm.) The Vision of God is partner to creation and companion to Providence, and is active in redemption as we have noted in different movements of the drama. The Spirit is the Power that brings newness to be at the beginning as well as at the end, and conceives the Son at the center of the Story. And in all the actions of Vision and Power is to be found the presence of the Envisioner.

As the Tale unfolds, certain attributes of God emerge which characterize all of the modes of the divine being. We shall identify them as the formal and material qualities. The academic nature of this kind of cataloguing grates on the proper sense of mystery that should attend our talk about God. Let all these descriptions be understood, therefore, as modest glances toward a Light whose inner reaches are finally "hid from our eyes."

FORMAL QUALITIES

Subjectivity

The God of the Christian Story is a Subject. The events we have traced rise out of a Self that purposes and chooses. The ground of these happenings and of all being is the inner spontaneity of the divine Subject. The forevision of God and the deeds done to consummate that intention bespeak freedom, awareness, self-direction. Here is the living, willing Spirit, and therefore the *personal* God (Exod. 3:14; Eph. 1:9, 11).

A cloud of ambiguity envelops many discussions about the divine subjectivity. A strong and important mystical tradition, in alliance with Hebraic and Reformed concern to protect the sovereignty of God, declares that all anthropomorphisms, including that of human selfhood, are not finally worthy of the God who is above all our formulas. That is eminently right. Both mystery and majesty require us to say about subjectivity, and all the other qualities we attribute to God, that they are analogies which faith employs to describe what is ultimately indescribable. However, either a certain kind of secularization or an extra-biblical mysticism disguised in these proper modesties also disavows anthropomorphism and counsels us to translate personal metaphors ("necessary for piety") into more literal philosophical descriptions of the divine, such as the absolute, all, depth, process, ground, etc. There is both methodological and theological error here. Methodologically, it assumes that faith supplies only the emotive symbols and philosophy the cognitive meanings. But faith is, as we have noted, both *assensus* and *fiducia,* both *assent* and *trust;* it uses *meaningful* metaphors which carry within them crucial, albeit not exhaustive, cognitive implications. Moreover, what are declared to be literal philosophical terms are themselves also metaphors, drawn from areas of experience that are consistently sub-personal.

While these might be reinterpreted themselves in personal terms, as in some forms of process philosophy, when the fundamental experiential matrix for the concept is sub-personal the word communicates more than that assertion with great difficulty. Theologically, the reserve about personal metaphors does not mean the denial of the real subjectivity of God. It signifies that while *at least* personal, God is inexhaustibly *more so.* God is not less than our own self-directing, purposive, free, choosing selves. The God of the Christian Story is an envisioning, acting Self, the abysmal depths and plenitude of whose subjectivity can only be hinted at by our frail figures.

Transcendence

All that we have said about God the Subject could be interpreted to mean a macrocosmic Person complete with body parts, as indeed Deity has been portrayed in three level cosmologies and in Mormon and Swedenborgian traditions. While the word *transcendence* is employed to mean a variety of things, a common refrain adaptable to our context is the understanding of God as incorporeal. The God who acts in our history is not one being among other beings, but Another who transcends space and time. God is a Spirit. The divine Other stands over against the world even while being a full participant in its history (John 4:24; Col. 1:15; I Tim. 1:17).

Transcendence includes two classic attributes: *infinity* and *eternity.* As Infinite, the God of the Story is not exhausted by finitude. God is not in space but space is in God. As Eternal, God is not in time but time is in God. While it is common to express this transcendence of space-time by speaking of God as "outside of space" and/or God as "before and after" time, both statements assert what they are seeking to deny, for they use spatial and temporal metaphors (outside, before, after) to express the non-spatiality and non-temporality of God. "Apophatic theology" may be the best way to deal with this enigma, using a negative statement to point toward our meaning: God is not spatialized or time-bound (Deut. 32:40; Job 11:7–9; Ps. 90:2; Matt. 6:13).

Immanence

While God does not have a body in the Christian Story, the psychosomatic unity of human selfhood does provide an analogy that expresses the immanence of God in the world. As human subjectivity expresses itself in, with, and throughout our bodies, so the transcendent subjectivity of God is immanent in the patterns, processes, and events of this world. The Christian narrative is unintelligible apart from the assumption of the busy presence of the purposing God in nature, selves, historical happenings and structures, and in a singular fashion in the Person and Work of Jesus Christ. Immanence is an abstract label for the sum of these involvements: the warm currents of grace that flow in the cosmos, holding it together, bringing it to new levels of creativity and wholeness, resisting the powers inimical to it, calling and claiming each individual through the traces of the Vision which we have not been able to expel from our consciousness, setting boundaries to the destructive powers of evil in history and nature, acting in the events and illuminations of Israel, taking flesh in Jesus Christ, displaying and living out the Vision and finally overcoming the assaults directed toward it, empowering the Church to see the Vision and bear witness to it, and coursing through the world with signs and portents that point toward the final coming together of all things. Immanence is our description of these happenings that were, and are, and are to be in our time and space. In this Story God has not willed to be God without, this relationship with us and participation in our world.

Immutability

The unchangeableness of God has been vigorously called into question in recent theological discussion. "Immutability" suggests the marks of the Greek philosophical climate with its high valuation of the dispassionate and ahistorical. As we have noted, this *apatheia* does not cohere with affirmations about the passion of Christ or the vulnerable responsive love of God intrinsic to the Story.

For all that, the quality of *steadfastness* at the heart of this ancient insistence on the unchanging nature of God is part and parcel of our Tale. While the philosophical categories and aristocratic cultural models of passionlessness do not adequately convey the meaning of the immutability, it is important to understand what they intended. Ancient gods were volatile and idiosyncratic (reflecting cultural dispositions and temperament). Classic theology was concerned to distinguish its understanding of God from these tendencies, and did so by seizing upon other metaphors in order to portray the undeviating thrust of God toward the fulfillment of the divine Vision. These cultural borrowings, while preserving the note of constancy, added to it the idea of impassibility and prevented the biblical understanding of divine vulnerability and relatedness from reaching theological consciousness. About this we shall say more presently. For now it is important to underscore the divine perseverance. God will not be deflected from the course. While the ways of pursuing the purpose may vary according to the resistance mounted by the world, the divine mind of Shalom does not change, and the intention to pursue this Vision to its end point remains unswerving. This Story is about a stubborn God, steadfast in purpose, immutable (Ps. 102:27; Mal. 3:6; James 1:17).

All-Sufficiency

The Christian Story discloses that God is able to accomplish the divine purpose. Deity has all that is necessary to fulfill the Vision. Herein is the belief in the *all-sufficiency* of God. The conviction has customarily been expressed in terms of three "omnis"—omnipresence, omniscience, and omnipotence.

Not infrequently traditional theology has expressed the all-sufficiency of God in terms of a speculatively established idea of what supreme Being ought to be like. Thus notions of power as it is manifest in human experience become the touchstone for defining divine power. Because we are limited to what we know in this world for our metaphors about God, we can do no other than begin with this raw data of human experience. But the Christian idea of God is not finally derived from general human experience, but from the deeds of God done in the midst of that experience. Therefore, our language about God undergoes a transformation in the light of that special history of God with us. We do not extrapolate the meaning of divine all-sufficiency from what we reason would be the highest form of it in our common life. Rather we interpret all-ness in terms of what God has done, is doing, and will do in this biography. All-sufficiency then does not mean a human quality to the nth power, but all-sufficiency as God defines it by the deeds done to accomplish the divine end. We shall interpret the omnis from within that framework provided by the Story.

Omnipresence: "Where can I flee from thy presence. . ." (Ps. 139:7). God is everywhere we choose to go in flight and in need. God tracks us to the ends of the earth. We are never out of reach. God moves in all things to achieve the Vision. Thus nature as well as history, the cosmos in its extent and depth, are penetrated by the Presence. Our discussion of the immanence of God has touched upon the range of God through the vastness of outer and inner space. God is there actively bringing Shalom to be. Thus God has all-sufficient presence to assure the divine purpose (Jer. 23:23–24; Acts 17:27–28).

Omniscience: God has all-sufficient knowledge to assure the divine purpose. The figure of the all-seeing Eye has been a favorite one in Christian art and interpretation. All that ever has been, touching the divine intention, is within the divine purview (Matt. 10:29–30; Acts 2:23; Rom. 11:33). To believe in the resurrection of the dead implies the preservation in the divine sensibility of all that comes within the range of that concern.

The divine knowledge in its all-sufficiency must include not only the awareness of things that have been, and the things that are, but also the things that will be. Knowledge includes foreknowledge, forevision. At this point we confront a major enigma. Does the foreknowledge of God mean that all we do in our presumed free-dom is charted and known beforehand? In its strictest construction the omniscience of God includes an omnipotence of God that has foreordained a yet-to-be-executed pattern which is therefore known by the divine omniscience. In a more modest form, the freedom to choose is really ours, but the all-seeing Eye knows what that choice is to be. If what is to be is to be, the distinction between these two scenarios seems to be little more than verbal.

Genuine freedom of choice in response to the divine beckoning requires that specifics of choice must have their own integrity, and therefore are hidden by God's choice, even from the divine Eye. Does the belief in the omniscience of God and the all-sufficiency of the divine knowledge require the kind of total exposure assumed by what is usually meant by foreknowledge? That would be so if foreknowledge were our human kind of knowing speculatively extended to its limits. But we have said this rational projection will not control our understanding of the attributes of God. Rather the frame of reference will be the Story as it unfolds. By this biblical criterion, foreknowledge means the grasp by God of the future in which the world shall be won to the divine purpose. God both foreknows and foreordains that Shalom shall be. The foreknowledge of God is grounded in the confidence God has in the Power of God, the Holy Spirit, to fulfill the eternal purpose of God. Further, that foreknowledge must include the range of options the world has to respond to the divine invitation, and therefore the resources God has to deal with those responses. The omniscience of God in this context is the foreknowledge of the possibilities of choice, the scenarios of divine response and the ultimate outcome of the struggle between the human No and the divine Yes. To believe in the all-sufficiency of God's knowledge to pursue the Story to its successful completion is to be prepared to affirm this much. What further is insisted upon has more to do with speculation about the Deity than close attention to the Storyline. What has been added over and above these affirmations grows out of a wedding of Christian faith with cultural assumptions about what "omni-ness" ought to mean and is therefore regularly influenced by imperial models of power. This is eminently true of notions of omnipotence with which we shall presently deal, but its effects are also to be seen here in the understanding of omniscience. Yet any notion of omniscience that takes the Story as its frame of reference must allow for the genuine freedom of the world to maneuver out of the range of the divine reach and for that lively set of moves and counter moves made by God to deal with this flight. All the "omnis" must be understood so as not to constrict the genuine overagainstness of the world as that is described in the divine drama. It is a real drama, and not a marionette show. God has all the knowledge needed to execute the divine purpose.

Omnipotence: "Almighty God. . . ." Intrinsic to Christian spirituality and inseparable from the Christian Story is the belief in the divine omnipotence. As with the other "omnis" we live with the tension between the world's conceptions of all-ness and the understanding of it from the perspective of the Christian faith, or more exactly, how the metaphors of absoluteness drawn from human experience are transmuted by the revelation in Jesus Christ. It is in the question of the omnipotence of God that the significance of this transmutation comes most forcefully home. And it is around the issue of theodicy that the Christian meaning of the power of God takes clearest form.

By extrapolating from a fragmentary human experience of power—the capacity to influence things—we are inclined to interpret omnipotence to mean the power to effect and control all things. In traditional discussions about omnipotence it is recognized, however, that this abstract notion of total power, if pressed to the limit, contradicts certain fundamental assumptions about God. Thus omnipotence cannot mean the power of God to sin, lie, or die, to draw a straighter line than that between two points, to make two and two equal five, and to make wrong right. In these recognitions it is being acknowledged that any power definition must be commensurate with the kind of God at work in this saga.

But there are other givens that also must be taken into account in the refinement of the understanding of omnipotence in Christian context. One of these is the narrative framework for understanding power. If this is a genuine drama, a real struggle, and therefore an unquestioned defiance by the world of God's intention, then omnipotence cannot be conceived as instant control everywhere. The all-ness of power is asserted to be on a time line thrusting toward a goal and climax. The almightiness of Deity is that God *shall* be all in all. And more, that on this time line God is even now thrusting toward this consummation of the divine purpose.

Our inclination to make Deity serve our own ends is such that we will not let this God of the Bible be who this God wills to be. So we smuggle into the Story our own scenarios. In these, God becomes the projection of our conceptions of power. In the ancient world the Oriental potentate furnished the model of omnipotence and so God becomes the one who by fiat and force exercises immediate and universal sway. Assumed here as well, as we are discovering lately, is an implicitly machismo image shaped by masculine self-percep- tions. But the God of the narrative we have explored is the God who is neither an autocratic regent or the lengthened shadow of John Wayne. This Creator gives the world the space and time it needs to be what it will be. This Liberator and Reconciler does not act by force or fiat but by a vulnerable Love. And this Redeemer and Consummator shall be all in all, but only so along a line of the stubborn Love that stretches into eternity itself.

When omnipotence is understood in this framework, and therefore eschatologically, the agonizing question of theodicy is put in correct perspective. Implicit in the traditional formulation of the problem of evil by Epicurus in the third century B.C. was the assumption of divine omnipotence according to the model of im- perial (and masculine) sovereignty. And this assumption has been unquestioned in much of the subsequent discussion of how the power of God, the goodness of God, and the reality of evil can be reconciled. No wonder the insistent question: What kind of God tolerates or ordains such horrendous historical, natural, and per- sonal evil? This quandary assumes the God made in our image of power. The God of this Story, not our own tale, is One whose act of creation comes out of the hope of Shalom which gives freedom to the creature to participate in the divine Vision, to be freely together with God. The power of God expressed in the act of creation was not only the power of creativity, but also of self-limitation. God willed the world to have a fiatless freedom, for in the Dream of God there is no solidarity that is not freely chosen, no community that is not consented to. That is the nature of the divine Love which, by definition, cannot program or robotize its responses. The self-limi- tation of God is the risk taken that the world will say No to the invitation to life together with God. Herein is the vulnerability of God. The history of God and the world in the Christian Story is the tale of what God does about the abuse of that freedom. Its center point is the act of ultimate vulnerability when God plunges into the world at Incarnation and receives the ultimate rebuke on the cross. Yet in so receiving it, God displays the sovereign power of this vulnerable love by overcoming on the cross and in the resurrection the resistance of sin, evil, and death, and beginning the process of winning the world in fact as well as in principle. "The weakness of God is stronger than men" (I Cor. 1:25 RSV). The eschatological faith of the Christian community is the hope that all the recalcitrance of the world shall be met and God shall overcome. This eschatological conquest includes the transformation of time and space and thus the final redemption of the world from sin and evil and their issue, death. The Almighty God is the One who has all the power necessary to fulfill this divine purpose. What kind of power that is—vulnerable Love—and how that power is exercised—on a time line and in a drama—is determined by that data of Christian faith and not our images of potency. The word in the Christian vocabulary for this power is the *Holy Spirit.* God as the Power to fulfill the Vision is the ultimate meaning of omnipotence in the Christian Story, the Spirit of the Son and the Father, and therefore the Spirit of suffering Love.

MATERIAL QUALITIES

Shalom

The purpose that emerges from the events of the Story, the content that fills the formal attributes of God, is the Vision of peace and freedom. Running like a red thread through the narrative is the beckoning of God to the world. This invitation presupposes the freedom of the world to respond, a gift of answerability granted in creation. And it is a gift given with the goal of communion in view. The freely chosen life together of God and the world is the end of this vast adventure.

The clarity of this Vision of the purpose and promise of God comes to us in the prophetic tradition; hence we use the Old Testament word to describe it (Ezek. 34:25–29; Isa. 32:16–17). In the prophet's imagery, the Vision is portrayed against the background of the world's resistance to the divine intent: swords beaten into plowshares, wolf and lamb together, the child with its hand over the viper's nest. Similarly the patriarch's Law is couched in "thou shalt nots" which also assume the resistance of the world. The Vision comes to us in our history with God as rescued from the enemies that have arisen to contest the divine purpose, and as overcoming the alienation that has set in between the world and God. The primal Vision of freedom and peace becomes, after the Fall, the hope of liberation and reconciliation. God's Yes related to the world's No becomes liberation from the bondage of sin, evil, and death and the reconciliation of humanity, nature, and God.

Implicit in the Vision of God as it expresses itself in the history of God and as interpreted by the biblical seers of that Vision are certain fundamental originating attributes. The purpose of Shalom is rooted in qualities in the abysmal Selfhood of God. If Shalom is the goal of the history of God, what is this ground of the history of God?

Love

The will-to-Shalom is the divine Love. Love is the caring intention from which the creation and redemption of the world arise. It is the Love of God that brings the world to be, preserves it, shares its Vision, enters into enemy territory, suffers its worst assaults, and never lets it go until it has won its response.

The depths of this Love are revealed in the face of the heights of our resistance to it. The divine Love is not only the quest for community with the world, but the faithful pursuit that is undeterred by the lovelessness of its object. God loves the enemies that destroy the enfleshed Vision and break the divine heart. God loves the sinner. Here is the in-spite-of, unconditional, unmerited Agape. The history of God is carried by this undeviating Agape, receiving into itself the world's hates and hurts. This is the Love that "bears all things. . ." but "never ends" (I Cor. 13). As such it is gracious Love, going before the world, and not turned aside by whatever No may be said to it by the world.

The care spilled out unreservedly on the world in each chapter of the Christian Story is a Love constitutive of the divine Life itself. This Love expressed in the mission of God from creation to consummation is a Love finally grounded in the inner-trinitarian Life itself.

The historical Love is the overspill of this inner plenitude. As we have made use of Augustine's psychological analogy in the Prologue to understand the origin of the narrative, so it is helpful here to use another Augustinian metaphor, this time an interpersonal one to express the inner life of Love. As God is Envisioner, Vision, and Power, so God is Lover, Loved, and Love. God the envisioning Lover eternally empowers by Love the beloved Vision. In the language of tradition, the unbegotten Father eternally begets the Son by the eternally processive Spirit. What we encounter in the deeds of God comes ultimately from the relationships within the Godhead. Within and without, "God is love" (John 3:16; I John 4:8–12).

Holiness

The Love of God in the Christian Story is not divine indulgence. The God who invites response is the God who holds the world responsible. The God who beckons into relationship holds accountable those who choose to turn aside. This is a righteous God with whom we have to do, a *holy* Love whose call is also expectation.

The accountability intrinsic to invitation is manifest in the Christian Story in the judgment of God that attends rebellious response. The wages of sin and evil are death. Thus the act of sin earns the rebuke of God in the fading of the divine Vision, the darkening of the image of God in us, and our loss of perception of the grace of God around us. The act of human sin in alliance with the fallen powers and principalities brings in its wake historical movements of a Providence that cast the mighty from their seats and call to account those who grind the faces of the poor. The Providence that watches over the divine Vision in history brings judgment on the selves and societies that attack it. The Old Testament with its profound sense of the limits that a righteous God sets to rebellion is a crucial perception of the "wrath of God." And this is eminently true of the acts of greatest benevolence, as in the Covenant itself where the heights of its accountability grow out of the depths of Love. The boundary set to the limits of rebellion is at work in both self and society as the "law of love" which takes its toll on the imperial ego or nation as that violates the mandate: "love or perish." The wrath of God is seen in the central chapter of the Christian Story in the bar of judgment on Calvary before which the world is called as a result of its ultimate assault on the Hope of God. And the subsequent accountability that grows from that on the day of judgment is also there. Death, as the futurelessness of rebellion, is integral to each chapter of the Christian Story. The divine righteousness brooks no challenge to its claims. No understanding of the love of God does justice to the deeds of God that does not also include the holiness of God (Deut. 32:4; I Pet. 1:16; Rev. 4:8).

Suffering

How can the just and judging God persist in love in the face of the world's rejection of the gracious invitation? This enigma has produced the predictable alternatives that sacrifice one of the attributes of this polarity: either God is finally holy and therefore an unloving consigner of the adjudged to the everlasting fires, or God is loving and withdraws the judgment that rebellion merits. Yet at the center of the Christian Story there is a more profound wrestling with this mystery. On the cross the judgment does fall on the world. The death we deserve comes to our world. Yet it is not we who receive it, but the God who comes among us in Jesus Christ. God suffers our punishment in the Person of Jesus Christ. The Vision of Shalom dies. Yet as a seed falls into the ground and is transformed (I Cor. 15:36), so the death in God of the divine Dream is transmuted into one reborn in suffering Love. The broken heart of God carries the world to its reunion with its purpose. Suffering Love is triumphant Love. The divine grace is not cheap indulgence of our recalcitrance, but a costly love whose passion and pain takes into itself our punishment. In the language of Luther, on the cross the blessing of God overcomes the curse, the love of God transcends the wrath of God, and a suffering and triumphant Love bears the world toward the promise of Shalom. Suffering Agape is the ground and Shalom is the goal of the history of God (Rom. 8:32; II Cor. 5:19; I Pet. 1:19–20; Rev. 13:8).

MYSTERY AND MEANING

Whatever we envision of the divine qualities, we see by the eye of faith as it perceives the deeds of God. The words and images we use to convey these visions are taken from our language and experience of presence, knowledge, power, love, justice, suffering. As such these carry with them all the limitations of the human matrix. Faith distinguishes them by an increase of magnitude—thus our impotence compared to God's omnipotence—and more important by reverse of their common valuations—our calculating love compared to God's unconditional Agape. Thus our words capture something of the meaning of the deeds of God, enough to allow us to see through the glass of vision what God has done, is doing, and will do, enough to bring us to our knees in repentance, faith, and adoration. It is the work of theology to be a resource to the preaching and teaching Church so that by the power of the Spirit that glass may be diaphanous to the divine Glory.

Yet when all the Story is said and all theological clarifications done, we do see through a glass darkly. Because this epic adventure is not yet over, it is only at its consummation that we shall see "face to face." What we say about the being and doing of God for now is in terms of the figures of time and not eternity. Christian theology does its work with a keen sense of its fragility and transiency. The telling of this Story in the language of this time and place bears the marks of this fragility and transiency. This time-bound, place-bound translation needs companions for other occasions and peoples. And whatever recounting is done will never exhaust the heights and depths of the divine Life. We are given enough Light to make our way, but we can make no claim to have penetrated the full reaches of that Glory. Living in this Pauline penumbra, we must finally echo the Apostle's words: "O depths of wealth, wisdom, and knowledge in God! How unsearchable his judgements, how untraceable his ways! Who knows the mind of the Lord? . . . Source, Guide, and Goal of all that is—to him be glory forever! Amen" (Rom. 11:33–34, 36).

Bibliography

The following works are the English literature recommended for more extensive investigation of each doctrinal area.

SYSTEMATIC THEOLOGIES AND GENERAL WORKS IN CHRISTIAN DOCTRINE

The Augsburg Confession. Translated and Edited by Theodore G. Tappert. Philadelphia: United Lutheran Publishing House, 1959.

Aulén, Gustaf. *The Faith of The Christian Church.* Translated by Eric H. Wahlstrom. Philadelphia: Fortress Press, 1960.

Barth, Karl. *Church Dogmatics.* Vol. I, i-iv, 4. General Editors, G. W. Bromiley and T. F. Torrance. Various Translators. Edinburgh: T. & T. Clark, 1936–1962.

_____. *Credo.* Foreword by Robert McAfee Brown. Translated by J. Strathearn McNab. New York: Charles Scribner's Sons, 1962.

_____. *Dogmatics in Outline.* Translated by G. T. Thompson. New York: Harper & Bros., 1959.

Berkhof, Louis. *Systematic Theology.* 2nd Revised and Enlarged Edition. Grand Rapids: Eerdmans Publishing Co., 1941.

Braaten, Carl S. *The Future of God.* New York: Harper & Row, 1969.

Brunner, Emil. *Dogmatics,* Vols. I–III, Translated by Olive Wyon. Philadelphia: Westminster Press, 1950–62.

Calvin, John. *The Institutes of the Christian Religion,* Vols. I and II. Translated by Henry Beveridge. Grand Rapids: Eerdmans Publishing Co., 1957.

Clarke, William Newton. *An Outline of Christian Theology.* New York: Charles Scribner's Sons, 1909.

Cochrane, Arthur C., Editor. *Reformed Confessions of the 16th Century.* Philadelphia: Westminster Press, 1965.

Documents of Vatican II. Austin P. Flannery, Editor. Grand Rapids: Eerdmans Publishing Co., 1975.

Evans, Robert and Parker, Thomas, Editors. *Christian Theology:* A Case Method. New York: Harper & Row, 1976.

Feiner, Johannes and Vischer, Lukas, Editors. *The Common Catechism.* New York: Seabury Press, 1975.

Gerhart, Emmanuel. *Institutes of the Christian Religion,* Vols. I and II. New York: A. C. Armstrong, 1891.

Gutierrez, Gustavo. *A Theology of Liberation.* Translated and Edited by Sister Caridad Inda and John Eagleson. Maryknoll, New York: Orbis Books, 1971.

Halverson, Marvin and Cohen, Arthur, Editors. *A Handbook on Christian Theology.* New York: Meridian Books, 1962.

The Heidelberg Catechism with Commentary, 400th Anniversary Edition. 1563–1963. Philadelphia: United Church Press, 1963.

Hendry, George S. *The Westminster Confession For Today.* Richmond: John Knox Press, 1960.

Hodge, Charles. *Systematic Theology.* Vols. I–III. Grand Rapids: Eerdmans Publishing Co., 1960.

Hodgson, Leonard. *For Faith and Freedom.* Vols. I and II. Oxford: Basil Blackwell, 1956, 1957.

The Interpreter's Dictionary of the Bible. Vols. I–IV. Edited by George Arthur Buttrick. New York: Abingdon Press, 1962.

Kaufman, Gordon D. *Systematic Theology:* A Historicist Perspective. New York: Charles Scribner's Sons, 1968.

Kittel, Gerhard and Friedrich, Gerhard, Editors. *The Theological Dictionary of the Bible.* Vols. I–IX. Translated and Edited by Geoffrey W. Bromiley. Grand Rapids: Eerdmans Publishing Co., 1964–1974. Vol. X, *Index* compiled by Robert E. Pitkin. Grand Rapids: Eerdmans Publishing Co., 1976.

Küng, Hans. *On Being a Christian.* Translated by Edward Quinn. New York: Doubleday & Co., 1976.

Leith, John H., Editor. *Creeds of the Churches.* Chicago: Aldine Publishing Co., 1963.

Lossky, Vladimir. *The Mystical Theology of the Eastern Church.* Translated by Members of the Fellowship of St. Albans and St. Sergius. London: James Clarke & Co., 1957.

—————. *The Small Catechism.* Minneapolis: Augsburg Publishing House, 1960.

Luther, Martin. *Large Catechism.* Translated by Robert Fischer. Philadelphia: Fortress Press, 1959.

Macquarrie, John. *Principles of Christian Theology,* Second Edition. New York: Charles Scribner's Sons, 1977.

Marty, Martin E. and Peerman, Dean G., Editors. *New Theology.* Nos. 1–10. New York: The Macmillan Co., 1964–1973.

Melanchthon, Philip. *Loci Communes.* Translated by Charles Leander Hill with Introduction by E. E. Flack. Boston: Meador Publishing Co., 1944.

Miller, Allen O. *Invitation to Theology.* Philadelphia: Christian Education Press, 1958.

A New Catechism: Catholic Faith for Adults. Translated by Kevin Smith. New York: Herder and Herder, 1969.

Pannenberg, Wolfhart. *The Apostles' Creed in the Light of Today's Questions.* Translated by Margaret H. Kohl. Philadelphia: Westminster Press, 1972.

_____. *Basic Questions in Theology,* Vols. I–II. Translated by George H. Kehm. Philadelphia: Fortress Press, 1970, 1971; Vol. III. Translated by R. A. Wilson. London: SCM Press, 1973.

Preparatory Report Volumes of World Council of Churches Assemblies. 1948–1975.

Proceedings. Consultation on Church Union. 1962–1978.

Rahner, Karl. *Theological Investigations.* Vols. I–XIV. Various Translators. Baltimore: Helicon Press, 1961–1977.

_____. *Foundations of Christian Faith.* Translated by William V. Dych. New York: Seabury Press, 1978.

Rahner, Karl, Editor, *Encyclopedia of Theology:* The Concise *Sacramentum Mundi.* New York: Seabury Press, 1975.

Schleiermacher, Friedrich. *The Christian Faith.* Edited by H. R. Mackintosh and J. S. Stewart. New York: Harper Torch Books, 1963. Introduction by Richard R. Niebuhr.

Shinn, Roger Lincoln and Williams, Daniel Day. *We Believe.* Philadelphia: United Church Press, 1966.

Stott, John R. *Basic Christianity.* Revised Edition. Grand Rapids: Eerdmans Publishing Co., 1965.

Strong, Augustus H. *Systematic Theology* (3 vols. in 1). New York: Fleming Revell Co., 1907.

Thielicke, Helmut. *I Believe: The Christian's Creed.* Translated by John W. Doberstein. Philadelphia: Fortress Press, 1968.

Thomas Aquinas. *Summa Theologica.* Translated by Fathers of the English Dominican Province. Vols. 1–22. London: Burns, Oates and Washbourne, 1912–1927.

Thomas, Owen. *Introduction to Theology.* Cambridge, Mass.: Greeno, Hadden & Co., 1973.

Tillich, Paul. *Systematic Theology.* Vols. 1–3. Chicago: University of Chicago Press, 1951–1963.

Vassady, Bela. *Light Against Darkness.* Philadelphia: Christian Education Press, 1961.

Walker, Williston. *The Creeds and Platforms of Congregationalism.* Introduction by Douglas Horton. Boston: Pilgrim Press, 1960.

Whale, J. S. *Christian Doctrine.* Cambridge: Cambridge University Press, 1941.

INTRODUCTION

Achtemeier, Paul. *An Introduction to the New Hermeneutic.* Philadelphia: Westminster Press, 1969.

Anderson, Gerald, Editor. *Asian Voices in Christian Theology.* Maryknoll, New York: Orbis Books, 1976.

Baillie, John. *Our Knowledge of God.* New York: Charles Scribner's Sons, 1939.

_____, Editor. *The Idea of Revelation in Recent Thought.* New York: Columbia University Press, 1956.

_____, and Hugh Martin, Editors. *Revelation.* New York: The Macmillan Co., 1937.

Barbour, Ian. *Myths, Models and Paradigms.* New York: Harper & Row, 1974.

Barclay, William. *By What Authority?* Valley Forge: Judson Press, 1976.

Barnhouse, Ruth Tiffany and Holmes, Urban T. III, Editors. *Male and Female: Christian Approaches to Sexuality.* New York: Seabury Press, 1976.

Barth, Karl. *Evangelical Theology.* Translated by Grover Farley. New York: Holt, Reinhart and Winston, 1963.

_____. *The Knowledge of God and the Service of God.* Translated by J. L. Haire and Ian Henderson. London: Hodder, 1938.

_____. *The Word of God and the Word of Man.* Translated by Douglas Horton. New York: Harper & Row, 1957.

Berger, Peter, *A Rumor of Angels.* Garden City, New York: Doubleday, 1969.

Berkouwer, G. C. *Holy Scripture.* Translated and Edited by Jack Rogers. Grand Rapids: Eerdmans Publishing Co., 1975.

Bloesch, Donald. *The Evangelical Renaissance.* Grand Rapids: Eerdmans Publishing Co., 1973.

Bonhoeffer, Dietrich. *Letters and Papers From Prison.* Edited by Eberhard Bethge, Translated by Reginald Fuller, Frank Clarke and John Bowden; Enlarged Edition. New York: The Macmillan Co., 1971.

Braaten, Carl E. *History and Hermeneutics.* Philadelphia: Westminster, 1968.

Brunner, Emil. *The Divine. Human Encounter.* Translated by Amandus W. Loos. Philadelphia: Westminster Press, 1943.

_____. *Revelation and Reason.* Translated by Olive Wyon. Philadelphia: Westminster Press, 1946.

Bultmann, Rudolf et al. *Kerygma and Myth.* Edited by H. W. Bartsch. Translated by Reginald H. Fuller. New York: Harper & Row, 1961.

_____. *Existence and Faith.* Selected, Translated, Edited and Introduction by Schubert M. Ogden. New York: Meridian Books, 1960.

Callahan, D., Oberman, H., O'Hanlon, D., Editors. *Christianity Divided.* New York: Sheed and Ward, 1961.

Casserley, Julian Victor Langmead. *Graceful Reason.* Greenwich, CT: Seabury Press, 1954.

Childs, Brevard. *Biblical Theology in Crisis.* Philadelphia: Westminster Press, 1970.

Cobb, John, Jr. and Griffin, David R. *Process Theology.* Philadelphia: Westminster Press, 1976.

Cragg, Gerald R. *Freedom and Authority.* Philadelphia: Westminster Press, 1975.

Dodd, C. H. *The Authority of the Bible.* London: Nisbet & Co., 1952.

Downing, Francis G. *Has Christianity a Revelation?* London: SCM Press, 1964.

Dulles, Avery. *The Survival of Dogma.* Garden City, New York: Doubleday & Co., 1971.

Ebeling, Gerhard. *The Nature of Faith.* Translated by Ronald Gregor Smith. Philadelphia: Muhlenberg Press, 1961.

Evans, Robert. *Intelligible and Responsible Talk About God.* Leiden: Brill, 1973.

Fackre, Gabriel. *Humiliation and Celebration.* New York: Sheed and Ward, 1969.

Farrer, Austin. *The Glass of Vision.* Westminster: Dacre Press, 1948.

Ferré, Frederick. *Language, Logic and God.* New York: Harper & Row, 1961.

Ferré, Nels F. S. *Reason in Religion.* London: Thomas Nelson & Sons, 1963.

Freire, Paulo. *Pedagogy of the Oppressed.* Translated by Myra Bergman Ramos. New York: Herder & Herder, 1972.

Geisler, Norman. *Christian Apologetics.* Grand Rapids: Eerdmans Publishing Co., 1976.

Hammer, Paul. *The Gift of Shalom.* Philadelphia: United Church Press, 1974.

Harris, Douglas. *Shalom: The Biblical Concept of Peace.* Grand Rapids: Baker Book House, 1970.

Hazelton, Roger. *Ascending Flame, Descending Dove.* Philadelphia: Westminster Press, 1975.

Herzog, Frederick, Editor. *Theology of the Liberating Word.* Nashville: Abingdon Press, 1971.

Herzog, Frederick. *Understanding God.* New York: Charles Scribner's Sons, 1966.

Hick, John. *Faith and Knowledge.* 2nd Edition. Ithaca, N.Y.: Cornell University Press, 1966.

Jenkins, Daniel. *The Christian Belief in God.* Philadelphia: Westminster Press, 1964.

Johnson, Robert Clyde. *Authority in Protestant Theology.* Philadelphia: Westminster Press, 1957.

Kelsey, Morton T. *Myth, History and Faith.* New York: Paulist Press, 1974.

Kierkegaard, Søren. *Concluding Unscientific Postscript.* Translated by

David Swenson and Walter Lowrie. Princeton: Princeton University Press, 1944.

Kirk, Kenneth. *The Vision of God.* London: Longmans, Green and Co., 1931.

Kuitert, H. M. *The Reality of Faith.* Translated by Lewis B. Smedes. Grand Rapids: Eerdmans Publishing Co., 1968.

Lossky, Vladimir. *The Vision of God.* Translated by Asheleigh Moorehouse. Preface by John Meyendorff. London: Faith Press, 1964.

Lonergan, Bernard. *Method In Theology.* New York: Herder & Herder, 1972.

_____. *Insight.* New York: Philosophical Library, 1958.

Machen, J. Gresham, *Christian Faith in the Modern World.* Grand Rapids: Eerdmans Publishing Co., 1967.

Manschreck, Clyde, Editor. *Erosion of Authority.* Nashville: Abingdon Press, 1971.

McKenzie, John L. *Authority in the Church.* New York: Sheed and Ward, 1966.

Micks, Marianne H. *An Introduction to Theology.* New York: Seabury Press, 1964.

Miller, Donald. *The Authority of the Bible.* Grand Rapids: Eerdmans Publishing Co., 1972.

McLaughlin, Eleanor L. "Christ My Mother: Feminine Naming and Metaphor in Medieval Spirituality," *St. Luke's Journal of Theology,* Vol. 18 (September, 1975), pp. 366–386.

Morris, George. *Shalom: A Vision of a New World.* Nashville: Tidings, 1974.

Morris, Leon. *I Believe in Revelation.* Grand Rapids: Eerdmans Publishing Co., 1976.

Moran, Gabriel. *Theology of Revelation.* New York: Seabury Press, 1966.

Niebuhr, H. Richard. *The Meaning of Revelation.* New York: The Macmillan Co., 1941.

Novak, Michael. *Belief and Unbelief.* New York: The Macmillan Co., 1965.

Nygren, Anders. *Meaning and Method.* Translated by Philip Watson. Philadelphia: Fortress Press, 1972.

Oman, John. *Vision and Authority.* New York: Harper & Row, 1929.

Pannenberg, Wolfhart. *Theology and the Philosophy of Science.* Translated by Francis McDonagh. Philadelphia: Westminster Press, 1976.

Pannenberg, Wolfhart, et al. *Revelation as History.* Translated by David Granskou. New York: The Macmillan Co., 1968.

_____, et al., *History and Hermeneutic.* Various Translators. New York: Harper & Row, 1967.

Pelikan, Jaroslav. *The Light of the World.* New York: Harper & Row, 1962.

Powers, Edward. *Signs of Shalom.* Philadelphia: United Church Press, 1973.

Rahner, Karl. *Visions and Prophecies.* Translated by Charles Henkey and Richard Strachan. New York: Herder & Herder, 1964.

Ramm, Bernard L. *Protestant Biblical Interpretation.* 3rd Revised Edition. Grand Rapids: Baker Book House, 1970.

Ramsey, Ian T. *Models and Mystery.* London: Oxford University Press, 1964.

_____. *Religious Language.* London: SCM Press, 1957.

Reid, J. K. S. *The Authority of Scripture.* London: Methuen, 1957.

Reuther, Rosemary Radford. *Religion and Sexism:* Images of Women in Jewish and Christian Religious Traditions. New York: Simon and Schuster, 1973.

Richardson, Alan. *Christian Apologetics.* London: SCM Press, 1947.

Robinson, James and Cobb, John B., Jr., Editors. *The New Hermeneutic.* New York: Harper & Row, 1964.

_____. *Theology as History.* New York: Harper & Row, 1967.

Russell, Letty M., Editor. *The Liberating Word.* Philadelphia: Westminster Press, 1976.

Schilling, Harold K. *Science and Religion.* New York: Charles Scribner's Sons, 1962.

Segundo, Juan Luis. *The Liberation of Theology.* Translated by John Drury. Maryknoll, New York: Orbis Books, 1976.

Shideler, Emerson. *Believing and Knowing.* Ames, Iowa: Iowa State University Press, 1966.

Söderblom, Nathan. *The Nature of Revelation.* Edited with an Introduction by Edgar Carlson. Translated by F. Pamp. Philadelphia: Fortress Press, 1966.

Sontag, Frederick. *How Philosophy Shapes Theology.* New York: Harper & Row, 1971.

Sölle, Dorothee. *Political Theology.* Translated with an Introduction by John Shelley. Philadelphia: Fortress Press, 1974.

Stotts, Jack L. *Shalom: The Search for a Peaceable City.* Nashville: Abingdon Press, 1973.

Terrien, Samuel. *The Bible and the Church.* Philadelphia: Westminster Press, 1962.

TeSelle, Sallie McFague. *Speaking in Parables.* Philadelphia: Fortress Press, 1975.

Thielicke, Helmut. *The Evangelical Faith.* Translated by G. W. Bromiley. Vol. I. Grand Rapids: Eerdmans Publishing Co., 1974.

Torrance, T. F. *Theology in Reconstruction.* London: SCM Press, 1965.

Tracy, David. *Blessed Rage for Order.* New York: Seabury Press, 1975.

Trible, Phyllis. "Depatriarchalizing in Biblical Interpretation," *Journal of American Academy of Religion,* Vol. XLI (1973), No. 1, pp. 30–48.

Urban, Wilbur. *Language and Reality.* New York: The Macmillan Co., 1939.

Walvoord, John F. *Inspiration and Interpretation.* Grand Rapids: Eerdmans Publishing Co., 1957.

Wilder, Ames Niven. *Theopoetic: Theology and the Religious Imagination.* Philadelphia: Fortress Press, 1976.

Wiles, Maurice. *The Making of Christian Doctrine.* London: Cambridge University Press, 1967.

——————. *The Remaking of Christian Doctrine.* London: SCM Press, 1973.

Wink, Walter. *The Bible in Human Transformation.* Philadelphia: Fortress Press, 1973.

Wiggins, James B. *Religion as Story.* New York: Harper & Row, 1975.

Wolf, William J. *Man's Knowledge of God.* Garden City: Doubleday & Co., 1955.

Wright, G. Ernest and Fuller, Reginald H. *The Book of the Acts of God.* Garden City, New York: Doubleday & Co., 1957.

Zahrnt, Heinz. *What Kind of God?* Translated by R. B. Wilson. Minneapolis: Augsburg Publishing House, 1972.

PROLOGUE AND EPILOGUE: GOD

Altizer, Thomas and Hamilton, William. *Radical Theology and the Death of God.* Indianapolis: Bobbs-Merrill Co., 1966.

Anderson, Ray S. *Historical Transcendence and the Reality of God.* Foreword by D. M. Mackinnon. London: G. Chapman, 1975.

Aulén, Gustaf. *The Drama and the Symbols.* Translated by Sydney Linton. Philadelphia: Fortress Press, 1970.

Augustinus, Aurelius. *On the Trinity.* Translated by A. W. Haddon (Nicene and Post-Nicene Fathers, First Series, Vol. III). New York: Charles Scribner's Sons, 1900.

Baillie, John. *The Sense of the Presence of God.* New York: Charles Scribner's Sons, 1962.

Basil of Caesarea. *On the Holy Spirit.* Translated by B. Jackson (Nicene and Post-Nicene Fathers, Second Series, Vol. VIII). New York: Charles Scribner's Sons, 1895.

Berkhof, Hendrikus. *The Doctrine of the Holy Spirit.* Richmond: John Knox Press, 1964.

Bertocci, Peter. *The Person God Is.* New York: Humanities Press, 1970.

Boman, Thorlief. *Hebrew Thought Compared with Greek.* Translated by Jules L. Moreau. London: SCM Press, 1960.

Bouquet, Alan C. *The Doctrine of God.* Cambridge: W. Heffer & Sons, 1934.

Bowie, Walter Russell. *Jesus and The Trinity.* Nashville: Abingdon Press, 1960.

Brightman, Edgar B. *Is God a Person?* New York: Association Press, 1932.

——————. *The Problem of God.* New York: Abingdon Press, 1930.

Brown, Robert McAfee. *The Pseudonyms of God.* Philadelphia: Westminster Press, 1972.

Cobb, John. *A Christian Natural Theology.* Based on the Thought of Alfred

North Whitehead. Philadelphia: Westminster Press, 1965.

Cousins, Ewart, Editor. *Process Theology.* New York: Newman Press, 1971.

Daane, James. *The Freedom of God.* Grand Rapids: Eerdmans Publishing Co., 1973.

Daly, Mary. *Beyond God the Father.* Boston: Beacon Press, 1973.

Daniélou, Jean. *God and the Ways of Knowing.* Translated by Walter Roberts. New York: Meridian Books, 1957.

Dewart, Leslie. *The Future of Belief.* New York: Herder & Herder, 1966.

Dillenberger, John. *God Hidden and Revealed.* Philadelphia: Muhlenberg Press, 1953.

Dunne, John S. *A Search for God in Time and Memory.* New York: The Macmillan Co., 1969.

Farley, Edward. *The Transcendence of God.* Philadelphia: Westminster Press, 1960.

Farmer, H. H. *Toward Belief in God.* New York: The Macmillan Co., 1943.

Farrer, Austin. *Finite and Infinite.* Westminster: Dacre Press, 1943.

Ferré, Nels F. S. *The Christian Understanding of God.* New York: Harper & Bros., 1951.

Fortman, Edmund J. *The Triune God.* Philadelphia: Westminster Press, 1972.

Franks, R. S. *The Doctrine of the Trinity.* London: Duckworth, 1953.

Gilkey, Langdon. *Naming the Whirlwind:* The Renewal of God Language. Indianapolis: Bobbs-Merrill Co., 1969.

Gollwitzer, H. *The Existence of God as Confessed by Faith.* Translated by James Leitch. Philadelphia: Westminster Press, 1965.

Grant, Robert. *The Early Christian Doctrine of God.* Charlottesville, Va.: University of Virginia, 1966.

Green, Edward Michael Banks. *I Believe in the Holy Spirit.* Grand Rapids: Eerdmans Publishing Co., 1975.

Gregory of Nyssa. *On The Holy Trinity.* Translated by H. A. Wilson (Nicene and Post-Nicene Fathers, Second Series, Vol. I). New York: Charles Scribner's Sons, 1893.

Gundry, Stanley N. and Johnson, Alan F. *Tension in Contemporary Theology.* Foreword by Roger Nicole. Chicago: Moody Press, 1976.

Hamilton, Kenneth. *Revolt Against Heaven.* Grand Rapids: Eerdmans Publishing Co., 1965.

Hartshorne, Charles. *Man's Vision of God.* Chicago: Willett, Clark, 1941.
_____. *The Divine Relativity.* New Haven: Yale University Press, 1948.

Hazelton, Roger. *Knowing the Living God.* Valley Forge: Judson Press, 1969.

Hedley, George P. *The Holy Trinity:* Experience and Interpretation. Philadelphia: Fortress Press, 1967.

Heim, Karl. *God Transcendent.* Translated by E. P. Dickie with Introduction and Revision by E. Bevan. New York: Charles Scribner's Sons, 1936.

Hendry, George S. *The Holy Spirit in Christian Theology.* Philadelphia: Westminster Press, 1956.

Hick, John, Editor. *The Existence of God.* New York: The Macmillan Co., 1964.

Hocking, William Ernest. *The Meaning of God in Human Experience.* New Haven: Yale University Press, 1912.

Hodgson, Leonard. *The Doctrine of the Trinity.* New York: Charles Scribner's Sons, 1944.

Jenkins, Daniel. *The Christian Belief in God.* Philadelphia: Westminster Press, 1963.

Jenson, Robert. *God after God.* Indianapolis: Bobbs-Merrill Co., 1969.

Jüngel, Eberhard. *The Doctrine of the Trinity.* Grand Rapids: Eerdmans Publishing Co., 1977.

Jones, William R. *Is God a White Racist?* Problems for a Black Theology. Garden City: Doubleday & Co., 1973.

Kaufman, Gordon. *God the Problem.* Cambridge: Harvard University Press, 1972.

Kitamori, Kazoh. *Theology of the Pain of God.* Richmond: John Knox Press, 1965.

Knudson, Albert. *The Doctrine of God.* New York: Abingdon Press, 1930.

Koyama, Kosuke. *Waterbuffalo Theology.* Maryknoll, New York: Orbis Books, 1974.

Lee, Jung Young. *God Suffers for Us.* The Hague: Martinus Nijhoff, 1974.

Lonergan, Bernard. *The Way to Nicea.* Translated by Conn O'Donovan, First Part of *De Deo Trino* . Philadelphia: Westminster Press, 1976.

MacGregor, Geddes. *He Who Lets Us Be.* New York: Seabury Press, 1975.

Mascall, E. L. *He Who Is.* London: Darton, Longman and Todd, 1966.

Maury, Pierre. *Predestination.* Translated by Edwin Hudson with a Foreword by Karl Barth and a Memoir by Robert Mackie. Richmond: John Knox Press, 1960.

Mbiti, John. *Concepts of God in Africa.* New York: Praeger Publishers, 1970.

Metz, Johannes B., Editor. *New Questions on God.* New York: Herder & Herder, 1972.

Moltmann, Jürgen. *The Crucified God.* Translated by R. A. Wilson and John Bowden. London: SCM Press, 1974.

Mozley, J. K. *The Impassibility of God.* Cambridge: University Press, 1926.

Niebuhr, H. Richard. *Radical Monotheism and Western Culture.* New York: Harper & Row, 1960.

Nygren, Anders. *Agape and Eros.* Translated by Philip Watson. London: SPCK, 1953.

Ogden, Schubert. *The Reality of God and Other Essays.* New York: Harper & Row, 1966.

Ott, Heinrich. *God.* Translated by Iain and Ute Nicol. Richmond: John Knox Press, 1973.

Pike, Nelson. *God and Timelessness.* New York: Schocken Books, 1970.

Prestige, George L. *God in Patristic Thought.* London: SPCK, 1952.

Rahner, Karl. *The Trinity.* Translated by Joseph Donceel. New York: Herder & Herder, 1970.

Richardson, Cyril. *The Doctrine of the Trinity.* New York: Abingdon Press, 1958.

Robinson, H. Wheeler. *Suffering, Human and Divine.* New York: The Macmillan Co., 1939.

Robinson, J. A. T. *Exploration into God.* London: SCM Press, 1967.
_____. *Honest to God.* Philadelphia: Westminster Press, 1963.

Sayers, Dorothy. *The Mind of the Maker.* London: Methuen, 1942.

Schilling, S. Paul. *God in an Age of Atheism.* Nashville: Abingdon Press, 1969.

Schwarz, Hans. *The Search for God.* Minneapolis: Augsburg Publishing Co., 1975.

Segundo, Juan Luis. *Our Idea of God.* In collaboration with the staff of the Peter Faber Center in Montevideo, Uruguay, translated by John Drury. Maryknoll, New York: Orbis Books, 1974.

Shinn, Roger. *Life, Death and Destiny.* Philadelphia: Westminster Press, 1957.

Sloyan, Gerald. *The Three Persons in One God.* Englewood Cliffs, New Jersey: Prentice-Hall, 1964.

Smith, Ronald Gregor. *The Doctrine of God.* Philadelphia: Westminster Press, 1970.

Teilhard de Chardin, Pierre. *The Phenomenon of Man.* Translation from the French. New York: Harper & Row, 1965.

Thielicke, Helmut. *The Evangelical Faith.* Vol. 2. The Doctrine of God and of Christ. Translated by G. W. Bromiley. Grand Rapids: Eerdmans Publishing Co., 1977.

Van Buren, Paul. *The Secular Meaning of the Gospel.* New York: The Macmillan Co., 1963.

Wainwright, Arthur W. *The Trinity in the New Testament.* Edited by Samuel G. Craig. London: SPCK, 1962.

Weil, Simone. *Waiting on God.* Translated by Emma Craufurd. London: Routledge and Kegan Paul, 1965.

Welch, Claude. *In This Name.* New York: Charles Scribner's Sons, 1952.

CREATION

Anderson, Bernhard W. *Creation Versus Chaos.* New York: Association Press, 1967.

Barbour, Ian. *Issues in Science and Religion.* Englewood Cliffs, New Jersey: Prentice-Hall, 1966.

Baum, Gregory. *Man Becoming.* New York: Herder & Herder, 1971.

Butterfield, Herbert. *Christianity and History.* London: G. Bell and Sons, 1954.

Cairns, David. *The Image of God in Man.* Revised Edition with Introduction by David E. Jenkins. London: Collins, 1973.

Cobb, John. *God and The World.* Philadelphia: Westminster Press, 1969.
Come, Arnold B. *Human Spirit and Holy Spirit.* Philadelphia: Westminster Press, 1959.
Dunne, John S. *How God Created.* Notre Dame: University of Notre Dame Press, 1960.
Florovsky, Georges V. *Creation and Redemption.* Belmont, Mass.: Nordlund Publishing Co., 1976.
Gilkey, Langdon. *Maker of Heaven and Earth.* Garden City, New York: Doubleday & Co., 1959.
_____. *Reaping the Whirlwind.* New York: Seabury Press, 1976.
Gundry, Robert H. *Soma in Biblical Theology.* New York: Cambridge University Press, 1976.
Hatt, Harold E. *Cybernetics and the Image of Man.* Nashville: Abingdon Press, 1968.
Hazelton, Roger. *God's Way with Man.* New York: Abingdon Press, 1956.
James, Edwin Oliver. *Creation and Cosmology.* Leiden: Brill, 1969.
Jewett, Paul K. *Man as Male and Female.* Grand Rapids: Eerdmans Publishing Co., 1975.
LeFevre, Perry. *Understandings of Man.* Philadelphia: Westminster Press, 1966.
Löwith, Karl. *Meaning in History.* Chicago: University of Chicago Press, 1949.
Miller, Alexander. *The Man in the Mirror.* New York: Doubleday & Co., 1958.
Moltmann, Jürgen. *Man.* Translated by John Sturdy. Philadelphia: Fortress Press, 1974.
Montefiore, Hugh, Editor. *Man and Nature.* Foreword by Michael Ramsey. London: Collins, 1975.
Moule, C. F. D. *Man and Nature in the New Testament.* London: University of London Athlone Press, 1964.
Nelson, J. Robert, Editor. *No Man is Alien.* Leiden: Brill, 1971.
Niebuhr, Reinhold. *Man's Nature and His Communities.* New York: Charles Scribner's Sons, 1965.
_____. *The Self and The Dramas of History.* New York: Charles Scribner's Sons, 1955.
Norris, Richard, Jr. *God and the World in Early Christian Theology.* New York: Seabury Press, 1965.
O'Connor, Daniel and Oakley, Francis, Editors. *Creation: The Impact of an Idea.* New York: Charles Scribner's Sons, 1969.
Pannenberg, Wolfhart. *What is Man?* Translated by Duane A. Priebe. Philadelphia: Fortress Press, 1970.
Prenter, Regin. *Creation and Redemption.* Translated by Theodore I. Jensen. Philadelphia: Fortress Press, 1967.
Reumann, John H. P. *Creation and New Creation.* Minneapolis: Augsburg Publishing House, 1973.
Scheffczyk, Leo. *Creation and Providence.* Translated by Richard Strachan. New York: Herder & Herder, 1970.

Shinn, Roger. *Christianity and the Problem of History.* New York: Charles Scribner's Sons, 1953.

—————. *Man: The New Humanism.* Philadelphia: Westminster Press, 1968.

Smith, Ronald Gregor. *The Whole Man: Studies in Christian Anthropology.* Philadelphia: Westminster Press, 1969.

Teilhard de Chardin, Pierre. *Hymn of the Universe.* Translated by Simon Bartholomew. New York: Harper & Row, 1965.

—————. *The Future of Man.* Translated by Norman Denny. New York: Herder & Herder, 1964.

von Balthasar, Hans Urs. *A Theology of History.* Translated from the German. New York: Sheed and Ward, 1963.

—————. *A Theological Anthropology.* Translated from the German. New York: Sheed and Ward, 1967.

Westermann, Claus. *Creation.* Translated by John J. Scullion. Philadelphia: Fortress Press, 1974.

Whitehead, Alfred North. *Process and Reality.* New York: The Macmillan Co., 1929.

Williams, Daniel Day. *God's Grace and Man's Hope.* New York: Harper & Row, 1949.

Wright, G. Ernest et al. *The Biblical Doctrine of Man in Society.* London: SCM Press, 1954.

Young, Norman. *Creator, Creation and Faith.* Philadelphia: Westminster Press, 1976.

FALL

Augustinus, Aurelius. *The Confessions of St. Augustine.* Translated by F. J. Sheed. New York: Sheed and Ward, 1943.

—————. *The Problem of Free Choice.* Translated and Annotated by Mark Pontifex. Westminster, Maryland: Newman Press, 1955.

Berkhof, Hendrikus. *Christ and the Powers.* Translated by John H. Yoder. Scottdale, Pa.: Herald Press, 1962.

Berkouwer, G. C. *Man—The Image of God.* Translated by Dirk W. Jellema. Grand Rapids: Eerdmans Publishing Co., 1962.

—————. *The Providence of God.* Translated by Lewis Smedes. Grand Rapids: Eerdmans Publishing Co., 1952.

—————. *Sin.* Translated by Philip Holtrop. Grand Rapids: Eerdmans Publishing Co., 1971.

Berdyaev, Nicolas. *Freedom and the Spirit.* Translated by Oliver Fielding Clarke. New York: Charles Scribner's Sons, 1935.

Bonhoeffer, Dietrich. *Creation and Fall.* Translated by John C. Fletcher. New York: The Macmillan Co., 1959.

Brunner, Emil. *Man in Revolt.* Translated by Olive Wyon. New York: Charles Scribner's Sons, 1939.

Caird, George. *Principalities and Powers.* Oxford: Clarendon Press, 1956.

Carus, Paul. *The History of the Devil and the Idea of Evil.* LaSalle, Illinois: Open Court Publishing Co., 1974.

Cherbonnier, Edmond La Beaume. *Hardness of Heart.* Garden City, New York: Doubleday & Co., 1955.

Dubarle, André Marie. *The Biblical Doctrine of Original Sin.* Translated by E. M. Stewart. New York: Herder & Herder, 1965.

Edwards, Jonathan. *Original Sin.* Edited by Clyde A. Holbrook. New Haven: Yale University Press, 1970.

Farrer, Austin. *Love Almighty and Ills Unlimited.* Garden City, New York: Doubleday & Co., 1961.

Ferré, Nels F. S. *Evil and the Christian Faith.* New York: Harper & Bros., 1947.

Fitch, William. *God and Evil.* London: Pickering and Inglis, 1969.

Galloway, Allan. *The Cosmic Christ.* London: Nisbet & Co., 1951.

Gelin, Albert and Descamps, Albert. *Sin in the Bible.* Translated by Charles Schaldenbrand. New York: Desclee Co., 1965.

Griffin, David Ray. *God, Power and Evil:* A Process Theodicy. Philadelphia: Westminster Press, 1976.

Harkness, Georgia Elma. *The Dark Night of the Soul.* New York: Abingdon Cokesbury Press, 1945.

_____. *The Providence of God.* New York: Abingdon Press, 1960.

Hick, John. *Evil and the God of Love.* London: Collins, 1968.

Holl, Adolf. *Death and the Devil.* Translated by Matthew J. O'Connell. New York: Seabury Press, 1976.

Kierkegaard, Søren. *The Concept of Dread.* Translated with Introduction by Walter Lowrie. Princeton: Princeton University Press, 1944.

_____. *The Sickness Unto Death.* Translated with an Introduction by Walter Lowrie. Princeton: Princeton University Press, 1944.

Leivestad, Ragnar. *Christ the Conqueror.* London: SPCK, 1954.

Lewis, C. S. *The Problem of Pain.* London: G. Bles, The Centenary Press, 1942.

Lewis, Edwin. *The Creator and the Adversary.* New York: Abingdon Press, 1948.

Menninger, Karl. *Whatever Became of Sin?* New York: Hawthorn Books, 1973.

Niebuhr, Reinhold. *The Nature and Destiny of Man.* New York: Charles Scribner's Sons, 1941.

_____. *Moral Man and Immoral Society.* New York: Charles Scribner's Sons, 1932.

Olson, Alan, Editor. *Disguises of the Demonic:* Contemporary Perspectives on the Power of Evil. New York: Association Press, 1970.

Ott, Heinrich. *Theology and Preaching:* Questions I–II of the Heidelberg Catechism. Translated by Harold Knight. Philadelphia: Westminster Press, 1965.

Outler, Albert C. *Who Trusts in God.* New York: Oxford University Press, 1968.

Palachovsky, V. *Sin in the Orthodox Church.* Translated by Charles Schaldenbrad. New York: Desclee Co., 1966.

Plantinga, Alvin. *God, Freedom and Evil.* New York: Harper & Row, 1974.

Pollard, W. G. *Chance and Providence.* New York: Charles Scribner's Sons, 1958.

Ricoeur, Paul. *Fallible Man.* Translated by Charles Kelbey. Chicago: Henry Regnery Co., 1965.

_____. *The Symbolism of Evil.* Translated by Emerson Buchanan. New York: Harper & Row, 1967.

Roberts, David E. *Psychotherapy and the Christian View of Man.* New York: Charles Scribner's Sons, 1950.

Schilling, S. Paul. *God and Human Anguish.* Nashville: Abingdon Press, 1977.

Segundo, Juan Luis. *Evolution and Guilt.* Translated by John Drury Marshall. Maryknoll, New York: Orbis Books, 1974.

Sontag, Frederick. *The God of Evil: An Argument From the Existence of the Devil.* New York: Harper & Row, 1970.

Stringfellow, William. *An Ethic for Christians and Other Aliens in a Strange Land.* Waco, Texas: Word, 1973.

Tennant, Frederick R. *The Sources of the Doctrines of Fall and Original Sin.* New York: Schocken Books, 1968.

Thelen, Mary Frances. *Man as Sinner in Contemporary American Realistic Theology.* New York: King's Crown Press, 1946.

Tillich, Paul. *The Interpretation of History.* Translated by N. A. Rasetzki and Elsa Talmey. New York: Charles Scribner's Sons, 1936.

Tsanoff, Radoslav A. *The Nature of Evil.* New York: The Macmillan Co., 1931.

Van Den Heuvel, Albert. *These Rebellious Powers.* New York: Friendship Press, 1965.

Weatherhead, Leslie. *The Will of God:* A Contemporary Interpretation of the Doctrine of Sin. New York: Abingdon-Cokesbury Press, 1944.

Whale, J. S. *The Christian Answer to the Problem of Evil.* New York: Abingdon Press, 1936.

Wiles, Maurice, Editor. *Providence.* London: SPCK, 1969.

Williams, N. P. *The Idea of the Fall and Original Sin.* New York: Longmans, Green and Co., 1927.

COVENANT

Achtemeier, Elizabeth Rice. *The Old Testament and the Proclamation of the Gospel.* Philadelphia: Westminster Press, 1973.

Achtemeier, Paul J. and Elizabeth. *The Old Testament Roots of our Faith.* Nashville: Abingdon Press, 1962.

Anderson, Bernhard W. *Understanding the Old Testament.* Second Edition. Englewood Cliffs, New Jersey: Prentice-Hall Publishing Co., 1966.

Anderson, Bernhard W., Editor. *The Old Testament and Christian Faith.* New York: Herder & Herder, 1969.

Baltzer, Klaus. *The Covenant Formulary.* Translated by David E. Green. Philadelphia: Fortress Press, 1971.

Baly, Denis et al. *God and History in the Old Testament.* New York: Harper & Row, 1976.

Bright, John. *Covenant and Promise.* Philadelphia: Westminster Press, 1976.

Brueggemann, Walter. *Living Toward a Vision:* Biblical Reflections on Shalom. Philadelphia: United Church Press, 1976.

_____. *Tradition for Crisis.* Richmond: John Knox Press, 1968.

Brueggemann, Walter and Wolff, Hans Walter. *The Vitality of Old Testament Traditions.* Atlanta: John Knox Press, 1976.

Childs, Brevard. *The Book of Exodus:* A Critical Theological Commentary. Philadelphia: Westminster Press, 1974.

Clements, Ronald E. *Prophecy and Covenant.* Naperville, Illinois: A. R. Allenson, 1965.

_____. *Prophecy and Tradition.* Atlanta: John Knox, 1975.

Eichrodt, Walter. *Theology of the Old Testament.* Translated by J. A. Baker. Vols. I and II. Philadelphia: Westminster, 1967.

Hasel, Gerhard. *Old Testament Theology:* Basic Issues in the Covenant Debate. Grand Rapids: Eerdmans Publishing Co., 1972.

Heschel, Abraham. *The Prophets.* Selected, Edited, and Introduced by Fritz A. Rothschild. New York: Harper & Row, 1962.

_____. *Between Man and Man.* Glencoe, Ill.: Free Press, 1965.

Holladay, William L. *Jeremiah: Spokesman Out of Time.* Philadelphia: United Church Press, 1974.

Jocz, Jakob. *The Covenant:* A Theology of Human Destiny. Grand Rapids: Eerdmans Publishing Co., 1968.

Köhler, Ludwig. *Old Testament Theology.* Translated by A. S. Todd. Philadelphia: Westminster, 1957.

Lindblom, J. *Prophecy in Ancient Israel.* Oxford: Basil Blackwell, 1962.

McCarthy, Dennis J. *Old Testament Covenant:* A Survey of Current Opinions. Richmond: John Knox Press, 1972.

McKenzie, John. *A Theology of the Old Testament.* New York: Doubleday & Co., 1974.

Moss, Robert V. "The Covenant Conception in Early Christian Thought." Ph.D. Dissertation, University of Chicago, 1954.

Mowinckel, Sigmund. *He That Cometh.* Translated by G. W. Anderson. Oxford: Basil Blackwell, 1956.

Muilenburg, James. *The Way of Israel.* New York: Harper & Bros., 1961.

Myers, Jacob. *Grace and Torah.* Philadelphia: Fortress Press, 1975.

Napier, B. Davie. *The Prophets in Perspective.* New York: Abingdon Press, 1963.

Pedersen, Johannes. *Israel, Its Life and Culture.* Vols. I and II. London: Oxford University Press, 1959.

Piper, Otto. *God in History.* New York: The Macmillan Co., 1939.

Reuther, Rosemary. *Faith and Fratricide.* With Introduction by Gregory Baum. New York: Seabury Press, 1974.

Rowley, H. H. *The Rediscovery of the Old Testament.* Philadelphia: Westminster Press, 1956.

Rust, Eric Charles. *Covenant and Hope.* Waco, Texas: Word Books, 1972.

Sanders, James. *Torah and Canon.* Philadelphia: Fortress Press, 1972.

von Rad, Gerhard. *Old Testament Theology.* Vols. I and II. Translated by D. M. G. Stalker. New York: Harper & Row, 1965.

Vriezen, Th. C. *An Outline of Old Testament Theology.* Oxford: Basil Blackwell, 1958.

White, Hugh. *Shalom in the Old Testament.* New York: United Church Board for Homeland Ministries, 1973.

Wright, G. Ernest. *The Old Testament and Theology.* New York: Harper & Row, 1969.

Yohn, David Waite. *The Christian Reader's Guide to the Old Testament.* Grand Rapids: Eerdmans Publishing Co., 1972.

Zimmerli, Walther. *The Old Testament and the World.* Translated by J. Scullion. Atlanta: John Knox Press, 1976.

_____. *Man and His Hope in the Old Testament.* Translated from the German. Naperville, Ill.: A. R. Allenson, 1971.

CHRIST

Aldwinckle, Russell. *More Than Man.* Grand Rapids: Eerdmans Publishing Co., 1976.

Anselm of Canterbury. *Basic Writings (Cur Deus Homo).* Translated by S. N. Deane with Introduction by Charles Hartshorne. LaSalle, Illinois: Open Court Publishing Co., 1962.

Athanasius, *On the Incarnation.* Translated and Edited by Religious of C.S.M.V. with Introduction by C. S. Lewis. London: A. R. Mowbray, 1953.

Aulén, Gustaf. *Christus Victor.* Translated by A. G. Hebert. New York: The Macmillan Co., 1951.

_____. *Jesus in Contemporary Historical Research.* Translated by I. H. Hjelm. Philadelphia: Fortress Press, 1976.

Baillie, D. M. *God Was in Christ.* New York: Charles Scribner's Sons, 1948.

Barth, Karl. *Christ and Adam.* Translated by T. A. Smail. New York: Harper & Bros., 1956.

_____. *The Humanity of God.* Translated by Thomas Weiser and John N. Thomas. Richmond: John Knox Press, 1960.

Barth, Markus and Fletcher, Vern. *Acquittal by Resurrection.* New York: Holt, Rinehart and Winston, 1964.

Berkhof, Hendrikus. *Christ: The Meaning of History.* Translated by L. Buurman. London: SCM Press, 1962.

Berkouwer, G. C. *The Person of Christ.* Translated by John Vriend. Grand Rapids: Eerdmans Publishing Co., 1954.

_____. *The Work of Christ.* Translated by Cornelius Lambregtse. Grand Rapids: Eerdmans Publishing Co., 1965.

Best, W. E. *Studies in the Person and Work of Jesus Christ.* Grand Rapids: Baker Book House, 1975.

Bloesch, Donald. *Jesus is Victor!* Nashville: Abingdon Press, 1976.

Bonhoeffer, Dietrich. *Christ the Center.* Translated by J. Bowden. New York: Harper & Row, 1966.

Bornkamm, Gunther. *Jesus of Nazareth.* Translated by Irene and Fraser McLuskey with James M. Robinson. New York: Harper & Bros., 1960.

Bowman, John Wick. *Which Jesus?* Philadelphia: Westminster Press, 1970.

Braaten, Carl E. and Harrisville, Roy A., Translators and Editors. *The Historical Jesus and the Kerygmatic Christ.* New York: Abingdon Press, 1964.

Brown, Raymond. *Jesus: God and Man.* Milwaukee: Bruce, 1967.

_____. *The Virginal Conception and Bodily Resurrection of Jesus.* New York: Paulist Press, 1973.

Brunner, Emil. *The Mediator.* Translated by Olive Wyon. Philadelphia: Westminster Press, 1947.

Bultmann, Rudolf. *Jesus and the Word.* Translated by Louise Pettibone Smith and Erminie Huntress Lantero. New York: Charles Scribner's Sons, 1958.

_____. *Jesus Christ and Mythology.* New York: Charles Scribner's Sons, 1958.

_____. *Theology of the New Testament.* Vols. I and II. Translated by Kendrick Grobel. New York: Charles Scribner's Sons, 1951–55.

Bushnell, Horace. *God in Christ.* Hartford: Brown & Parsons, 1849.

Carlston, Charles. *The Parables in the Triple Tradition.* Philadelphia: Fortress Press, 1975.

Cave, Sydney. *The Doctrine of the Work of Christ.* Nashville: Cokesbury Press, 1937.

_____. *The Doctrine of the Person of Christ.* London: Duckworth Press, 1925.

Cobb, John. *Christ in a Pluralistic Age.* Philadelphia: Westminster Press, 1975.

Cone, James H. *God of the Oppressed.* New York: Seabury Press, 1975.

Conzelmann, Hans. *Jesus.* Translated by Raymond Lord and Edited with Introduction by John Reumann. Philadelphia: Fortress Press, 1973.

_____. *An Outline of the Theology of the New Testament.* Translated by John Bowden. New York: Harper & Row, 1969.

Cullmann, Oscar. *The Christology of the New Testament.* Translated by

Shirley Guthrie and Charles Hall. Philadelphia: Westminster Press, 1959.

_____.*Jesus and the Revolutionaries.* Translated by Gareth Putnam. New York: Harper & Row, 1970.

Curtis, A. H. *The Vision and Mission of Jesus.* Edinburgh: T. & T. Clark, 1954.

Daly, Robert J. *Christian Sacrifice:* The Judeo-Christian Background up to Origen. Washington: Catholic University of America Press, 1978.

_____. *The Origin of the Christian Doctrine of Sacrifice.* Philadelphia: Fortress Press, 1977.

Deschner, John. *Wesley's Christology, an Interpretation.* Dallas: Southern Methodist University Press, 1960.

Dillistone, F. W. *The Christian Understanding of the Atonement.* Welwyn, Herts: Nisbet & Co., 1968.

Dodd, C. H. *The Interpretation of the Fourth Gospel.* London: Cambridge University Press, 1953.

_____. *The Founder of Christianity.* New York: The Macmillan Co., 1970.

Downing, Francis G. *A Man for Us and a God for Us.* London: Epworth Press, 1968.

Farmer, H. H. *The Work of Reconciliation.* London: Nisbet & Co., 1966.

Ferré, Nels F. S. *Christ and the Christian.* New York: Harper & Bros., 1958.

Forsyth, P. T. *The Cruciality of the Cross.* London: Independent Press, 1948.

_____. *The Person and Place of Jesus Christ.* London: Independent Press, 1909.

_____. *The Work of Christ.* London: Collins, 1965.

Franks, Robert S. *The Work of Christ.* London: Thomas Nelson and Sons, 1962.

Frei, Hans. *The Identity of Jesus Christ.* Philadelphia: Fortress Press, 1975.

Fuchs, Ernst. *Studies of the Historical Jesus.* Translated by A. Scobic. London: SCM Press, 1964.

Fuller, Reginald H. *The Foundations of New Testament Christology.* New York: Charles Scribner's Sons, 1965.

Gogarten, Friedrich. *Christ the Crisis.* Translated by R. A. Wilson. Richmond: John Knox Press, 1972.

Griffin, David R. *A Process Christology.* Philadelphia: Westminster Press, 1973.

Grillmeier, Aloys. *Christ in Christian Tradition.* Vol. I. 2nd Revised Edition. Translated by J. S. Bowden. London: A. R. Mowbray & Co., 1975.

Gustafson, James. *Christ and the Moral Life.* New York: Harper & Row, 1968.

Hanson, Anthony. *Grace and Truth.* London: SPCK, 1975.

Hardy, E. R. and Richardson, Cyril C., Editors. *Christology of the Later*

Fathers. Library of Christian Classics, Vol. III. Philadelphia: West-minster Press, 1954.

Hayes, John H. *Son of God to Superstar.* Nashville: Abingdon Press, 1976.

Heim, Karl. *Jesus the Lord.* Translated by D. H. van Daalen. Edinburgh: Oliver Boyd, 1959.

Hendry, George S. *The Gospel of the Incarnation.* Philadelphia: Westminster Press, 1958.

_____. "Christology" in Alan Richardson. *Dictionary of Christian Theology.* Philadelphia: Westminster Press, 1969.

Hengel, Martin. *The Son of God.* Translated by John Bowden. Philadelphia: Fortress Press, 1976.

Henry, Carl F. H., Editor. *Jesus of Nazareth: Saviour and Lord.* Grand Rapids: Eerdmans Publishing Co., 1966.

Hodge, Archibald. *The Atonement.* Grand Rapids: Baker Book House, 1974.

Hodgson, Leonard. *The Doctrine of the Atonement.* London: Nisbet Press, 1951.

Hodgson, Peter. *Jesus—Word and Presence.* Philadelphia: Fortress Press, 1973.

Hunter, Archibald M. *The Work and Words of Jesus.* Revised Edition. London: SCM Press, 1973.

Jenkins, David. *The Glory of Man.* London: SCM Press, 1967.

Jeremias, Joachim. *The Parables of Jesus.* Translated by S. H. Hooker. London: SCM Press, 1963.

Kähler, Martin. *The So-Called Historical Jesus and the Historic Biblical Christ.* Translated and Edited with an Introduction by C. Braaten. Foreword by Paul Tillich. Philadelphia: Fortress Press, 1964.

Käsemann, Ernst. *Essays on New Testament Themes.* Translated by W. J. Montague. London: SCM Press, 1964.

_____. *Jesus Means Freedom.* Translated by Frank Clarke. Philadelphia: Fortress Press, 1970.

Kasper, Walter. *Jesus the Christ.* New York: Paulist Press, 1976.

Keck, Leander E. *A Future for the Historical Jesus.* Nashville: Abingdon Press, 1971.

Kelly, J. N. D. *Early Christian Doctrines.* New York: Harper & Bros., 1958.

_____. *Early Christian Creeds.* London: Longmans, Green, 1950.

Knox, John. *The Humanity and Divinity of Christ.* Cambridge: University Press, 1967.

_____. *The Death of Christ.* Nashville: Abingdon Press, 1958.

_____. *Jesus: Lord and Christ.* New York: Harper & Bros., 1958.

Kümmel, Werner G. *Theology of the New Testament.* Translated by John Steely. Nashville: Abingdon Press, 1973.

Ladd, George E. *A Theology of the New Testament.* Grand Rapids: Eerdmans Publishing Co., 1974.

Mackintosh, H. R. *The Doctrine of the Person of Christ.* New York: Charles Scribner's Sons, 1914.

Martin, Malachi. *Jesus Now.* New York: Dutton, 1973.

Marxsen, Willi. *The Beginnings of Christology.* Translated by Paul Achtemeier. Philadelphia: Westminster Press, 1969.

Mascall, E. L. *Christ, the Christian and the Church.* London: Longmans, 1955.

Mathews, W. R. *The Problem of Christ in the 20th Century.* London: Oxford University Press, 1940.

McIntyre, John. *The Shape of Christology.* London: SCM Press, 1966.

Moltmann, Jürgen. *The Crucified God.* Translated by R. A. Wilson and J. Bowden. New York: Harper & Row, 1974.

Moule, C. F. D., Editor with an Introduction. *The Significance of the Message of the Resurrection for Faith in Jesus Christ.* London: SCM, 1968.

Newbigin, Lesslie. *The Finality of Christ.* London: SCM Press, 1969.

Niebuhr, Richard R. *Resurrection and Historical Reason.* New York: Charles Scribner's Sons, 1951.

Norris, Richard. *Manhood and Christ: A Study in the Christology of Theodore of Mopsuestia.* Oxford: Clarendon Press, 1967.

Nygren, Anders. *The Essence of Christianity.* Translated by Philip Watson. London: Epworth Press, 1960.

O'Collins, Gerald. *The Calvary Christ.* Philadelphia: Westminster Press, 1977.

Ogden, Schubert M. *Christ Without Myth.* New York: Harper & Row, 1961.

O'Grady, John F. *Jesus, Lord and Christ.* New York: Paulist Press, 1973.

Otto, Rudolf. *The Kingdom of God and the Son of Man.* Translated by Floyd V. Filson and Bertram Lee Wolf. New and Revised Edition. London: Lutterworth Press, 1943.

Pannenberg, Wolfhart. *Jesus—God and Man.* Translated by Lewis L. Wilkins and Duane A. Priebe. Philadelphia: Westminster Press, 1963.

Paul, Robert. *The Atonement and the Sacraments.* Nashville: Abingdon Press, 1960.

Pelikan, Jaroslav. *The Christian Tradition, Vol. I.* Chicago: U. of Chicago Press, 1971.

_____, Editor. *The Finality of Christ in an Age of Universal History.* London: Lutterworth Press, 1965.

Perrin, Norman. *Jesus and the Language of the Kingdom.* Philadelphia: Fortress Press, 1976.

_____. *A Modern Pilgrimage in New Testament Christology.* Philadelphia: Fortress Press, 1974.

Pittenger, W. Norman. *Christology Reconsidered.* London: SCM Press, 1970.

_____. *The Word Incarnate.* New York: Harper & Bros., 1959.

_____, Editor. *Christ For Us Today.* London: SCM Press, 1968.

Rahner, Karl. "Incarnation," "Jesus Christ." *Sacramentum Mundi,* III. New York: Herder & Herder, 1969.

Ramsey, Arthur Michael. *The Resurrection of Christ*. London: G. Bles, The Centenary Press. 2nd Edition, 1946.

Relton, Herbert. *A Study in Christology*. London: SPCK, 1917.

Richardson, Alan. *The Political Christ*. London: SCM Press, 1973.

Robinson, J. A. T. *The Human Face of God*. Philadelphia: Westminster, 1973.

Robinson, James M. *A New Quest of the Historical Jesus*. London: SCM Press, 1959.

Routley, Erik. *The Man for Others*. Oxford: Oxford University Press, 1964.

Rupp, George. *Christologies and Cultures*. The Hague: Mouton, 1974.

Schillebeeckx, Edward and van Iersel, Bas, Editors. *Jesus Christ and Human Freedom*. New York: Herder & Herder, 1974.

——————. *Jesus: An Experiment in Christology*. New York: Seabury Press, 1977.

Schmaus, Michael. *Dogma 3: God and His Christ*. Kansas City: Sheed and Ward, 1971.

Schoonenberg, Piet. *The Christ*. Translated by Della Couling. New York: Herder & Herder, 1972.

Schweitzer, Albert. *The Quest of the Historical Jesus*. Translated by N. Montgomery. London: Black, 1910.

Singh, Surjit. *Christology and Personality*. Philadelphia: Westminster Press, 1961.

Skärd, Bjarne. *The Incarnation*. Translated by Herman Jorgensen. Minneapolis: Augsburg Publishing House, 1960.

Smedes, Lewis. *All Things Made New*. Grand Rapids: Eerdmans Publishing Co., 1970.

Sölle, Dorothee. *Christ the Representative*. Translated by David Lewis. London: SCM Press, 1970.

Sykes, S. W. and Clayton, J. P., Editors. *Christ, Faith and History*. Cambridge: University Press, 1972.

Taylor, Vincent. *The Person of Christ in New Testament Teaching*. New York: The Macmillan Co., 1958.

——————. *The Atonement in New Testament Teaching*. London: Epworth Press, 3rd ed., 1958.

TeSelle, Eugene. *Christ in Context*. Philadelphia: Fortress Press, 1975.

Thornton, Lionel S. *The Incarnate Lord*. New York: Longmans, Green, 1928.

Torrance, Thomas F. *Space, Time and Incarnation*. London: Oxford University Press, 1969.

Van Buren, Paul. *Christ in Our Place*. Grand Rapids: Eerdmans Publishing Co., 1957.

Van Beeck, Frans Jozef. *Christ Announced: Christology As Rhetoric*. Unpublished Manuscript, 1977.

Vawter, Bruce. *This Man Jesus*. Garden City: Doubleday & Co., 1973.

Via, Dan Otto, Jr. *The Parables*. Philadelphia: Fortress Press, 1967.

Vincent, John. *Secular Christ*. Nashville: Abingdon Press, 1968.

Visser 't Hooft, W. A. *The Kingship of Christ.* New York: Harper & Bros., 1948.

Warfield, Benjamin B. *Person and Work of Christ.* Philadelphia: Presbyterian and Reformed Publishing House, 1950.

Whale, J. S. *Victor and Victim.* Cambridge: University Press, 1960.

Williams, Sam K. *Jesus' Death as Saving Event.* Missoula, Montana: Scholars Press, 1975.

Wolf, William J. *No Cross, No Crown.* New York: Doubleday & Co., 1957.

CHURCH

Anderson, Wilhelm. *Towards a Theology of Mission.* London: SCM Press, 1958.

Anderson, Gerald, Editor. *The Theology of Christian Mission.* Nashville: Abingdon Press, 1961.

Anderson, Gerald and Stransky, Thomas, Editors. *Mission Trends,* I–IV. Grand Rapids: Eerdmans Publishing Co., 1974–77.

Aulén, Gustaf. *Eucharist and Sacrifice.* Translated by Eric H. Wahlstrom. Philadelphia: Muhlenberg Press, 1958.

Augustinus, Aurelius. *The City of God.* A New Translation by Henry Bettenson with Introduction by David Knowles. Harmondsworth: Penguin Books, 1972.

Baillie, D. M. *The Theology of the Sacraments.* New York: Charles Scribner's Sons, 1957.

Barclay, William. *The Promise of the Spirit.* Philadelphia: Westminster, 1960.

Barth, Karl. *The Teaching of the Church Regarding Baptism.* Translated by Ernest A. Payne. London: SCM Press, 1948.

Berkouwer, G. C. *The Church.* Translated by J. E. Davison. Grand Rapids: Eerdmans Publishing Co., 1976.

Blauw, Johannes. *The Missionary Nature of the Church.* New York: McGraw-Hill, 1962.

Bloesch, Donald. *The Reform of the Church.* Grand Rapids: Eerdmans Publishing Co., 1970.

Bonhoeffer, Dietrich. *The Communion of Saints.* New York: Harper & Row, 1963.

_____. *Life Together.* Translated with Introduction by John W. Doberstein. New York: Harper & Bros., 1954.

Brilioth, Yngve. *Eucharistic Faith and Practice:* Evangelical and Catholic. Translated by A. G. Hebert. New York: The Macmillan Co., 1939.

Brown, Robert McAfee. *The Significance of the Church.* Philadelphia: Westminster Press, 1956.

Brunner, Emil. *The Misunderstanding of the Church.* Translated by Harold Knight. London: Lutterworth Press, 1952.

Buttrick, George Arthur. *Prayer.* New York: Abingdon-Cokesbury Press, 1942.

Casteel, John L. *Rediscovering Prayer.* New York: Association Press, 1955.

Christians, Clifford, et al. *Who in the World?* Grand Rapids: Eerdmans Publishing Co., 1972.

Church of South India. *The Sacraments.* Madras: Christian Literature Society, 1956.

Come, Arnold. *Agents of Reconciliation.* Revised and Enlarged Edition. Philadelphia: Westminster Press, 1964.

Cooke, Bernard. *Ministry of Word and Sacraments.* Philadelphia: Fortress Press, 1976.

Costas, Orlando E. *The Church and Its Mission.* Wheaton, Illinois: Tyndale House, 1974.

Cullmann, Oscar. *Baptism in the New Testament.* Translated by J. K. S. Reid. London: SCM Press, 1950.

Cullmann, Oscar and Leenhardt, F. J. *Essays on the Lord's Supper.* Translated by J. G. Davies. Richmond: John Knox Press, 1958.

Cully, Kendig Brubaker, Editor. *Confirmation:* History, Doctrine, Practice. Greenwich, Connecticut: Seabury Press, 1962.

_____. *Sacraments: A Language of Faith.* Philadelphia: Christian Education Press, 1961.

Daly, Mary. *The Church and the Second Sex.* With a New Feminist Post-Christian Introduction by the Author. New York: Harper & Row, 1975.

Detroit Ordination Council. *Women and Catholic Priesthood: An Expanded Vision.* Edited by Ann Marie Gardner. New York: Paulist Press, 1976.

Dillistone, F. W. *Christianity and Symbolism.* Philadelphia: Westminster Press, 1955.

Dittes, James. *The Church on the Way.* New York: Charles Scribner's Sons, 1967.

Dix, Dom Gregory. *The Shape of the Liturgy.* London: Dacre Press, 1945.

Doely, Sarah Bentley, Editor. *Women's Liberation and the Church.* New York: Association Press, 1970.

Dulles, Avery. *Dimensions of the Church.* Westminster, Maryland: Newman Press, 1965.

_____. *Models of the Church.* Garden City, New York: Doubleday & Co., 1974.

Dunkerley, Roderic, Editor. *The Ministry and the Sacraments.* London: SCM Press, 1937.

Elert, Werner. *The Lord's Supper Today.* Translated by Martin Bertram. St. Louis: Concordia Publishing House, 1973.

Fackre, Gabriel. *The Pastor and the World.* Philadelphia: United Church Press, 1964.

_____. *Secular Impact.* Philadelphia: United Church Press, 1968.

_____. *Word in Deed:* Theological Themes in Evangelism. Grand Rapids: Eerdmans Publishing Co., 1975.

Farley, Edward. *Ecclesial Man.* Philadelphia: Fortress Press, 1975.

Fisher, Wallace. *Because We Have Good News.* Nashville: Abingdon, 1974.
_____. *From Tradition to Mission.* Nashville: Abingdon Press, 1965.

Flew, R. Newton, Editor. *The Nature of the Church.* New York: Harper & Bros., 1952.

Forsyth, P. T. *The Church and the Sacraments.* 2nd Edition. London: Independent Press, 1947.

Gibbs, Mark and Morton, T. Ralph. *God's Frozen People.* Philadelphia: Westminster Press, 1965.

Green, Edward Michael Banks. *Evangelism in the Early Church.* Grand Rapids: Eerdmans Publishing Co., 1970.

Hageman, Alice L., Editor. *Sexist Religion and Women in the Church.* New York: Association Press, 1974.

Hageman, Howard G. *Pulpit and Table.* Richmond: John Knox Press, 1962.

Hamilton, Michael, Editor. *The Charismatic Movement.* Grand Rapids: Eerdmans Publishing Co., 1975.

Hanson, Anthony. *The Pioneer Ministry.* Philadelphia: Westminster Press, 1961.

Heiler, Friedrich. *Prayer.* Translated by Samuel McComb with assistance of J. Edgar Park. New York: Oxford University Press, 1932.

Heitman, Claus and Mühlen, Herbert, Editors with Charles A. M. Hall, Translator and General Editor. *The Theology and Experience of the Holy Spirit.* Philadelphia: Fortress Press, 1976.

Heyward, Carter. *A Priest Forever.* New York: Harper & Row, 1976.

Hoekendijk, J. C. *The Church Inside Out.* Edited by L. A. Hoedemaker and Pieter Tjimes and Translated by Isaac C. Rottenberg. Philadelphia: Westminster Press, 1966.
_____. *Horizons of Hope.* Nashville: Tidings, 1970.

Hollenweger, Walter. *The Pentecostals.* Translated by R. A. Wilson with Revisions by the Author. Minneapolis: Augsburg Publishing Co., 1972.

Jenkins, Daniel T. *The Nature of Catholicity.* London: Faber, 1942.
_____. *The Protestant Ministry.* Garden City, New York: Doubleday & Co., 1958.
_____. *The Strangeness of the Church.* Garden City, New York: Doubleday & Co., 1955.

Jeremias, Joachim. *Infant Baptism in the First Four Centuries.* Translated by David Cairns. Philadelphia: Westminster Press, 1960.

Knox, John. *The Church and the Reality of Christ.* New York: Harper & Row, 1962.

Kraemer, Hendrik. *A Theology of the Laity.* Philadelphia: Westminster Press, 1958.

Küng, Hans. *The Church.* Translated by Ray and Rosaleen Ockenden. New York: Sheed and Ward, 1967.

Lampe, G. W. *The Seal of the Spirit.* 2nd Edition with Corrections and a New Introduction. London: SPCK, 1967.

MacGregor, Geddes. *Corpus Christi, The Nature of the Church According to the Reformed Tradition.* Philadelphia: Westminster Press, 1959.

Manson, T. W. *The Church's Ministry.* London: Hodder and Stoughton, 1948.

Margull, Hans. *Hope in Action.* Translated by Eugene Peters. Philadelphia: Muhlenberg Press, 1962.

Marty, Martin E. *Protestantism.* New York: Holt, Rinehart and Winston, 1972.

Mascall, Eric L. *Christ, the Christian and the Church.* London: Longmans, Green, 1946.

McBrien, Richard. *Church: The Continuing Quest.* Paramus, N.J.: Newman Press, 1970.

——————. *The Remaking of the Church.* New York: Harper & Row, 1973.

McLeod, George. *Only One Way Left.* Glasgow: Iona Community, 1956.

Miller, Donald. *The Nature and Mission of the Church.* Richmond: John Knox Press, 1957.

Minear, Paul. *Images of the Church in the New Testament.* Philadelphia: Westminster Press, 1960.

Moltmann, Jürgen. *The Church in the Power of the Spirit.* Translated by Margaret Kohl. New York: Harper & Row, 1977.

Mouw, Richard J. *Political Evangelism.* Grand Rapids: Eerdmans Publishing Co., 1973.

Mudge, Lewis. *One Church: Catholic and Reformed.* Philadelphia: Westminster Press, 1963.

Neill, Stephen. *Salvation Tomorrow.* Nashville: Abingdon Press, 1976.

Nelson, J. Robert. *The Realm of Redemption.* Chicago: Wilcox & Follett Co., 1951.

Nevin, John W. *The Mystical Presence and Other Writings on the Eucharist.* Edited by Bard Thompson and George Bricker. Philadelphia: United Church Press, 1966.

Newbigin, Lesslie. *The Household of God.* New York: Friendship Press, 1954.

Nichols, James Hastings, Editor. *The Mercersburg Theology.* New York: Oxford University Press, 1966.

Niebuhr, H. Richard. *The Purpose of the Church and its Ministry.* New York: Harper & Bros., 1956.

Niebuhr, H. Richard and Williams, Daniel D. *The Ministry in Historical Perspective.* New York: Harper & Bros., 1956.

Nygren, Anders and Aulén, Gustaf, Editors. *This is the Church.* Translated by Carl C. Rasmussen. Philadelphia: Muhlenberg Press, 1952.

O'Connor, Elizabeth J. *Inward Journey, Outward Journey.* New York: Harper & Row, 1968.

Osborn, Ronald E. *In Christ's Place:* Christian Ministry in Today's World. St. Louis: Bethany Press, 1967.

O'Shea, William J. *Sacraments of Initiation.* Englewood Cliffs, N.J.: Prentice-Hall, 1966.

Paul, Robert. *Ministry.* Grand Rapids: Eerdmans Publishing Co., 1965.

Prenter, Regin. *Spiritus Creator.* Translated by John M. Jensen. Philadelphia: Muhlenberg Press, 1953.

Quere, Ralph W. *Evangelical Witness.* Minneapolis: Augsburg Publishing House, 1975.

Quick, Oliver. *The Christian Sacraments.* New York: Harper & Bros., 1927.

Rahner, Karl. *The Church and the Sacraments.* Translated by W. J. O'Hara. New York: Herder & Herder, 1963.

Raines, Robert. *The Secular Congregation.* New York: Harper & Row, 1968.

Rendtorff, Trutz. *Church and Theology.* Translated by Reginald Fuller. Philadelphia: Westminster Press, 1971.

Rouner, Arthur A. *The Free Church Today.* New York: Association Press, 1968.

Schaff, Philip. *The Principle of Protestantism.* Translated by John W. Nevin. Edited by Bard Thompson and George Bricker. Philadelphia: United Church Press, 1964.

Schillebeeckx, Edward. *The Mission of the Church.* Translated by N. D. Smith. New York: Seabury Press, 1973.

Schillebeeckx, Edward and Willems, Boniface, Editors. *The Sacraments in General: A New Perspective.* New York: Paulist Press, 1968.

Schlink, Edmund. *The Doctrine of Baptism.* Translated by Herbert J. A. Bouman. St. Louis: Concordia Publishing House, 1972.

Segundo, Juan Luis. *The Community Called Church.* Translated by John Drury. Maryknoll, New York: Orbis Books, 1973.

Skydsgaard, K. E. *One in Christ.* Translated by Axel C. Kildegaard. Philadelphia: Muhlenberg Press, 1957.

Spike, Robert. *Safe in Bondage.* New York: Friendship Press, 1960.

Swete, Henry B. *The Holy Spirit in the New Testament.* London: The Macmillan Co., 1919.

Symanowski, Horst. *The Christian Witness in an Industrial Society.* Translated by George Kehm. Philadelphia: Westminster Press, 1964.

Taylor, John V. *The Go-Between God.* Philadelphia: Fortress Press, 1973.

Underhill, Evelyn. *Worship.* New York: Harper & Bros., 1937.

Webber, George W. *The Congregation in Mission.* New York: Abingdon Press, 1964.

Welch, Claude. *The Reality of the Church.* New York: Charles Scribner's Sons, 1958.

Wieser, Thomas, Editor. *Planning for Mission.* New York: U.S. Conference for the World Council of Churches, 1966.

Williams, Colin. *Where in the World?* National Council of Churches, 1963.
_____. *The Church.* Philadelphia: Westminster Press, 1968.

World Council of Churches. *A Theological Reflection on the Work of Evangelism.* Geneva: WCC, 1959.
_____. *The Church for Others and the Church for the World.* Geneva: World Council of Churches, 1971.

_____. *One Lord, One Baptism.* Minneapolis: Augsburg Publishing House, 1961.

SALVATION

Adams, James Luther. *On Being Human Religiously.* Edited and Introduced by Max L. Stackhouse. Boston: Beacon Press, 1976.
_____. *Taking Time Seriously.* Glencoe, Illinois: Free Press, 1957.
Alves, Rubem. *A Theology of Human Hope.* Washington: Corpus Books, 1969.
Assmann, Hugo. *Practical Theology of Liberation.* Translated by Paul Burns. London: Search Press, 1975.
Baillie, John. *Baptism and Conversion.* New York: Charles Scribner's Sons, 1963.
Barclay, William. *Turning to God:* A Study of Conversion in the Book of Acts. Philadelphia: Westminster Press, 1964.
Barth, Karl. *The Epistle to the Romans.* Translated by E. C. Hoskyns. London: Oxford University Press, 1933.
Barth, Markus. *Justification.* Translated by A. M. Woodruff, III. Grand Rapids: Eerdmans Publishing Co., 1971.
Bennett, John Coleman. *The Radical Imperative:* From Theology to Social Ethics. Philadelphia: Westminster Press, 1975.
Berkouwer, G. C. *Faith and Justification.* Translated by Lewis B. Smedes. Grand Rapids: Eerdmans Publishing Co., 1954.
Bernard of Clairvaux. *On the Love of God.* Translated by a Religious of C.S.M.V. London: A. R. Mowbray & Co., 1961.
Birch, Bruce C. and Rasmussen, Larry L. *Bible and Ethics in the Christian Life.* Minneapolis: Augsburg Publishing House, 1976.
Bloesch, Donald G. *The Christian Life and Salvation.* Grand Rapids: Eerdmans Publishing Co., 1967.
Bonhoeffer, Dietrich. *Ethics.* Edited by Eberhard Bethge and Translated by Neville Horton Smith. New York: The Macmillan Co., 1955.
_____. *The Cost of Discipleship.* Revised and Enlarged Edition. Translated by R. H. Fuller. New York: The Macmillan Co., 1959.
Bonino, Jose Miguez. *Doing Theology in a Revolutionary Situation.* Philadelphia: Fortress Press, 1975.
Brown, Robert McAfee. *The Spirit of Protestantism.* New York: Oxford University Press, 1961.
_____. *Is Faith Obsolete?* Philadelphia: Westminster Press, 1974.
Brunner, Emil. *The Divine Imperative.* Translated by Olive Wyon. New York: The Macmillan Co., 1937.
Calhoun, Robert Lowry. *God and the Common Life.* New York: Charles Scribner's Sons, 1935.
Catherine of Siena. *The Dialogue of the Seraphic Vision.* Translated by Algar Thorold. Westminster, Md.: The Newman Bookshop, 1943.

Collins, Sheila D. *A Different Heaven and Earth.* Valley Forge: Judson Press, 1974.

Cone, James. *A Black Theology of Liberation.* Philadelphia: J. B. Lippincott & Co., 1970.

Cox, Harvey. *The Secular City.* New York: The Macmillan Co., 1965.

Cullmann, Oscar. *Christ and Time.* Revised Edition. Translated by Floyd Filson. Philadelphia: Westminster Press, 1964.

_____. *Salvation in History.* Translated by Sidney Sowers. New York: Harper & Row, 1967.

Dussell, Enrique D. *History and the Theology of Liberation.* Translated by John Drury. Maryknoll, New York: Orbis Books, 1976.

Ebeling, Gerhard. *Word and Faith.* Translated by James W. Leitch. Philadelphia: Fortress Press, 1963.

Edwards, Jonathan. *Freedom of the Will.* Edited by Paul Ramsey. New Haven: Yale University Press, 1957.

Eller, Vernard. *The Promise: Ethics in the Kingdom of God.* Garden City, New York: Doubleday & Co., 1970.

Ellul, Jacques. *The Meaning of the City.* Translated by Dennis Pardee. Grand Rapids: Eerdmans Publishing Co., 1970.

_____. *The Ethics of Freedom.* Translated and Edited by G. W. Bromiley. Grand Rapids: Eerdmans Publishing Co., 1976.

_____. *Violence.* Translated by Cecelia G. Kings. New York: Seabury Press, 1969.

Ernst, Cornelius. *The Theology of Grace.* Notre Dame: Fides Publishers, 1974.

Farmer, H. H. *The Word of Reconciliation.* Nashville: Abingdon Press, 1966.

Flew, R. Newton. *The Idea of Perfection in Christian Theology.* London: Oxford University Press, 1934.

Fortman, Edmund J., Editor. *The Theology of Man and Grace: Commentary.* Milwaukee: Bruce Publishing Co., 1966.

Gardner, C. Clinton. *Biblical Faith and Social Ethics.* New York: Harper & Row, 1960.

Green, Edward Michael Banks. *The Meaning of Salvation.* Philadelphia: Westminster Press, 1965.

_____. *I Believe in the Holy Spirit.* Grand Rapids: Eerdmans Publishing Co., 1976.

Gustafson, James M. *Christ and the Moral Life.* New York: Harper & Row, 1968.

Gustafson, James M. and Laney, James T., Editors. *On Being Responsible: Issues in Personal Ethics.* New York: Harper & Row, 1968.

Hardman, Oscar. *The Christian Doctrine of Grace.* New York: The Macmillan Co., 1947.

Harned, David Baily. *Faith and Virtue.* Philadelphia: United Church Press, 1973.

Haroutunian, Joseph. *God With Us.* Philadelphia: Westminster Press, 1965.

273

Henry, Carl F. H. *Christian Personal Ethics*. Grand Rapids: Eerdmans Publishing Co., 1957.

Herrmann, Wilhelm. *The Communion of the Christian with God*. Edited with Introduction by Robert Voelkel. Philadelphia: Fortress Press, 1971.

Hertz, Karl, Editor. *Two Kingdoms and One World*. Minneapolis: Augsburg Publishing House, 1976.

Herzog, Frederick. *Liberation Theology*. New York: Seabury Press, 1972.

"Humanization and Mission," *International Review of Mission*, Vol. LX, No. 237 (January, 1971).

Jones, Major J. *Black Awareness*: A Theology of Hope. Nashville: Abingdon Press, 1971.

Julian of Norwich. *The Revelation of Divine Love*. Translated by James Walsh. St. Meinrad, Indiana: Abbey Press, 1974.

Laurentin, René. *Liberation, Development and Salvation*. Translated by Charles Quinn. Maryknoll, New York: Orbis Books, 1972.

Lehmann, Paul. *Ethics in a Christian Context*. New York: Harper & Row, 1963.

Luther, Martin. *Three Treatises*. Translated by C. M. Jacobs, A. T. Steinhaeuser, and W. A. Lambert. Philadelphia: Muhlenberg Press, 1943.

Mackintosh, H. R. *The Christian Experience of Forgiveness*. London: Collins, 1927.

Metz, Johannes B. *Theology of the World*. Translated by William Glen-Doepel. New York: Herder & Herder, 1971.

Michaelson, Carl. *Worldly Theology*. New York: Charles Scribner's Sons, 1967.

Miller, Alexander. *The Renewal of Man*. Garden City, New York: Doubleday & Co., 1955.

Miller, Allen O., Editor. *Reconciliation in Today's World*. Grand Rapids: Eerdmans Publishing Co., 1970.

Minear, Paul. *And Great Shall Be Your Reward*: The Origin of Christian Views of Salvation. New Haven: Yale University Press, 1941.

Moffatt, James. *Grace in the New Testament*. New York: Ray Long and Richard R. Smith, 1932.

Muelder, Walter. *Foundations of the Responsible Society*. New York: Abingdon Press, 1959.

Newbigin, Lesslie. *Sin and Salvation*. Philadelphia: Westminster Press, 1957.

Niebuhr, H. Richard. *Christ and Culture*. New York: Harper & Row, 1951.
——————. *The Responsible Self*. New York: Harper & Row, 1963.

Niebuhr, Reinhold. *An Interpretation of Christian Ethics*. New York: Harper & Bros., 1935.
——————. *Beyond Tragedy*. New York: Charles Scribner's Sons, 1937.
——————. *Faith and History*. New York: Charles Scribner's Sons, 1949.
——————. *Justice and Mercy*. Edited by Ursula M. Niebuhr. New York: Harper & Row, 1974.

Rauschenbusch, Walter. *A Theology for the Social Gospel.* New York: The Macmillan Co., 1917.

Reuther, Rosemary Radford. *Liberation Theology.* New York: Paulist Press, 1972.

Richards, George W. *Christian Ways of Salvation.* New York: The Macmillan Co., 1923.

Ritschl, Albrecht. *The Christian Doctrine of Justification and Reconciliation.* Edited by H. R. Mackintosh and A. B. Macauley. Edinburgh: Clark, 1902.

Roberts, J. Deotis. *A Black Political Theology.* Philadelphia: Westminster Press, 1974.

_____. *Liberation and Reconciliation.* Philadelphia: Westminster Press, 1971.

Rogers, Jack, et al. *Case Studies in Christ and Salvation.* Philadelphia: Westminster Press, 1977.

Routley, Erik. *The Gift of Conversion.* Philadelphia: Muhlenberg Press, 1960.

Russell, Letty M. *Human Liberation in a Feminist Perspective.* With a Foreword by Elisabeth Moltmann-Wendel and Jürgen Moltmann. Philadelphia: Westminster Press, 1974.

Salvation Today and Contemporary Experience. Geneva: World Council of Churches, 1973.

"Salvation Today II," *International Review of Mission,* Vol. LXI, No. 241 (January, 1972).

"Secularization and Conversion," *Study Encounter,* Vol. I, No. 2 (1965).

Segundo, Juan Luis. *Grace and the Human Condition.* Translated by John Drury. Maryknoll, New York: Orbis Books, 1973.

Sölle, Dorothee. *Suffering.* Translated by Everett R. Kalin. Philadelphia: Fortress Press, 1975.

_____. *Political Theology.* Translated with an Introduction by John Shelley. Philadelphia: Fortress Press, 1974.

Sovik, Arne. *Salvation Today.* Minneapolis: Augsburg Publishing House, 1973.

Stackhouse, Max L. *Ethics and the Urban Ethos.* Boston: Beacon Press, 1972.

Stevens, George Barker. *The Christian Doctrine of Salvation.* New York: Charles Scribner's Sons, 1905.

Stott, John. *Christian Missions in the Modern World.* London: Falcon Press, 1975.

Stringfellow, William. *A Private and Public Faith.* Grand Rapids: Eerdmans Publishing Co., 1962.

Taylor, Vincent. *Forgiveness and Reconciliation.* London: The Macmillan Co., 1941.

Thielicke, Helmut. *Theological Ethics.* Edited by William H. Lazareth, Vols. I and II. Philadelphia: Fortress Press, 1966.

Thomas, M. M. *Salvation and Humanisation.* Madras: Christian Institute for the Study of Religion and Society, 1971.

Tillich, Paul. *Love, Power, and Justice.* New York: Oxford University Press, 1960.

_____. *Political Expectation.* Translated and Edited by James Luther Adams. New York: Harper & Row, 1971.

van Leeuwen, Arend Th. *Christianity in World History.* Translated by H. H. Hoskins. New York: Charles Scribner's Sons, 1964.

Verkuyl, J. *The Message of Liberation in our Age.* Translated by Dale Cooper. Grand Rapids: Eerdmans Publishing Co., 1970.

Watson, Philip S. *The Concept of Grace.* Philadelphia: The Muhlenberg Press, 1959.

Wesley, John. *A Plain Account of Christian Perfection.* London: Epworth Press, 1968.

Whale, J. S. *The Protestant Tradition.* Cambridge: University Press, 1962.

Williams, Daniel Day. *God's Grace and Man's Hope.* New York: Harper & Row, 1949.

_____. *The Spirit and the Forms of Love.* Welwyn, Herts: Nisbet & Co., 1968.

Yoder, John Howard. *The Politics of Jesus.* Grand Rapids: Eerdmans Publishing Co., 1972.

CONSUMMATION

Aldwinckle, Russell. *Death in the Secular City.* Grand Rapids: Eerdmans Publishing Co., 1974.

Badham, Paul. *Christian Belief about Life after Death.* New York: Harper & Row, 1976.

Baillie, John. *And the Life Everlasting.* New York: Charles Scribner's Sons, 1933.

Ball, Brian. *A Great Expectation:* Eschatological Thought in English Protestantism to 1660. London: Brill, 1975.

Becker, Ernest. *The Denial of Death.* New York: Free Press, 1973.

Benoit, Pierre and Murphy, Roland. *Immortality and Resurrection.* New York: Herder & Herder, 1970.

Berdyaev, Nicholas. *The Beginning and the End.* Translated by R. M. French. London: Geoffrey Bles, 1952.

Berkhof, Hendrikus. *Well-Founded Hope.* Richmond: John Knox Press, 1969.

Berkouwer, G. C. *The Return of Christ.* Translated by James Van Oosterom and Edited by Marlin Van Elderen. Grand Rapids: Eerdmans Publishing Co., 1972.

Boros, Ladislaus. *The Mystery of Death.* Translated by Gregory Bainbridge. New York: Herder & Herder, 1965.

Braaten, Carl. *Christ and Counter-Christ.* Philadelphia: Fortress Press, 1971.

_____. *Eschatology and Ethics.* Minneapolis: Augsburg Publishing House, 1974.

Braaten, Carl and Jenson, Robert. *The Futurist Option.* New York: Newman Press, 1970.

Bright, John. *The Kingdom of God.* New York: Abingdon Press, 1953.

Brunner, Emil. *Eternal Hope.* Translated by Harold Knight. Philadelphia: Westminster Press, 1954.

Bultmann, Rudolf. *History and Eschatology.* Edinburgh: University Press, 1957.

Calian, Samuel. *The Significance of Eschatology in the Thought of Nicholas Berdyaev.* Leiden: Brill, 1965.

Capps, Walter H. *The Future of Hope.* Philadelphia: Fortress Press, 1970.

Cargas, Henry J. and White, Ann, Editors. *Death and Hope.* New York: Corpus Books, 1971.

Charles, R. H. *Eschatology.* With Introduction by George Wesley Buchanan. New York: Schocken Books, 1963.

Chauncy, Charles and Mather, Samuel. *All Men will be Saved and All Men Will Not be Saved Forever.* Reprint Edition with Introduction by Conrad Wright. Hicksville, N.Y.: The Regina Press, 1975.

Choran, Jacques. *Death and Western Thought.* New York: The Macmillan Co., 1963.

Cousins, Ewert, Editor. *Hope and the Future of Man.* Philadelphia: Fortress Press, 1972.

Edwards, David L. *The Last Things Now.* London: SCM Press, 1969.

Elert, Werner. *Last Things.* Translated by M. Bertram. Edited by R. Norden. St. Louis: Concordia Publishing House, 1974.

Eliade, Mircea. *Death, Afterlife and Eschatology.* New York: Harper & Row, 1974.

Ellul, Jacques. *Apocalypse: The Book of Revelation.* Translated by George W. Shreiner. New York: Seabury Press, 1977.

_____. *Hope in a Time of Abandonment.* Translated by C. Edward Hopkin. New York: Seabury Press, 1973.

Erickson, Millard J. *Contemporary Options in Eschatology.* Grand Rapids: Baker Book House, 1977.

Fackre, Gabriel. *The Rainbow Sign.* Grand Rapids: Eerdmans Publishing Co., 1969.

Fison, J. *The Christian Hope:* The Presence and the Parousia. New York: Longmans, Green, 1954.

Greeley, Andrew. *Death and Beyond.* Chicago: Thomas More Press, 1976.

Heim, Karl. *The World: Its Creation and Consummation.* Translated by R. Smith. Edinburgh: Oliver and Boyd, 1952.

Herzog, Frederick, Editor. *The Future of Hope.* New York: Herder & Herder, 1970.

Hick, John·H. *Death and Eternal Life.* New York: Harper & Row, 1976.

Jüngel, Eberhard. *Death, the Riddle and the Mystery.* Translated by Iain and Ute Nicol. Philadelphia: Westminster Press, 1975.

Lewis, C. S. *The Great Divorce.* New York: The Macmillan Co., 1946.

Lindbeck, George. *The Future of Roman Catholic Theology.* Philadelphia: Fortress Press, 1970.

Margull, Hans J. *Hope in Action.* Translated by Eugen Peters. Philadelphia: Muhlenberg Press, 1962.

Marsh, John. *The Fullness of Time.* London: Nisbet, 1952.

Martin, James. *The Last Judgment in Protestant Theology from Orthodoxy to Ritschl.* Edinburgh: Oliver and Boyd, 1963.

Mbiti, John S. *New Testament Eschatology in an African Background.* London: Oxford University Press, 1971.

Meeks, M. Douglas. *Origins of the Theology of Hope.* Philadelphia: Fortress Press, 1974.

Minear, Paul. *Christian Hope and the Second Coming.* Philadelphia: Westminster Press, 1954.

Moltmann, Jürgen. *Theology of Hope.* Translated by J. Leitch. New York: Harper & Row, 1967.

_____. *The Experiment Hope.* Edited and Translated with Foreword by M. Douglas Meeks. Philadelphia: Fortress Press, 1975.

_____. *Religion, Revolution and the Future.* Translated by M. Douglas Meeks. New York: Charles Scribner's Sons, 1969.

Moody, Dale. *The Hope of Glory.* Grand Rapids: Eerdmans Publishing Co., 1964.

Muckenhirn, Maryellen, Editor with Introduction. *The Future as the Presence of Shared Hope.* New York: Sheed and Ward, 1968.

Niebuhr, H. Richard. *The Kingdom of God in America.* New York: Harper & Bros., 1937.

Pelikan, Jaroslav. *The Shape of Death.* New York: Abingdon Press, 1961.

Pieper, Joseph. *Death and Immortality.* New York: Herder & Herder, 1969.

Pittenger, W. Norman. *The Last Things in Process Thought.* London: Epworth Press, 1970.

Polak, Frederick. *The Image of the Future.* Translated by Elsie Boulding. New York: Elsevier Scientific Publication Co., 1973.

Rahner, Karl. *On the Theology of Death.* Translated by Charles H. Henkey. London: Burns & Oates, 1961.

Reuther, Rosemary Radford. *The Radical Kingdom:* The Western Experience of Messianic Hope. New York: Harper & Row, 1970.

Robinson, J. A. T. *In the End God.* London: Collins, 1968.

_____. *Jesus and his Coming.* London: SCM Press, 1957.

Rosenstock-Huessy, Eugen. *The Christian Future.* New York: Harper & Row, 1966.

Schillebeeckx, Edward and Willems, Boniface, Editors. Various Translators. *The Problem of Eschatology.* New York: Paulist Press, 1969.

_____. *God the Future of Man.* Translated by N. D. Smith. New York: Sheed and Ward, 1968.

Schwarz, Hans. *On the Way to the Future.* Minneapolis: Augsburg Publishing House, 1972.

Stendahl, Krister, Editor. *Immortality and Resurrection*. New York: The Macmillan Co., 1965.

Taylor, A. E. *The Christian Hope of Immortality*. New York: The Macmillan Co., 1947.

Thielicke, Helmut. *Death and Life*. Translated by Edward Schroeder. Philadeiphia: Fortress Press, 1970.

Torrance, T. F. *Eschatology*. Edinburgh: Oliver and Boyd, 1953.

Towner, W. Sibley. *How God Deals with Evil*. Philadelphia: Westminster Press, 1976.

Vos, Geerhardus. *The Pauline Eschatology*. Grand Rapids: Eerdmans Publishing Co., 1952.

Wilder, Amos. *Eschatology and Ethics in the Teaching of Jesus*. New York: Harper & Bros., 1936.

World Council of Churches. *The Evanston Report,* Second Assembly of the World Council of Churches. London: SCM Press, 1955.

Subject Index

81